QUARTZ WATCHES

'Eventually everything connects – people, ideas, objects.
The quality of the connections is the key to quality per se.'
Charles Eames

CLÉMENT MAZARIAN

QUARTZ WATCHES

From early quartz to the Apple Watch, 90 ingenious electric watches explored

PHOTOGRAPHY BY
HENRY LEUTWYLER

MITCHELL BEAZLEY

MADE BY EMEXAG ZURICH
EMEX RU-106
PATENTED
WATER RESISTANT

PREFACE
BY NICOLAS GODIN

For my generation, a quartz watch was an absolute icon – consigning our trusty old analogues to a drawer, we got ready to fully embrace the 1980s. For me, this came in the form of a magnificent Seiko A638–5000 in brushed steel that I received on Christmas Day 1982 and never tired of admiring. As is so often the case, a happy union of technology and design had given birth to a classic; for me, on the cusp of adolescence, it was a revelation.

The appearance of quartz watches on our wrists heralded a sea change in everyday electronic devices; the synthesizer market was the same. Some analogue models had already featured an LED display, but these were soon supplanted by digital instruments that, with their oscillators, frequencies and even resonance, had a vocabulary much in common with electronic watches. The point of no return for musical instrument manufacturers came in 1983 with the advent of the Yamaha DX7 synthesizer; this was the year that musicians – much like the owners of Seikos and Casios, who had no further use for rotary winding crowns – stopped twiddling knobs and started pressing buttons.

In the recording studio, everything had to be immaculate and pristine; precision and accuracy were the standards to which musical production aspired – or became the constraints by which it was bound, depending on whether you saw yourself in the futurist or old-school camp. Personally, I have always refused to choose between them.

In the 1990s, the new technology of digital sampling allowed my generation of musicians to combine musical influences from any number of eras on a single recording; releases such as Portishead's *Dummy*, Beck's *Odelay* or, in my case, Air's *Moon Safari*, still bear witness to this joyous free-for-all.

Therefore, both my recording studio and my watch collection are now home to objects of desire from different decades, each distinct in their technology and their features – two inseparable aspects guaranteeing a functionality that will ensure they never end their days in a design museum.

FOREWORD

Exceptional Watches, my first book, saw us take a journey together through the ages to explore the watchmaking complications they spawned. This voyage of discovery showed us that watchmaking is not just about creating utilitarian objects; as we turned the pages of history we saw that this noble industry has brought the world a gift far greater than simple tools to count the hours – in short, watches do a lot more than just tell the time.

Humanity's quest for precision has never let up; our need to know for certain has remained an element of essential, indeed existential, importance to most human beings, companies and areas of activity. Electronic watches were invented in response to this need to anchor ourselves with absolute accuracy, to tell the exact time. Although their story begins with electric watches in the 1950s, it was to take its most important turn two decades later, with the advent of quartz movements. This tiny oscillator was solely responsible for revolutionizing the industry, shaking up the established order and bringing the mighty Swiss watchmaking empire to its knees – to the benefit of ambitious and creative Japanese entrepreneurs with a passion for technology. It is this unparalleled period in history (known variously as the quartz crisis and the quartz revolution), its origins, consequences and lessons, that this new volume will explore though a selection of watches.

The choices made for *Quartz Watches* will always be coloured by the subjectivity of the author, his relationship with their history, and his own taste in...well, watches. Just as in *Exceptional Watches*, each piece has been captured by the expert lens of Henry Leutwyler; many of them bear the marks of time and some have even ceased to measure the minutes for eternity. As the illustrious Nicolas Godin, one half of the band Air, has pointed out, 'It is precisely at the moment a watch stops working that a collection becomes art.' This is all the more true as great names such as Dieter Rams, Giorgetto Giugiaro, Gae Aulenti, Keith Haring and the like have left their mark on the iconic timepieces presented on these pages.

Whether you devour this book in a single sitting or explore it at a slower pace, I hope you will find everything you are looking for in its pages, from taking a deep dive into the electrifying history of these watches to using it as a useful support in which to prop open the case that displays your personal collection!

TIMELINE

From the first electric watch – unveiled to the public in 1952 – to the Apple Watch, the history of these timepieces is a rich one. Take a look back over many years of exceptional creativity and skill.

1927 **FIRST QUARTZ CLOCK**
W Marisson and J W Horton of Bell Laboratories invent the Crystal Clock

1952 **INTRODUCTION OF THE FIRST ELECTRIC WATCH**
Calibre R27 (LIP) and calibre 722 (Elgin)

1957 **HAMILTON | 500**
First electric watch to be sold globally

1958 **LIP | R27**
Calibre R27 brought to market in the LIP Electronic
—
FIRST QUARTZ TRAVEL CLOCK
Patek Philippe unveils a forerunner of the Naviquartz

1960 **BULOVA | ACCUTRON**
Introduction of the diapason (tuning-fork) movement

1961 **LAUNCH OF THE FIRST SWISS ELECTRIC MOVEMENT**
Ébauches SA/Landeron Calibre L-4750

1967 **CEH BETA PROTOTYPES**
July 1967: Beta 1
August 1967: Beta 2
—
ÉBAUCHES SA | DYNOTRON
Cal. 9150: first Swiss movement with a balance system using a transistor

1969 **SEIKO | ASTRON**
First quartz watch launched on 25 December 1969

1970 **CEH | BETA 21**
10 April 1970: first mass-produced Swiss quartz movement, incorporated into around 20 models from various brands associated with the Centre Électronique Horloger (CEH)

1971 **LONGINES | ULTRA-QUARTZ**
This model had been initially introduced and marketed in 1969

1972 **DAINI SEIKOSHA | CAL. 39**
—
GIRARD-PERREGAUX | GP350
First movement to feature a quartz crystal oscillating at a frequency of 32,768Hz
—
GOLAY | MICRO QUARTZ
—
INTRODUCTION OF THE FIRST LCD WATCHES
1972 saw Optel, Texas Instruments and Microma launch various projects using dynamic display technology
—
PULSAR
The first digital watch with an LED display comes to market

1973 **INVENTION OF THE FIELD EFFECT LCD**
This technique, initially used by Gruen for its Teletime model, was subsequently adopted by other brands

1973 **FIRST LCD WATCH WITH A SIX-DIGIT DISPLAY**
Seiko LC V.F.A. 06LC

1974 **CASIO | CASIOTRON**
First Casio wristwatch (LCD)
—
OMEGA | MEGAQUARTZ 2400
Calibre 1500 high-frequency Megaquartz. The 1511 variant featured in the first wristwatch to be certified as a marine chronometer.
—
OMEGA | MEGAQUARTZ 32KHz
Calibre 1300
—
SUWA SEIKOSHA | CAL. 48

1975 **DERBY | SWISSONIC**
—
PULSAR | CALCULATOR
First calculator watch with a digital display (LED)

1976 **BULOVA | COMPUTRON**
—
GIRARD-PERREGAUX | CASQUETTE
—
LIP | MACH 2000 LED
—
OMEGA | CHRONO-QUARTZ
First chronograph with a digital (LCD) and an analogue display
—
TISSOT | IDEA 2001 LCD
1971: launch of the IDEA 2001 range featuring a mechanical movement made of plastic
—
ZENITH | FUTURE TIME COMMAND
Analogue watch with an LED display for seconds

1977 **CARTIER | MUST**
—
OMEGA | 4.2 MHZ PROTOTYPES
—
EBEL | SPORT CLASSIC
—
ROLEX | OYSTERQUARTZ

1978 **SEIKO | QUARTZ DIVER**
—
SUWA SEIKOSHA | KING TWIN QUARTZ

1979 **DELIRIUM TREMENS**
Forerunner of the Swatch
—
SEIKO | WORLD TIME ATLAS

1981 **CHROMACHRON | COLOUR TIME**
Launch of quartz models after a short run of mechanical watches

1982 **AM RADIO**
This model was used by prop-makers to create the famous K.I.T.T. Commlink watch for the *Knight Rider* television series
—
BULOVA | THERMATRON
—
SEIKO | TV WATCH

1983 **CASIO | G-SHOCK**
A new range from Casio that became an icon of ruggedness, water resistance and extended battery life

1983 **SEIKO | 7A28**
Robust and repairable quartz movement developed over many years
—
SEIKO | 7A38
Same architecture as the 7A28, with day/date display
—
SEIKO | DATA 2000
LCD watch with a programmable memory
—
SWATCH

1984 **SEIKO | FIELD MASTER 'CONTRA'**

1985 **CASIO | DATABANK**
Calculator watch with an LCD display and data storage capacity
—
TISSOT | ROCKWATCH

1986 **SEIKO | 8T23**
Hand-wound quartz watch
—
SEIKO | GOLDEN TUNA 1,000M
1975: Automatic Hi-Beat 'Grandfather Tuna'
1978: Quartz 300m 'Tuna' and 600m 'Golden Tuna'

1987 **FLIK FLAK**

1988 **JUNGHANS | MEGA**
Radio-controlled digital watch allowing reception of time from atomic clock. It was launched as a digital/analogue watch in 1991.
—
LE PHARE-JEAN D'EVE SAMARA
Automatic quartz
—
LOUIS VUITTON | MONTEREY
—
SEIKO | KINETIC
AGM (automatic generating movement) technology introduced in 1986 and marketed in 1988 as AGS (automatic generating system)

1989 **BRAUN | AW 10**
—
CASIO | F-91 LCD
Today this is the world's bestselling watch

1990 **SEIKO | 7T**
Quartz movement capable of measuring time to one-hundredth of a second

1993 **IWC PORSCHE DESIGN TRAVEL**

1996 **SHELLMAN | COMPLICATIONS**

2007 **CATHODE CORNER NIXIE WATCH**

2015 **APPLE WATCH**

2017 **EONE BRADLEY**

2019 **CITIZEN 0100**
Movement varying by +/- one second per year

2022 **SWATCH | MOONSWATCH**

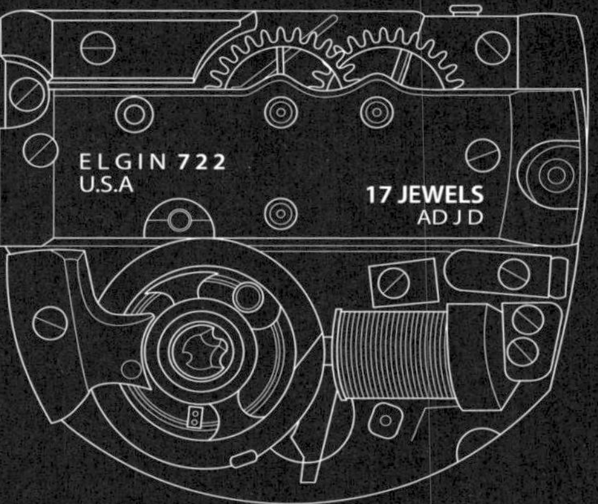
ELGIN 722
U.S.A
17 JEWELS
AD J D

THE PRE-QUARTZ ERA

CHAPTER 1

ELECTRIC WATCHES

THE PRE-QUARTZ ERA

ELECTRIC WATCHES

At a time in the dim and distant past, between the invention of traditional mechanical watches and the advent of entirely electronic quartz watches, experts and the public alike were beguiled by a now almost-forgotten technology: electric watches.

ELECTRIC VS ELECTRONIC

Within the broader history of watchmaking, the period referred to in this book as the pre-quartz era corresponds with the arrival of the first electric watches. Despite the name, such watches still measured time mechanically, relying on a balance wheel or a metal diapason (tuning fork). But they nonetheless differed from the movements that preceded them in their source of energy: the mainspring had been replaced by an electric current.

Electronic watches, which appeared later, should not be confused with their electric counterparts. These used electronic circuitry and were regulated by a quartz crystal resonator (hence they were known as quartz watches). This crystal oscillator generates a precise time signal of an accuracy far superior to that of mechanical watches (see page 72).

BALANCE SPRING OR TUNING FORK

Although there are many different kinds, electric watches with balance springs all retain a regulating component similar to that used in classic watches: a balance wheel attached to a spiral spring oscillating at a frequency of around 3Hz. In a classic mechanical movement, the balance wheel functions only as a regulator limiting the movement of the escape wheel. In an electric movement, it also functions as a motor and it drives the entire mechanism.

The electric diapason watch first appeared in the form of the Bulova Accutron, invented by Max Hetzel. Before this development, the balance wheel of an electric watch had been almost identical to that of a classic watch, with almost no gain in precision – although this didn't stop the manufacturers of the time making accuracy part of their sales pitch.

Hetzel was determined to do better, and designed another component to regulate a movement, a 24.85mm-long metal tuning fork with a frequency fixed at 360Hz that improved accuracy. Watches with this feature had two essential characteristics: the second hand swept evenly, rather than advancing in fractions of a second, and the usual tick-tock associated with the traditional escapement was replaced by a gentle vibration. This was so distinctive that the US advertising campaign presented the Accutron as 'the watch that hums'.

DISAPPEARANCE WITH QUARTZ

Many brands played a role in the rise of electric watches during the 20th century: LIP in France (see page 18), Hamilton in the United States (see page 22) and Ébauches SA in Switzerland (see page 24), for those based on a balance system; Bulova in the United States (see page 34) for those based on a metal tuning fork. All of these were in fact electromechanical watches.

Clockmakers wasted no time in incorporating electric power into their creations, however; the first timepiece with an electric balance wheel was designed by Alexander Bain in 1840. More than eight decades later, in 1921, the Shortt clock introduced a free-swinging pendulum in a vacuum chamber unconnected to the mechanism, the operation and display of which were electromechanical. For a long time this was the most accurate way to measure time. In another development, in 1934 LIP and Ericsson worked together to bring to market a desk clock with a mechanical escapement powered by an electric motor. Ultimately it was electric wristwatches that broadened the appeal of these movements slightly by miniaturizing their components, coils and contacts, but the sector gradually faded away with the advent of electronic quartz models.

ELECTROMECHANICAL WATCHES

FACT SHEET N°1

Unlike mechanical watches, electromechanical watches derive their power from a source of electricity rather than a mainspring. Despite this fundamental difference in energy supply, the way they measure time, which relies on a balance wheel or a metal tuning fork, is still mechanical.

BALANCE-DRIVEN ELECTRIC WATCH

The first research into electric watches dates back to the end of World War II. At the time, in the absence of a miniature, metal tuning fork (which would be invented and developed over the next few decades) efforts were concentrated on the creation of balance-driven electric watches. While the exploration of this technology gave rise to a range of different models, they all retained one common feature – a regulator similar to that found in traditional watches; that is, a balance wheel connected to a spiral spring that oscillated at a frequency around 3Hz.

What was new here was the way the movement was driven by the balance wheel through the addition of an electromagnet.

In a traditional mechanical movement, the balance wheel does no more than act as a regulator limiting the movement of the escape wheel; in a balance-driven electric movement, however, the balance plays the dual role of powering and triggering the entire mechanism. There are two kinds of balance-driven electric watch: those with moving coils and those with fixed coils.

FIXED COIL AND MOVING COIL

Moving coils (see page 22) were launched in 1957 by Hamilton. It produced watches featuring its calibre 500 in which the electromagnet was contiguous to the balance wheel; two wires mounted on the main plate made contact with brushes fixed to the balance, resulting in a current that passed through the coil and generated an attraction via a magnet mounted on the main plate. This created continuous motion. It did not take long for this new kind of engineering to attract the attention of other brands, starting with Russia's Slava, which copied the movement invented by Hamilton, and Timex, which built it into affordable electric watches.

The fixed coil was launched by LIP with its calibre R27 in 1958 (see page 18) and then by Ébauches SA in 1961, with the calibre L-4750 (see page 28). In these models, the electric circuit is made and broken in alternation (see illustration opposite), opening when the balance wheel, driven by the spiral spring, is in normal motion, but closing when the balance wheel arrives at a horizontal position and the plate to which it is attached displaces the contact wire. In this position, the assembly made up of the magnetic core and the balance form a circuit in which the coils act as electromagnets.

As a final touch, there is a diode that prevents any electric discharge of too violent a nature when the circuit is broken again.

THE TRANSISTOR

Whether using coils that were fixed or in motion, the movements of this first generation of electromechanical watches all suffered from the same major Achilles heel: the spark produced at the end of the contact wire with each alternation of the balance wheel entailed a high consumption of electricity, limiting the life of the batteries.

The second generation of fixed-coil movements overcame this flaw by eliminating mechanical contact. Instead, the magnet passed over the coils, inducing a very weak current that was amplified by a transistor. This crucial component had been invented at the end of the 1940s and, from 1954, was initially used in portable radio receivers before being adopted by other sectors such as clockmaking. Although the system had been used by LIP in its calibre R50, the invention of the balance-driven movement using a transistor is credited to Ébauches SA with its calibre ESA 9150, known as the Dynotron (see page 30).

EXPLODED VIEW OF A LANDERON L-4750 ELECTRIC MOVEMENT

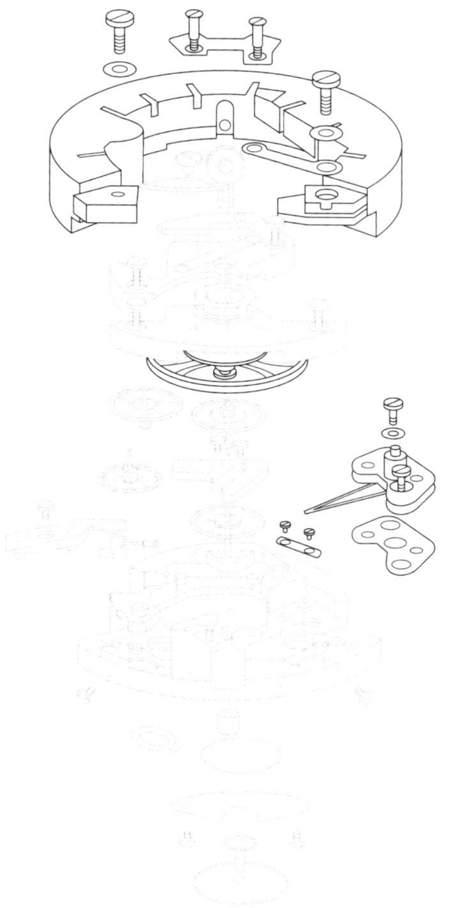

The electric parts of the movement are shown in bold. The other components are mechanical, so this was known as an electromechanical movement.

OPERATION OF A FIXED-COIL, BALANCE-DRIVEN ELECTRIC WATCH

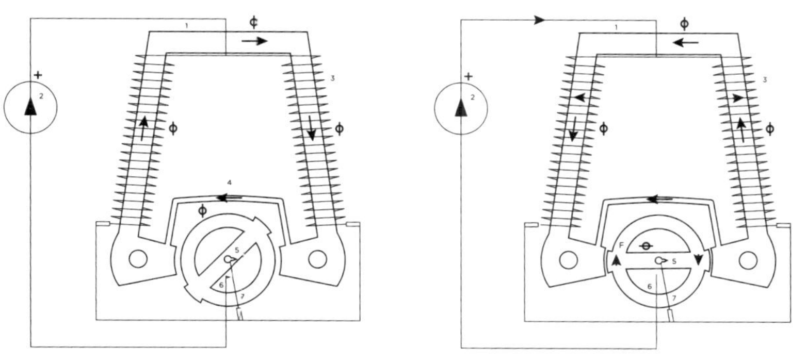

ELECTRIC CIRCUIT OPEN ELECTRIC CIRCUIT CLOSED

1 magnetic core 2 batteries 3 coil 4 permanent magnet
5 contact plate 6 contact finger 7 wire

ELECTRONIC R27

LIP – 1958

The first working prototype of the calibre R27 movement was unveiled in 1952. It was sold commercially from 1958 and was made popular by 'General de Gaulle' but was something of a misnomer – it was actually electromechanical.

MANUFACTURER	LIP

1. SEE OPPOSITE

YEAR	1954 MODEL
MODEL	NO NAME
CALIBRE	R27
MOVEMENT	ELECTROMECHANICAL
PRODUCTION	PROTOTYPE
MATERIAL	CHROMED BRASS
STRAP	N/A

2. SEE OVERLEAF

YEAR	1958 MODEL
MODEL	ELECTRONIC DE GAULLE
CALIBRE	R27
MOVEMENT	ELECTROMECHANICAL
PRODUCTION	SOLD COMMERCIALLY
MATERIAL	YELLOW GOLD
STRAP	LEATHER

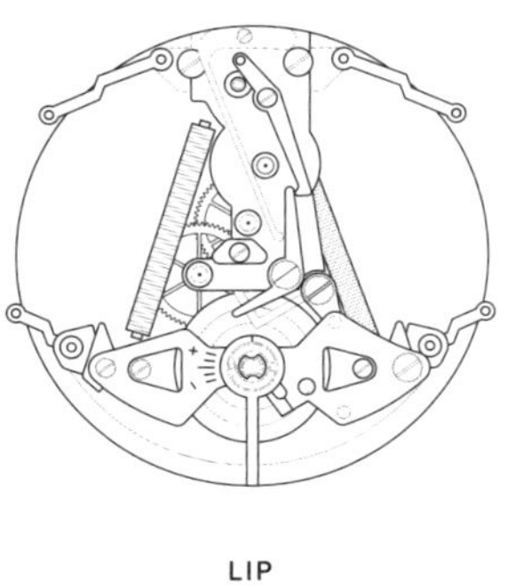

LIP
CALIBRE R27

First electric movement presented to the public. The electric circuit is closed when the bar-shaped balance wheel is in a horizontal position.

1952: THE FIRST ELECTRIC WRISTWATCH

Founded in Besançon in 1867, LIP is a French watchmaking manufacturer whose reputation is based on the mechanical watches and bold choices it has made over the years. Having gravitated towards electric power from the mid-1930s, it forged a partnership with the telecommunications firm Ericsson that gave rise to an electric desk clock with a mechanical escapement powered by an electric motor. Research and development for an electric wristwatch moved up a gear after World War II, but miniaturization remained a tough challenge as the batteries were so large and with insufficient voltage. LIP was aiming for a service life of a year and, to achieve this, the brand developed a hybrid mechanism (see page 16) in which the oscillation of the traditional spiral balance wheel was powered electrically. The initial (electric) part of the movement was made up of two fixed coils, a diode, an electric circuit and two batteries, while the other (mechanical) section featured the classic set-up of an escapement and a wheel train; the balance wheel served to link the two. While its competitors were still focusing on new automatic watches, LIP (in collaboration with Elgin in the United States) unveiled the world's first electric wristwatch on 19 March 1952.

1958: MARKET LAUNCH OF THE CALIBRE R27

The model presented in 1952 was still a prototype, however, and the design of the batteries and coils remained a tricky issue. A relentless research programme was continued, first led by Jean-Georges Laviolette and Paul Dargier de Saint-Vaulry, and then by Jean Pommier, under conditions of the strictest secrecy – the entrance to the laboratory was even kept under armed guard. The first electric watch to be made in Europe, incorporating the calibre R27 movement, was not launched until 1958. Elgin launched an electric version featuring the calibre 722 in the United States a year after the moving-coil Hamilton 500 (see page 22). The case for the LIP R27 was designed to be circular, with bean-shaped batteries, but was eventually adapted and extended to accommodate an adaptor with circular batteries that were more reliable than their predecessors. This was a highly appropriate stylistic quirk for a watch named Electronic even though, in reality, it was one of the first electromechanical watches.

ON THE WRIST OF CHARLES DE GAULLE

In 1958, the French president General Charles de Gaulle received two models of this watch directly from the hands of Fred Lip, the brand's visionary chairman; one to be worn and the second to be kept in the office so that the general always had the correct time to hand. The LIP R27 was also gifted to Dwight D Eisenhower, the president of the United States, joining the Rolex Day-Date and the Vulcain Cricket (see *Exceptional Watches*) in the elite ranks of US presidential watches. It should be noted that the 'General de Gaulle' model featured in the LIP collection at the time of publication is a reproduction of a 1970s model, not the 1958 version.

LIP
ELECTRONIC

LIP MODEL
SIMILAR TO THE GENERAL DE GAULLE MODEL

Fred Lip, the iconic chairman of the Besançon watchmaking firm LIP, presented one of these watches to General de Gaulle, and later to the his American counterpart, General Eisenhower.

ELECTRONIC
INCABLOC
PATENTS PENDING
21409

H500

HAMILTON – 1957

With its moving-coil, balance-driven movement, the Hamilton 500 was the first electric calibre to be sold commercially. Notably it was featured in the Ventura model created by the American designer Richard Arbib.

SEE OPPOSITE	1957 MODEL
MANUFACTURER	HAMILTON
MODEL	VENTURA
CALIBRE	H500
MOVEMENT	ELECTROMECHANICAL
PRODUCTION	SOLD COMMERCIALLY
MATERIAL	WHITE GOLD
STRAP	LEATHER

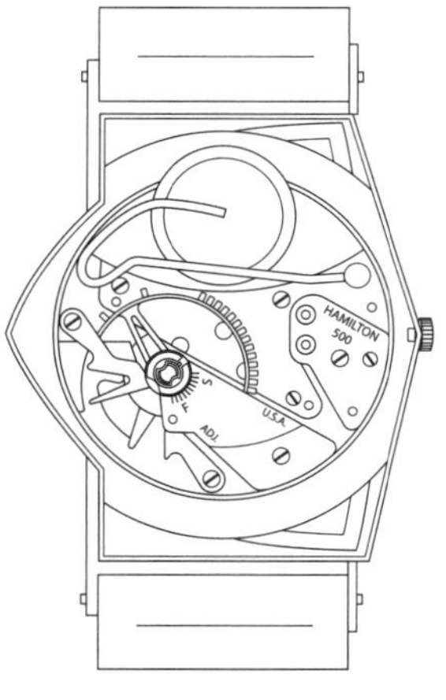

HAMILTON
CALIBRE H500

The first electric movement to be sold commercially. Two wires attached to the main plate are positioned to make contact with brushes mounted on the balance wheel.

DEVELOPING THE CALIBRE H500

Under the leadership of George Luckey, the Hamilton brand set about designing a moving-coil electromechanical watch (see page 16) in 1946. Of the two prototype versions constructed at this time, the company's management chose the one created by head physicist Philip E Biemiller and master technician James H Reese, which went by the name of Project X. A team was then formed around research director John Van Horn to build this watch, which was as revolutionary as it was complex. The principal technological challenge was essentially to find a battery suitable to supply the movement with electricity, and the brand turned to the National Carbon Company (now Energizer, and a global household name) to address this shortcoming. They nonetheless decided to produce all the components apart from the case in-house.

1957: COMMERCIAL LAUNCH OF THE FIRST ELECTRIC WATCH

After 11 years on the drawing board, Hamilton unveiled its creation on 3 January 1957 with much pomp and circumstance, including a press conference attended by more than 120 international journalists at the prestigious Savoy Plaza Hotel in New York City. Amazed by the electric timepiece that had been revealed to them, the reporters immediately dubbed it the 'watch of the future' – and rightly so, as the device amounted to no less than the greatest technological breakthrough in the field in centuries. Contemporary press reports even described it as the 'first improvement in watchmaking' in the 477 years of the craft's history (taking as their starting point the invention of the watch by Peter Henlein at the turn of the 16th century (a date that has since been called into question). This revolution was all the more radical as it managed to keep its promises; despite occasional recourse to the company's after-sales service, customers found that the Hamilton 500 worked well and it became a resounding commercial success.

RICHARD ARBIB AND ELVIS PRESLEY

More than 11,500 watches fitted with the calibre 500 were sold between 1957 and 1963, with both the innovative technology and the cutting-edge design of the Everest, Pacer and Ventura models appealing to fans. These had been dreamt up by the industrial designer Richard Arbib and were worn by A-list celebrities; the Ventura notably made an appearance on the wrist of Elvis Presley in the musical film *Blue Hawaii* (1961). Thirty-six years later, the electromechanical model passed the Hollywood baton on to the quartz version that was worn by the characters in the movie *Men in Black*.

HAMILTON
ELECTRIC
PAT. PENDING

PRÉ 475

ÉBAUCHES SA – 1954

Following its launch in 1952, the LIP R27 paved the way for electric watches. It inspired the Swiss to develop electromechanical movements of their own, and Ébauches SA led the field.

SEE OPPOSITE	1954 MODEL
MANUFACTURER	ÉBAUCHES SA
MODEL	NO NAME
CALIBRE	PRÉ 475
MOVEMENT	ELECTROMECHANICAL
PRODUCTION	PROTOTYPE
MATERIAL	BRASS
STRAP	LEATHER

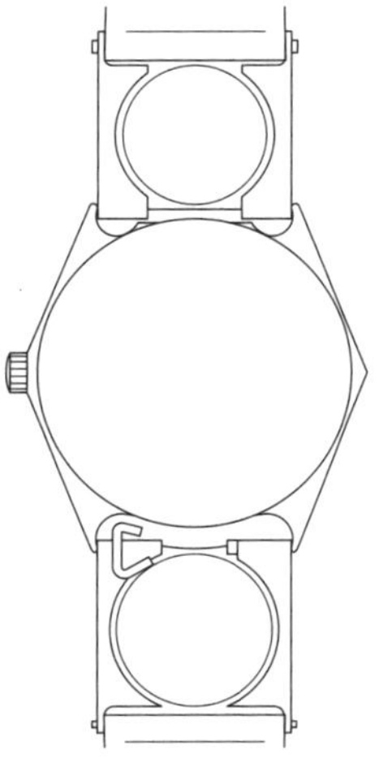

ÉBAUCHES SA
BATTERY-POWERED PRÉ 475

The earliest known Swiss electric watch with an electromechanical movement. The batteries are located on the strap, above and below the case.

ÉBAUCHES SA

The French term *ébauche* has a very particular meaning in watchmaking. It refers to the components that go to make up the movement of a watch, with or without jewels, but not including the regulating mechanism, mainspring, dial and hands. In 1927, a number of Swiss firms specializing in the manufacture of watch parts decided to join forces and found a holding company. Its name – Ébauches SA – was a fairly obvious choice. The conglomerate began pooling knowledge and, from the end of the 1940s, took an interest in electronics and semi-conductors, with the upshot that one of its divisions, Oscilloquartz, was even involved in creating large atomic clocks using caesium. This was enough to cement the reputation of Ébauches SA's mechanical parts, and the firm took an active interest in the development of electric wristwatches from the early 1950s.

THE OBJECTIVE: TO CREATE A SWISS ELECTRIC MOVEMENT

It must be said that its timing was propitious. France's LIP and the Elgin in the US had unveiled the world's first balance-driven electric wristwatch in 1952 (see page 16), and Max Hetzel had filed a patent in Switzerland for the Accutron a year later. This electric watch used a metal tuning fork instead of a balance wheel to regulate its mechanism (see page 34), but the system to be used in this future watch was still being developed by a research and development division in New York, the American bastion of watch manufacturing. This was not enough to satisfy Ébauches SA, whose aim was clear: the company had set its heart on developing the first electric movement of 100 per cent Swiss origin, little caring that other major Swiss manufacturers were fighting shy of the technology, considering it a diversion and, frankly, less than reliable. The pioneering spirits at Ébauches SA had an unshakable faith in the principle and set about creating a balance-driven electric watch that used fixed coils.

SWISS

ESA 475

ÉBAUCHES SA – 1958

Playing catch-up on the French and Americans, the Swiss unveiled their first electric movement in 1954 with a range from Ébauches SA that featured an electromechanical solution involving some rather original designs.

SEE OPPOSITE	1958 MODEL
MANUFACTURER	ÉBAUCHES SA
MODEL	MONTRE A COUILLES ('WATCH WITH BALLS')
CALIBRE	ESA 475
MOVEMENT	ELECTROMECHANICAL
PRODUCTION	PROTOTYPE
MATERIAL	BRASS
STRAP	N/A

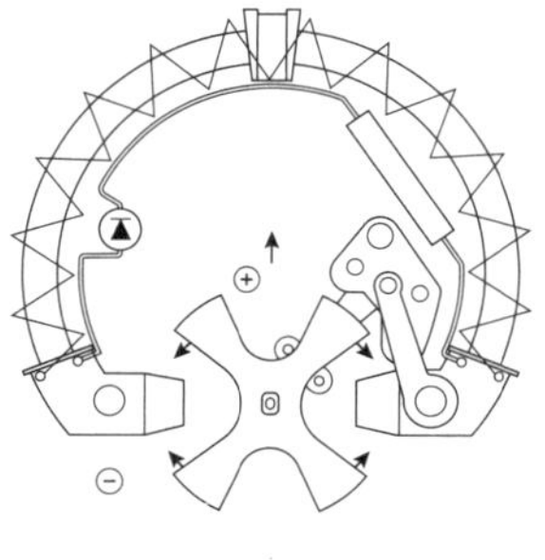

ÉBAUCHES SA
CALIBRE ESA 475

Here, the batteries are located to the left of the case. The operating principle is similar to that of the R27, but with a cruciform balance wheel.

INSPIRED RESEARCH

When research for this movement began in 1952, the spec sheet was unambiguous. The developers wanted and needed to create a watch at a price point less than or equal to that of an automatic watch – but with satisfactory timekeeping. The research, led by André Beyner and René Besson, was conducted in collaboration with Landeron, a subsidiary of Ébauches SA. After an exploratory phase lasting a year, the project presented viable prototypes that, both mechanically and in appearance, were closely similar to those produced by LIP. However, the look that the Swiss researchers eventually settled on was unexpected in both the differences it introduced and the reaction it elicited.

SURPRISING ELECTROMECHANICAL SOLUTIONS

Despite their similarities, these watches embodied an originality of design that bordered on the eccentric. The electric circuits and the battery that replaced the mainspring as the energy source ensured the regular oscillation of the balance wheel by mechanical means, which entailed a surprising choice of location for the batteries. While an electromechanical movement does not require any great changes to the calibre, the batteries do have to go somewhere, and the cells of the time were as large as they were low-voltage.

The solution chosen by the engineers was to site the batteries outside the case. In the first-generation prototypes, they were built into the strap, as LIP had also intended. In other versions, the batteries were located on the side of the case, giving the whole thing a shape that was anatomically somewhat suggestive and inspired a vulgar but amusing nickname among collectors, who called them *montres à couilles*, or 'watches with balls'. Other – more discreet – versions featured a solution that included a rechargeable cell (manufactured by Leclanché) built into the back of the case rather than the side array.

ELECTRIC
475
B
SWISS MADE

ELECTRO-CHRON

WITTNAUER-LONGINES – 1961

After years of research, the first electric movement of Swiss origin was finally brought to market as the calibre L-4750. It was built into models by a number of different brands, including Wittnauer.

SEE OPPOSITE	1961 MODEL
MANUFACTURER	WITTNAUER-LONGINES
MODEL	ELECTRO-CHRON 'ELECTRIC'
CALIBRE	L-4750
MOVEMENT	ELECTROMECHANICAL
PRODUCTION	SOLD COMMERCIALLY
MATERIAL	STEEL
STRAP	N/A

FIRST COMMERCIAL SALES

1957 HAMILTON 500 (USA)

1961 L-4750 (SWITZERLAND)

DESIGNING AND MARKETING THE L-4750

In the quest for the first electric movement of Swiss origin, Landeron produced a succession of prototypes under the supervision of André Beyner and René Besson. This division of Ébauches SA eventually filed its first patent (CH345611) on 27 March 1959. This was followed by a second (CH346828), granted on 20 April 1960. Both were inspired by the same ambition – to present the first electric watches of 100 per cent Swiss origin at the Basel trade fair, which opened its doors on 15 April 1961.

The L-4750 electromechanical movement featured a balance wheel that was both a regulator and a motor. The power to drive the movement of such a calibre can come from two different sources: a battery or a rechargeable cell. Unlike the prototypes that preceded it, the L-4750 featured batteries that were built into part of the case, a feat made possible only by the use of miniature batteries, manufactured by Leclanché and housed in a sealed compartment.

THE WITTNAUER ELECTRO-CHRON

Many brands, including Arsa, Angelus, Blancpain, Camy, Dulux, Enicar, Invicta, Leonidas, Mira, Reusser, Schild, Sandoz and Silvana, presented electric watches equipped with the L-4750 at the famous Basel trade fair, but one brand in particular stood out from this panoply of offerings: the Wittnauer-Longines Electro-Chron. It initially featured the word 'Electric' on its dial but this was soon replaced by another inscription, 'Electro-Chron'. The name was more modern and more technophile, but this was merely a detail; it was the lightning-shaped hands and the overall design that caught the attention of the journalists of the day. And so, in the wake of its French (LIP, see page 18) and US (Hamilton and Bulova) competitors (see pages 22 and 34), the story of the first Swiss electric watch began. This tale was unfortunately brought to an abrupt end by the appearance of quartz technology on the market but, though a relic of a bygone era, the Electro-Chron is still much sought-after by collectors.

WITTNAUER
ELECTRIC

DYNOTRON

ÉBAUCHES SA – 1967

The innovative calibre 9150 created by Ébauches SA featured a transistor and was available until the rise of digital technology.

SEE OPPOSITE	1967 MODEL
MANUFACTURER	ÉBAUCHES SA
MODEL	DYNOTRON
CALIBRE	ESA 9150
MOVEMENT	ELECTROMECHANICAL, TRANSISTOR
PRODUCTION	PROTOTYPE
MATERIAL	YELLOW GOLD
STRAP	N/A

ÉBAUCHES SA
CALIBRE ESA 9150 DYNOTRON

The energy source consists of a miniature battery that delivers a stable voltage. The electric current generated by the battery is supplied via an electric circuit featuring a transistor.

THE INTRODUCTION OF TRANSISTORS

The story of the transistor begins even earlier than its introduction in 1961, the year in which some fifteen different brands (see page 28) brought the Ébauches SA (ESA) L-4750 movement to market. For its inventors, André Beyner and René Besson, the magnitude of this success was matched only by its ephemerality. However, fierce competition from brands such as LIP (see page 18) essentially forced the Swiss firm to abandon the first electromechanical calibres it had created. It was obliged to take a longer view – and invent the future itself. At the time, the future went by the name 'transistor', a term both workmanlike yet oddly poetic for a small invention that was to usher in a new era of calibres thanks to its ability to amplify electric current. After six years of research and development, the technology was installed in the calibre 9150 Dynotron, the first Swiss commercial balance-driven movement to use a transistor. It was also the first in history to sport the ESA logo on the main plates of its movements.

MECHANISM AND PRODUCTION

Like many of its predecessors, the calibre 9150 Dynotron used a fixed-coil, balance-driven movement, although the magnet that is part of its balance wheel avoids any mechanical contact. As it passes the coils, it induces a current in them that is amplified by the transistor. The movement was in production until the 1970s, and found ever greater popularity in wristwatches for women as mechanisms became more and more compact.

THE CUTTING EDGE OF DIGITAL TECHNOLOGY

In addition to these versions for women, the calibre 9150 Dynotron was available in a number of different variants (including ESA 9154, ESA 9157 and ESA 9158), three of which are of particular note. First, there was the calibre ESA 9159 with which the brand Gruen marketed a jumping-hour watch. Even more astonishingly, there was the Certina Biostar, the calibre ESA 9156, which displayed the daily biorythms of the wearer, a global first at the time. Finally, there was the direct display electronic watch incorporating the calibre 9176 used in the Swissonic model; although functionally electromechanical, this watch featured an entirely digital read-out (see page 141).

dynotron
29
SWISS MADE LIC ATO

THE TUNING FORK

FACT SHEET N°2

The electric tuning fork watch invented by the Swiss engineer Max Hetzel in the 1950s was a watershed in the history of watchmaking, as this high-frequency mechanism achieved the singular feat of eliminating the balance wheel.

MAX HETZEL'S INVENTION

Max Hetzel was an inventor to the core. Born in Basel in 1921 and educated in the physics department of ETH in Zurich, he went on to join the Biel branch of the Bulova company in 1950 and was then appointed head of research. His ambition was nothing less than to revolutionize watchmaking, and he explored many different avenues over the years, trying to make a breakthrough and filing some 20 patents. Nonetheless, the scepticism he encountered from the Swiss watchmaking industry eventually forced him into exile in the United States and it was here, in a land so deeply in love with inventors, that he was to make his mark.

The work he did after his promotion to the role of head physicist at the Bulova Watch Company in New York unleashed a watchmaking revolution. On 25 October 1960, the brand unveiled the first electric tuning-fork movement, the calibre 214, which featured in the Bulova Accutron (see page 34), a name created by combining ACCUracy and ElecTRONic. Instead of a balance wheel, this innovative movement used a metal tuning fork controlled by a transistor.

MECHANISM

The resonator in this type of watch was no longer a balance wheel, but a 24.85mm-long metal tuning fork that vibrated at a preset frequency of 360Hz. With each pulse, a built-in ratchet moved a notched index wheel 3.54mm in diameter. The 300-tooth wheel completed 1.2 rotations every second, which was enough to guarantee significantly greater precision than any mechanical watch, with a maximum mean variation rate of about +/- one minute per month.

REVOLUTIONARY – IF SHORT-LIVED – SUCCESS

The story of Max Hetzel did not, however, stop there. In 1963, he left Bulova to become head of the LSRH watchmaking research laboratory in Neuchâtel in Switzerland, which was working in close collaboration with the Centre Électronique Horloger (CEH). Spurred on by his experience and innovative imagination, he went on to file four patents and create the CEH-Swissonic, a variant of his tuning-fork watch for the Swiss market that ultimately never went into production. Hetzel took an increasingly active role in research between 1966 and 1969, and was more or less directly involved in the development of innovative movements.

In 1969, he was appointed CEO of Elresor SA, a subsidiary of Omega, and led its development and manufacturing divisions, from which he filed eight patents and oversaw the design of the Omega Megasonic 720Hz diapason watch (see page 98). Despite these undeniable successes, some of his inventions would be eclipsed by the commercial launch of the Seiko Astron in 1969 (see page 64).

DIAPASON WATCH COMPONENTS

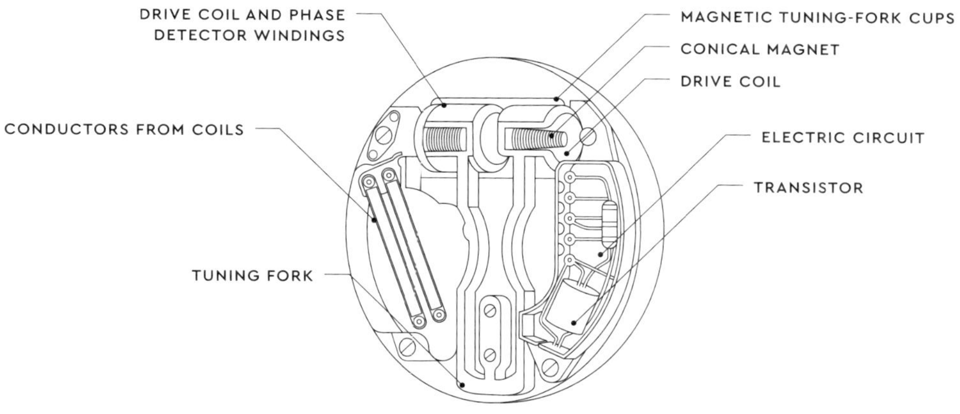

DIAL SIDE

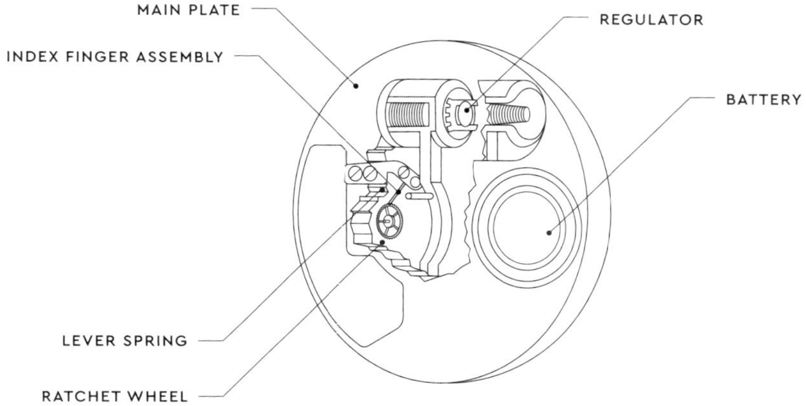

REVERSE

ELECTRIC DIAPASON WATCH MECHANISM

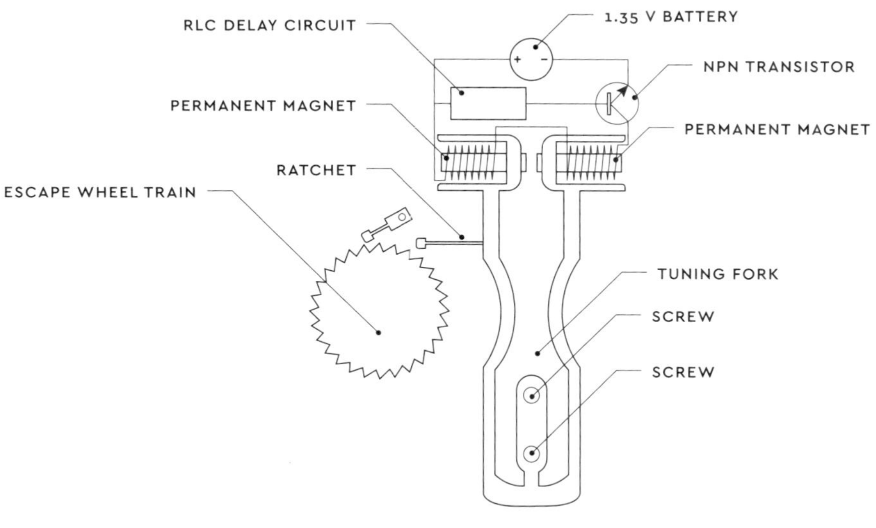

ACCUTRON

BULOVA - 1960

When the Accutron was unveiled in 1960, it represented the second generation of electric watches. The movement was fitted with a metal tuning fork rather than a balance wheel, and benefited from the considerable improvement in accuracy that this major advance brought with it.

SEE OPPOSITE	1960 MODEL
MANUFACTURER	BULOVA
MODEL	ACCUTRON
CALIBRE	214
MOVEMENT	TUNING FORK
PRODUCTION	SOLD COMMERCIALLY
MATERIAL	STEEL/YELLOW GOLD
STRAP	N/A

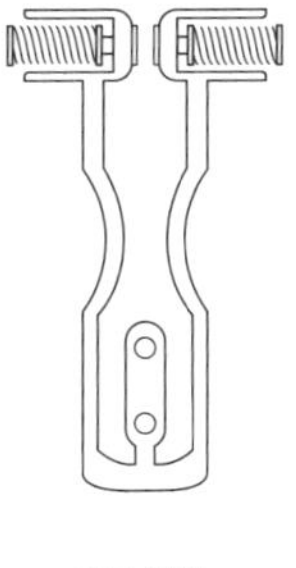

BULOVA
DIAPASON

The tuning fork is 24.85mm in size and vibrates at 360Hz, a frequency far higher than that of a traditional balance wheel.

THE SECOND GENERATION OF ELECTRIC WATCHES

Switzerland's watchmaking industry saw its predominance under threat in the wake of World War II, as more adventurous brands like LIP in France and Hamilton in the United States introduced their innovations. So much so that, when these companies announced their battery-powered watch in 1952, the Swiss took it as a personal insult – although this did not prevent them from working on similar developments. Such watches used batteries and coils (both fixed and moving) to transfer energy but retained the balance wheel used in mechanical watches.

The first generations of these Hamilton and LIP models did not, however, live up to their initial promise. The spark generated by each and every movement of the balance wheel caused their energy consumption to skyrocket, drastically reducing the lifespan of the battery – and while the overall power reserve may nonetheless have been boosted, it did nothing for accuracy.

BULOVA AND MAX HETZEL

In 1950, Bulova recruited the engineer Max Hetzel to automate its Swiss manufacturing and then conduct a feasibility study for an electric watch. Having been appointed head of the Accutron programme, he constructed a prototype using a block of wood into which he built the first low-voltage germanium transistor. The Raytheon CK722, which had recently appeared on the American market, increased the accuracy of the movement. The balance wheel was replaced with a tuning fork located beside the transistor, and this small metal part (consisting of two parallel arms soldered to form a U-shape extended with a rod magnet) vibrated at 360Hz, a frequency greater than that achieved by a traditional balance wheel.

MARKETING

The first working prototype appeared in 1954, before the final version of the calibre 214 was delivered by William O Bennett, another American engineer working at Bulova, in 1959. The first tuning-fork movement was launched in the revolutionary Accutron on 25 October 1960.

These watches were sold from 1961 and enjoyed considerable success until the 1970s (with 350,000 sales in 1965). The Spaceview model (famed for the absence of a dial, thereby exposing the action of its tuning fork and electric components) was to become particularly popular, so much so that most owners converted their models by removing the dials (see page 36). Bulova even became a supplier to NASA for clocks on board space missions. During the Faith 7 mission in 1963, one of these even saved astronaut Gordon Cooper, who experienced an electrical problem on board his capsule. He used his Accutron 'Astronaut' model to time reignition of the engines for his return to Earth. The original tuning-fork Accutron was nonetheless forced off the market by the advent of a quartz movement built into an updated Accutron version.

ACCUTRON

BULOVA

CALIBRE 214 ACCUTRON

In later years, the cutting-edge design and aesthetics of the mechanism have prompted many owners to remove the dials of these watches to enable them to fully admire the movement.

ROLEX S.A.
GENEVA
SWISS
155V
11
ELEVEN
JEWELS
5035
ADJUSTED
TEMPERATURE
+
−

SWISS QUARTZ

CHAPTER 2

THE DEVELOPMENT OF QUARTZ MOVEMENTS

SWISS QUARTZ

THE DEVELOPMENT OF QUARTZ MOVEMENTS

As Japanese watchmaking gained ground during the 1950s, the first electric watches appeared in various markets. The Centre Électronique Horloger (CEH) was founded in Switzerland in 1962 and gradually recognized the revolutionary potential of quartz for watchmaking.

A STIMULATING ENVIRONMENT

The 1950s proved to be a decisive crossroads in the history of the Swiss watchmaking industry – a time when innovative technologies revolutionized both energy reserves and balance wheels and disrupted the sales of traditional mechanical watches. France's LIP (see page 18) and America's Hamilton (see page 22) had even announced the bold possibility of substituting tiny electric batteries for the usual mechanical main springs. Spurred on – cut to the quick, even – by these strange ideas, the Swiss Ébauches SA (see page 24) enthusiastically threw itself into the development of an electric movement of its own.

THE THREAT FROM JAPAN

The rivalry between manufacturers from Switzerland and its competitor countries did not begin with the arrival of electric watches. In Japan, it was part of a broader historical narrative that described the emergence of the industry at the end of the 19th century. After decades spent slowly building up a skill base, the Japanese companies Hattori Seiko Co. and Citizen Watch Co. (see page 103) managed to establish themselves as competitors on the global market. The quest for accuracy was the main source of competition between watchmakers in a country where electronics had been recognized as an issue of major importance since the 1950s, and Japanese thinking was that mastery of this technology would allow them to outdo the Swiss. A decade later, when the electronic quartz watch was still in its infancy, the output of Japan's watchmaking manufacturers amounted to 24 per cent of that of its Swiss competitors.

THE CRUSADE OF THE CENTRE ÉLECTRONIQUE HORLOGER

To counter such competition, in 1959 Switzerland's Fédération Horlogère (FH) watchmaking association mandated its president Gérard Bauer – who was neither a watchmaker nor an engineer – to set up a structure capable of technologically and commercially developing an electronic Swiss watch. To achieve this, he enlisted the help of Roger Wellinger, who came directly from General Electric Company, and recruited Swiss engineers from the United States and the technical school attached to Lausanne University. These were all driven by an unshakable motivation that was only compounded by the launch of the Accutron by the American company Bulova (see page 34): an electric watch based on a metal tuning-fork resonator that had been invented by Max Hetzel, a native of Basel (see page 32).

The Centre Électronique Horloger (CEH) was officially created on 30 January 1962, after Gérard Bauer convinced some 20 or so Swiss manufacturers (including Ébauches SA) to pool their resources. Their mission was simple: to 'develop an electric wristwatch with at least one advantage over existing electric watches'. And they worked in the greatest secrecy. Two main wristwatch projects emerged from the crowd in 1964. The first, known as Alpha and led by Heinz Waldburger, used a metal tuning fork shaped like the number '8'. Project Beta, under the aegis of Max Forrer, also plumped for a metal tuning fork but decided to couple it with a series of electronic frequency dividers driving a stepping motor. The second hand did not move in a smooth fashion but jumped, which gave rise to its famous tick-tock sound. Neither of these was to see the light of day, but elements of project Beta were incorporated into the later quartz movement developed through the efforts of two CEH employees, Armin Frei and Rolf Lochinger (see page 42). Despite initial scepticism from the board, its director Roger Wellinger announced on 26 November 1965 that a quartz wristwatch would now be the group's main aim. A crucial moment in the history of Swiss watchmaking was in the offing.

BETA 21

FACT SHEET N°3

The Beta 21 was born of the determination of a group of men of vision and arose from numerous experiments carried out in succession in the 1960s. It was the first quartz movement watch to be produced on an industrial scale by the CEH, a consortium of Swiss watchmakers.

BETA 1: THE FIRST QUARTZ MOVEMENT

On 7 May 1965, Armin Frei and Rolf Lochinger – two of the boffins behind the CEH – unveiled a hare-brained scheme involving the adoption of a quartz oscillator linked to an electronic frequency divider system that recalled Max Forrer's Beta project (see page 41). In 1967, after two years of research, the Beta 1, the very first quartz movement, made its debut – a feat of ingenuity that was achieved using a quartz crystal vibrating at 8,192Hz. The energy running through a binary electronic circuit ultimately produced an oscillation rate of 0.5Hz, or one beat every two seconds. Each half-oscillation fired a 60-position stepping motor that moved the hand once a second, creating the symphony of the famous tick-tock. This was later to become the very heart of the quartz watch. A first prototype, the CEH 1020, was unveiled in July 1967 thanks to the efforts of two CEH engineers, Jean Hermann and François Niklès. A month later, the Beta 1 movement, nestling in its square case, set off to do battle in the arena of the Neuchâtel Observatory International Chronometer Competition. It is considered to be the first fully functional quartz wristwatch.

BETA 2: AN ALTERNATIVE PROJECT

However, the Beta 1 movement suffered from one fatal flaw: its batteries had too short a lifespan. Its successor, the Beta 2, used a five-stage frequency reduction process that drove a motor vibrating at 256Hz, rather like a tuning-fork movement. This resulted in a smoothly sweeping second hand like that in the Accutron. The technology also improved energy efficiency, extending the battery life to more than a year. The prototype Beta 2 appeared in August 1967 (less than a month after the advent of Beta 1) under the guidance of Max Forrer, who was in no doubt about the advantages of the tuning-fork system (see page 32).

1967: CHRONOMETER COMPETITION

The Beta 1 was too energy-hungry to be produced commercially, but nonetheless swept the board in the tests carried out by the Neuchâtel Observatory in 1967, achieving a timekeeping accuracy of 0.189 (with 0 indicating absolute exactitude) and leaving all its competitors in the shade (in particular, the ubiquitous Bulova Accutron, see page 34). The nine other first places were also taken by CEH quartz watches, while the four showcased by Seiko appeared in the top fifteen.

MARKETING THE BETA 21

Nine months after Longines announced its Ultra-Quartz (see page 66) and four months after the launch of the Seiko Astron (see page 64), which employed a stepping movement similar to that used in the Beta 1 project, the Beta 21 movement was unveiled. The launch happened under a range of different brands at the Basel trade fair on 10 April 1970. A quartz crystal vibrating at 8,192Hz deftly marshalled a total of 110 electronic components that were all contained on a chip less than 2mm thick, a considerable feat of technique and technology for the time. Its originality lay in the use of a motor vibrating at 256Hz, inherited from the Beta 2, which ensured the second hand executed a sweep rather than a tick-tock motion (a sequence broken up into seconds). This was thought to achieve the best of both worlds for an electronic quartz watch. At the heart of this breakthrough was both the Beta 21's use of a control circuit that was used to maintain and drive the quartz resonator, and a counting circuit that played the crucial role of frequency divider. However, only 6,000 Beta 21 movements were produced before the Swiss industry turned its back on the notion of joint manufacturing. Behind the scenes, watchmaking companies had begun to take steps to create quartz movements of their own.

THE BETA 21 MECHANISM

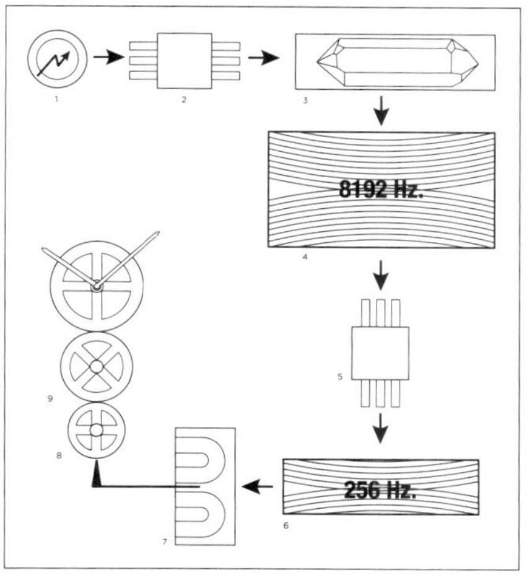

ENERGY TRANSMISSION

A 1.35-volt battery [1] powers the circuit maintaining the quartz [2] and causes the quartz crystal [3] to vibrate at 8,192 Hz [4]. The frequency divider [5] reduces this frequency to 256Hz [6] for the vibration motor [7]. This uses a ratchet [8] to engage the wheel train [9].

VIEW OF THE MAIN PLATE

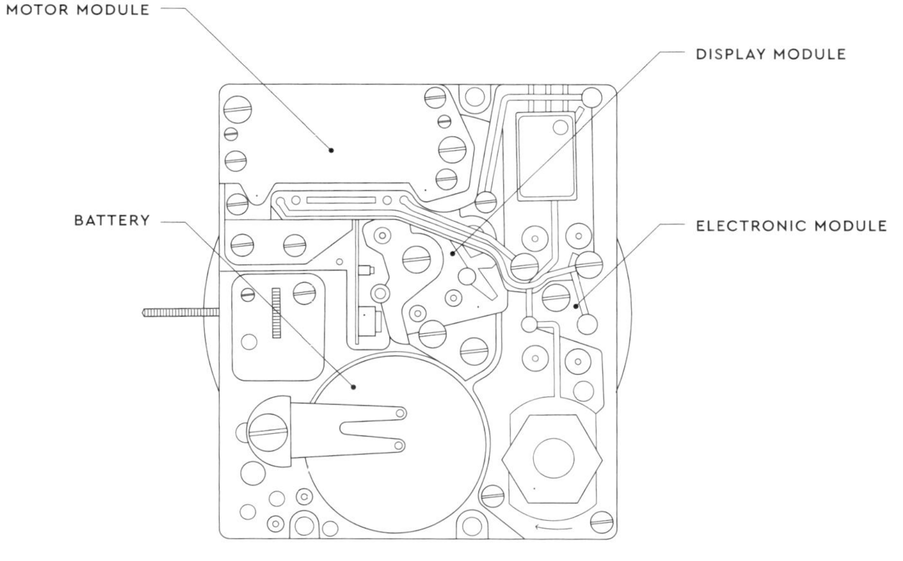

The Beta 21, officially unveiled at the Basel trade fair on 10 April 1970, was a large, thick watch movement with a strikingly original mechanism. Instead of using a traditional quartz stepping motor, it featured a vibration motor similar to a tuning fork.

PROTOTYPE BETA 21

CEH – 1969

On 15 February 1968, the Neuchâtel Observatory published the results of the tests it had carried out on the Beta 1 and Beta 2 the previous year. They were sufficiently exceptional to prompt genuine celebrations and to kickstart research to convert the technology used in the prototypes into an industrial product.

SEE OPPOSITE	1969 MODEL
MANUFACTURER	CEH
MODEL	BETA 21
CALIBRE	BETA 21
MOVEMENT	QUARTZ
PRODUCTION	PROTOTYPE
MATERIAL	NICKEL-PLATED BRASS
STRAP	N/A

BETA 21 TIMELINE

MAY 1965	RESEARCH BEGINS
JULY 1967	BETA 1
AUGUST 1967	BETA 2
APRIL 1970	LAUNCH OF THE BETA 21

BETA 2.1

The tests carried out by Neuchâtel Observatory were unambiguous, and the conclusions reached by Henri Oguey and Henri Schneider, engineers at the CEH, were equally clear: 'In light of the experience acquired through the prototypes, only the Beta 2 system was considered to guarantee battery life greater than a year'. The Beta 21 (actually called the Beta 2.1) was its direct successor and, having inherited its 256-Hz vibration motor, the movement pulsed harmoniously thanks to a quartz crystal vibrating at 8,192Hz, precisely coordinating 110 electronic components that are all neatly contained on a chip less than 2mm thick.

A MOVEMENT REIMAGINED

The Beta 21 was not merely a successor to the Beta 2; it was also a reinvention, designed by CEH engineers in the face of the realities of industrial production. Unlike its predecessor, the Beta 21 contained two refined integrated circuits: a control system in charge of managing the quartz and feeding the quartz resonator, and a counting system that played the crucial role of frequency divider. A quickset date complication – considered essential for a luxury quartz watch by some members of the CEH – was even added to the spec sheet of the new prototypes. While a little basic by current standards, the design of the movement was a real feat for its time.

PROTOTYPES PRECEDING INDUSTRIAL PRODUCTION

The first murmurings of the calibre Beta 21 emerged from the bowels of the CEH in the summer of 1969, although the components were constructed using adapted tools while the laboratory waited for new machinery. The watches themselves were assembled by hand. The movements were enclosed in nickel-plated brass cases with an acrylic caseback, but were not all identical: some of the prototypes had a date function, others had none. These experimental creations also made it possible to address the unresolved shortcomings of the Beta 1 and Beta 2 versions, such as the sensitivity of quartz to knocks and bumps during daily use. In so doing, the prototypes were submitted to newly introduced dynamic testing by the CEH and the Neuchâtel Observatory, and were assessed by the engineers who proudly wore them on their wrists.

Release of the movement was initially intended for the end of 1969, but was postponed for a few months because of major production challenges. The movements had run into significant snagging problems, from manufacture of the movement itself to assembly issues. However, a batch of 6,000 units eventually saw the light of day, beginning on 10 April 1970 for the Basel trade fair – four months after Seiko's Astron 35SQ. Only a handful of Swiss firms, all of which were leading members of the CEH, went on to launch watches incorporating the prestigious calibre Beta 21.

CEH
SWISS MADE
CEH - SWISS - 321
CEH
ODC04

ACCUQUARTZ

BULOVA – 1970

In the vast range of Accuquartz watches sold by Bulova before 1976, one yellow-gold model stood out from the others – because it featured the famous calibre Beta 21.

SEE OPPOSITE	1970 MODEL
MANUFACTURER	BULOVA
MODEL	ACCUQUARTZ
CALIBRE	BETA 21
MOVEMENT	QUARTZ
PRODUCTION	SOLD COMMERCIALLY
MATERIAL	YELLOW GOLD
STRAP	LEATHER

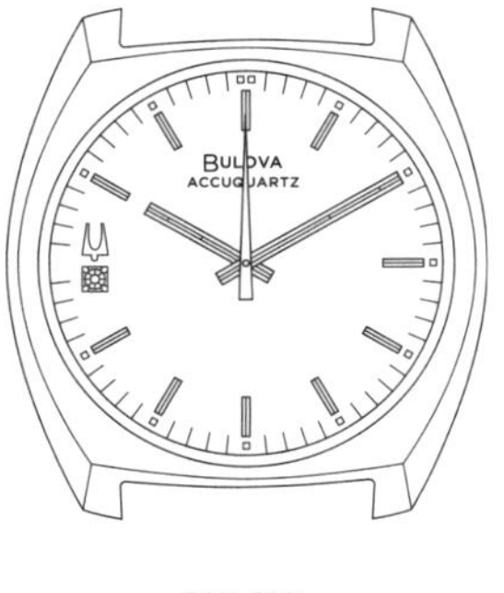

BULOVA
ACCUQUARTZ CAL. 224

The classic Accuquartz movement was created by combining a tuning fork and a 32-kHz quartz regulator.

A THREAT TO TUNING FORKS

Bulova found success in the 1960s with the Accutron, and thanks to its tuning-fork movement (see page 32), the company soon achieved a commanding position within the industry, selling millions of watches equipped with this revolutionary innovation. It was so successful that it even acquired its Swiss rival, Universal Genève, to further boost sales. However, the supremacy of the tuning fork as the most accurate movement on the market was soon to be undermined by the advent of quartz movements, which represented a serious threat to the brand.

ACCUQUARTZ BETA 21

The name Accuquartz was first given to a hybrid quartz/tuning-fork desk clock in 1969, heralding the dawn of an era of innovation. This clock movement used a quartz crystal as a cybernetic control unit for a tuning fork, the precise vibrations of which drove the wheel train by means of a ratchet, much in line with the Accutron movement launched nine years previously. A year later (1970), the members of the Beta 21 group at the CEH brought a series of quartz wristwatches to market that were all powered by this revolutionary movement; they included an Accuquartz model made by Bulova. Despite its name, the watch used a CEH Beta 21 movement rather than the new system that combined quartz with a tuning fork. There were two aspects that made it stand out: its imposing size, which was typical of watches equipped with the Beta 21, and the choice of a chunky but elegant rectangular yellow-gold case. Such accuracy and sophistication came at a price that was considerable for the time: $1,325.

USE OF THE BETA 21 COMES TO AN END

Bulova finally unveiled its production Accuquartz watch at the end of 1971. To create this, the company had bidden farewell to the Beta 21 and partnered the Accutron calibre with a 32-kHz quartz regulator to create a cybernetic system. In so doing, it had undoubtedly drawn inspiration from what Longines had achieved with its 1969 Ultra-Quartz model (see page 66); the tuning fork drove the mechanical components while the quartz crystal guaranteed accuracy. This kind of quartz-regulated Accutron movement could be mass-produced, and also made the Accuquartz more affordable (in fact, when it was launched the retail price was a far more accessible $395). The cunning design also allowed Bulova to create a thinner watch that outperformed the oversized quartz movements produced by other companies. A year later, the Accuquartz would be on sale for $250, less than half the price of some competitor quartz movements. Until 1972, it was also the only quartz watch available in the United States. In November 1974, Bulova introduced a digital watch with an LED display (see page 143) under the Accuquartz brand. Whatever the name might suggest, this was a modern integrated circuit movement with no tuning fork. Before the range was withdrawn completely in 1976, Bulova had expanded its collection with no fewer than 25 Accuquartz models.

BULOVA
ACCUQUARTZ
14

DA VINCI

IWC – 1970

The saga of IWC's Da Vinci collection began with a world first – the launch of the first model in the range to proudly sport the calibre Beta 21.

SEE OPPOSITE	1970 MODEL
MANUFACTURER	IWC
MODEL	DA VINCI 3501
CALIBRE	BETA 21
MOVEMENT	QUARTZ
PRODUCTION	SOLD COMMERCIALLY
MATERIAL	WHITE GOLD
BRACELET	INTEGRATED

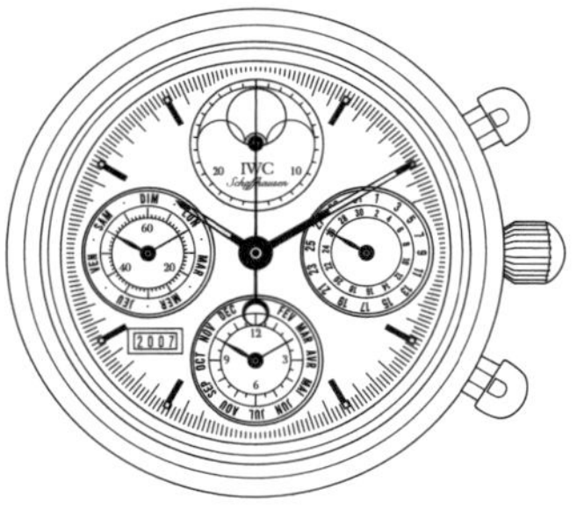

IWC
DA VINCI QP

This perpetual calendar chronograph launched in 1985 was invented by Kurt Klaus and used only 81 parts, propelling the Schaffhausen manufacturer to the pinnacle of high-end watchmaking.

THE DA VINCI COLLECTION: BEAUTY AND INNOVATION

The International Watch Company (better known under the abbreviation IWC) is a watch manufacturer based in Schaffhausen, Switzerland, that contributed to the development of the Beta 21, the very first Swiss quartz movement released in 1970. This innovative movement was incorporated into the first generation of a line the company called Da Vinci. With its reference to the most famous artist and inventor in human history, the name of the range symbolizes both beauty and technological innovation, and although the collection mostly owes it fame to the legendary perpetual calendar designed by Kurt Klaus, its inaugural model was also worthy of note for its incorporation of the famed Beta 21 quartz movement.

REFERENCE 3501: BREATHTAKING FUTURISM

The Beta 21 made its remarkable debut in the world of watchmaking in 1970, notably in the first Da Vinci. Listed as reference 3501, the watch movement was enclosed in an eye-catching and imposing hexagonal gold case. David Seyffer, the curator of the IWC Museum, speaks of it in glowing terms: 'This major achievement marks the birth of a watchmaking range that has no equal in combining the inventiveness and creativity of the engineers at IWC with a highly advanced aesthetic sensibility.' The first Da Vinci, which was available in a yellow or white gold version before being made in steel, elicited considerable amazement with its astonishing futurism and technological appearance, perfectly matching the spirit of the 1970s.

A QUARTZ WATCH OF GENUINE LUXURY

Other leading watchmakers such as Rolex and Patek Philippe (who were also members of the CEH consortium) also saw fit to launch creations showcasing the Beta 21 (see pages 54 and 60). The IWC Da Vinci Beta 21 should not be thought inferior in quality to these top-of-the-range models. There was no doubt that the reference 3501, which boasted a gold case with an integrated strap, generous proportions and dials finished in shades that ranged from champagne to sky blue, could hold its head high as a luxury quartz watch.

International Watch Co
SCHAFFHAUSEN
QUARTZ ELECTRONIC
Da Vinci
SWISS

ELECTROQUARTZ

OMEGA – 1970

Omega caused a sensation at the 1970 Basel trade fair when it revealed its Beta 21 model. The calibre 1300, which was housed in a case that soon acquired the evocative nickname 'Pupitre' (or 'writing desk') had caught every eye and put its competitors in the shade even before it was refined for larger-scale production.

SEE OPPOSITE	1970 MODEL
MANUFACTURER	OMEGA
MODEL	'PUPITRE'
CALIBRE	BETA 21
MOVEMENT	QUARTZ
PRODUCTION	UNIQUE PIECE
MATERIAL	STEEL
STRAP	N/A

A 'DESK' AT THE BASEL TRADE FAIR

Although some 20 watchmaking companies were initially involved in the development of the Beta 21 movement via the Centre Électronique Horloger (CEH), not all of them progressed to the production stage, and many failed to present a watch at the 1970 Basel trade fair. The Omega brand did make a showing (with its calibre 1300), however, with a model that made its debut under the name Electroquartz. The case design in particular stood out, as it was wider at the top than the bottom, earning it the appropriate nickname 'Pupitre', meaning 'writing desk'. Five examples in 18-carat gold with an integrated strap were on display at the fair in what was to be a notable year in the industry, and they all sold. They were arranged in a line, each showing the same time, to demonstrate their extreme accuracy.

WIDESPREAD USE OF THE BETA 21

The Electroquartz hit the retail market sometime after the fair, first in 18-carat gold, then in stainless steel, and as models that were proud recreations of the famous 'Pupitre' design. Some 6,000 Beta 21 movements were produced between 1970 and 1972, with Omega standing out as the brand that produced and used the greatest number (2,487, of which 1,850 were incorporated into models stamped with its prestigious logo). The Beta 21 later underwent some alterations, such as the adoption of a thinner battery and the addition of new, more advanced, regulating systems.

THE EVOLUTION OF LUXURY QUARTZ

This second generation of the calibre Beta 21 was dubbed the Beta 22, and tens of thousands were produced. Designated at Omega as calibre 1301 (or 1302 for the version with no second hand or date), they were available until 1977. The movement was marketed in various versions during this production period, and the Electroquartz was even included in the luxury Constellation collection – with some justification, as many of the models were made of precious metals, which meant they would automatically qualify as high-end watches. The Electroquartz series became so sought-after that Omega was able to bring out three or four new iterations every year, despite the existence of other quartz series such as the Megaquartz (see page 90).

OMEGA
12

QUARTZ CHRON

LONGINES – 1970

Longines' long history with electronics breaks down into two very distinct periods: the in-house development of its own model and the role it played in the CEH consortium with its Beta 21 model, known as the Quartz Chron.

SEE OPPOSITE	1970 MODEL
MANUFACTURER	LONGINES
MODEL	QUARTZ CHRON 8444
CALIBRE	BETA 21
MOVEMENT	QUARTZ
PRODUCTION	SOLD COMMERCIALLY
MATERIAL	STEEL
STRAP	LEATHER

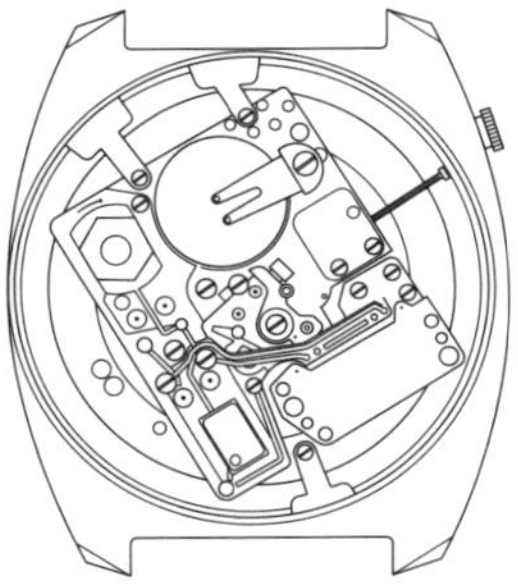

LONGINES
CALIBRE BETA 21 QUARTZ CHRON

Longines elected to rotate the movement by 45 degrees in the model it equipped with the Beta 21, thus displacing the crown and the date window.

LONGINES AND ELECTRONICS

Like many other Swiss firms, Longines took an early interest in developing electronic quartz timepieces. It had demonstrated its expertise in the field from the 1950s, creating innovative pieces of equipment such as the Chrono-Camera, the Photogines and the Chronocinégines, which combined electronic technology and photographic timing. This field was still in its infancy, but was growing in tandem with sporting events such as the Olympic Games. Two decades later, the brand teamed up with Omega to create the specialist Swiss Timing company, which exists to this day. The miniaturization of quartz movements was made possible through the partnership Longines forged with Bernard Golay SA in 1964 (see page 70), a collaboration that initially gave rise to prototype pocket watches. Two years later, the partners signed an agreement to define their roles, with Longines taking charge of the mechanical side and Golay dealing with the electronics; the quartz resonators were ordered from Ébauches SA's Oscilloquartz division. It was nonetheless the CEH (of which Longines was a member) that made history by creating the world's first prototype quartz wristwatch (see page 41).

QUARTZ CHRON BETA 21

Proudly sporting the CEH's Beta 21 movement, the Quartz Chron reference 8444 made its remarkable debut at the 1970 Basel trade fair. Inspired by a desire to push the envelope, the brand made a bold choice for this model, rotating the movement by 45 degrees and lending the watch a very particular appearance. The crown was located at 4 o'clock rather than the traditional 3 o'clock and the date window was located at 4.30. Longines had created a timepiece that stood out. And its innovations did not stop there. It unveiled the Ultra-Quartz model it had developed in-house with Bernard Golay SA (see page 66) at the same time.

THE RACE TO COMMERCIAL PRODUCTION

The CEH 1020 was the first quartz watch prototype and the Seiko Astron 35SQ was the first quartz watch to be brought to market, but the first marketing announcement connected with a quartz watch was made by Longines for its Ultra-Quartz model. In August 1969, well in advance of the 1970 Basel trade fair, four months before Seiko and eight months before any of the Swiss companies, Longines called the press to Geneva to announce its upcoming watch. Dubbed the Ultra-Quartz, it was praised for its electronic movement, which was called cybernetic as it lacked an integrated circuit. Longines had adopted an innovative approach whereby two oscillating circuits stabilized one another with an electronic array of 14 transistors, 19 resistors and 7 capacitors. The first oscillator was a quartz crystal vibrating 9,350 times a second, while the second was a motor pulsing at 170Hz and mounted on a torsion bar. The hands were moved by a ratchet wheel inspired by the Accutrons made by Bulova. Progression from prototype to production proved difficult, however, and it took two years to complete the journey – which was just long enough for Seiko to launch its first Astrons and for members of the CEH to industrially produce its Beta 21.

LONGINES
QUARTZ CHRON
16
T SWISS MADE T

TV WATCH

PATEK PHILIPPE – 1970

In 1970, Patek Philippe unveiled its vision for the luxury quartz watch of the future: the reference 3587, christened the TV Watch for its impressive size. The Grande Ellipse followed three years later.

SEE OPPOSITE	1970 MODEL
MANUFACTURER	PATEK PHILIPPE
MODEL	'TV WATCH' 3587
CALIBRE	BETA 21
MOVEMENT	QUARTZ
PRODUCTION	SOLD COMMERCIALLY
MATERIAL	WHITE GOLD
STRAP	LEATHER

PATEK PHILIPPE
GRANDE ELLIPSE

At the time, Patek Philippe had so much faith in the potential of the Beta 21 that the company used it in a number of different references, including a variation of the Ellipse, its flagship model.

THE PATEK PHILIPPE OF THE FUTURE

An unprecedented revolution took place in the 1970s, a high point in the quest for accuracy that seemed to sound the death knell of traditional watchmaking – or so many market observers seemed to think at the time. This was precisely the moment that Patek Philippe, which was at the cutting edge of watchmaking technology, chose to join other Swiss companies and set out on the adventure of designing the Beta 21 by contributing to the research carried out by the CEH. Each brand breathed its own aesthetic into its creations, transforming each watch into a bold vision of how the future of watchmaking might look. While some firms proudly highlighted the use of quartz on their dials, Patek Philippe refused to be drawn; the Patek Philippe of tomorrow preferred to keep its cards close to its chest.

REFERENCE 3587 'TV WATCH'

The reference 3587, Patek Philippe's first Beta 21 watch, turned heads with its introductory price of $3,500 – a considerable sum, even compared to the $2,200 asked for the reference 2499 (the famous perpetual calendar mechanical chronograph owned by John Lennon). It was still a tempting investment; the model now changes hands for six-figure sums – and for good reason. Even after more than 50 years the world of watchmaking has not forgotten the electrifying design of the reference 3587, going so far as to call it the 'TV Watch'. The case, designed in two parts by Ateliers Réunis, was thick enough to accommodate the movement, and the dial, made from the same blue gold as the Ellipse model, was a skilful Stern Frères creation bearing the mark 'Aprior' (Association pour la Promotion Industrielle de l'Or), often called the 'sigma' after the Greek letter, at six o'clock. It also featured a two-tone sunburst finish, with a satin centre and a matte outer edge punctuated by green indices for the seconds. Two other dial variants were available (gold and silver sunburst) and enthusiasts could also choose from several strap options besides leather.

GRANDE ELLIPSE REFERENCE 3603

Patek Philippe unveiled the reference 3603, a further version to incorporate the Beta 21, in 1973. Following on from the wave of enthusiasm sparked by the Ellipse watch, this new creation skilfully married the case and dial design of this popular icon with the new quartz movement. Called Grande Ellipse, it received a warm welcome even though it was manufactured in only limited numbers. It went on to feature in the firm's catalogue until 1983, coexisting with other models based on a quartz movement. With its two-part case (designed by Ateliers Réunis), the 3603 resembled the ref. 3587, but broke new ground with a clip-on (rather than screw-down) caseback. The options for the dial followed the classic lines of the Ellipse range, with shades ranging from blue to gold to a rarer chestnut brown. A wide choice of straps was available, including an integrated three-link version. Collectors have come to respect these models for their unique place in the history of the company as well as their typical 1970s look.

PATEK PHILIPPE
GENEVE
19
SWISS

RECTANGLE

PIAGET – 1970

Piaget, a manufacturer renowned for the sophistication of its mechanical watches, was also involved in the project to create the calibre Beta 21. It enthusiastically took up the challenge of integrating this impressive movement into a range of highly elegant watches.

SEE OPPOSITE	1970 MODEL
MANUFACTURER	PIAGET
MODEL	RECTANGLE
CALIBRE	BETA 21
MOVEMENT	QUARTZ
PRODUCTION	SOLD COMMERCIALLY
MATERIAL	WHITE GOLD
STRAP	LEATHER

PIAGET
POLO

Designed for the jet set in 1979, Piaget's gold Polo watch featured a calibre 7P quartz movement and was popularized by Ursula Andress.

FROM REFINEMENT TO QUARTZ

Piaget is a Swiss manufacturer of great renown; its timepieces are noted for their exceptional elegance, the natural stone that adorns their dials and their incredibly thin movements. In 1957, the brand introduced the calibre 9P, a manual-wind mechanical movement of considerable refinement. Three years later, it pushed the envelope even further with the calibre 12P, which was no more than 2.3mm thick and took pride of place as the thinnest automatic movement of its day. Always with an eye to the future, the company joined the CEH consortium and was involved in developing and manufacturing the Beta 21. With its specialization in extra-thin watches, however, the firm faced a challenge of its own: incorporating the outsize movement (dubbed the calibre Piaget XP4) into its understated timepieces.

A NO-DATE BETA 21

Because of the imposing size of the Beta 21, the cases for the models designed by Piaget took on unexpected forms. The brand playfully turned this constraint into a feature, creating solid gold cases with a three-step bezel surround. The cases featured dials that contained no reference to quartz, merely the brand's prestigious logo. Of these creations, the 'Black Tie' (reference 15101, 43mm in diameter and a so-called 'cushion' shape) stood out in particular, winning the heart of the artist Andy Warhol in 1972. Another model was a further example of Piaget's desire to design sophisticated watch: the reference 14101 Rectangular, with its slightly modified calibre XP4 Beta 21, did away with a date window and second hand – a choice that was all the bolder given that most other watchmaking firms were retaining this hand to showcase the accuracy of the Beta 21.

THE CALIBRE 7P

Like many of its partners in the Swiss consortium, Piaget set about developing a quartz movement of its own. Since its birth in La Côte-aux-Fées, the brand had always stayed true to its reputation and, in 1976, it unveiled the calibre 7P, a quartz movement of exceptional sophistication that represented the finest of its generation. This remarkable movement was incorporated into the Polo in 1979. This gold watch was highly fashionable at the time and was created by Yves G Piaget, the company's fourth generation of management, himself. The Polo, which was no more than 3.1mm thick, became a classic and one of the brand's iconic models.

Even as the dreaded quartz crisis loomed large on the horizon, the calibre 7P quartz movement pulled Piaget's irons out of the fire. Buoyed up by this innovation, the firm not only weathered the storm but prospered, creating a range of watches noted for their refinement in the choice of materials used and the harmony of their proportions.

PIAGET
SWISS

RADO
QUARTZ 8192

With a reputation established by cutting-edge designs and the use of innovative materials, Rado also stood out as a pioneer in the adoption of quartz with the Beta 21.

BUCHERER
QUARTZ

With its octagonal case and generous dimensions (50.5 × 46mm / 2 × 1¾in), the unique Bucherer Quartz stood out from all other watches incorporating the Beta 21 movement.

TEXANO

ROLEX – 1970

Rolex, was also a member of the CEH consortium. It unveiled a model of its own incorporating the calibre Beta 21; it was called the reference 5100 and featured several iconic innovations.

SEE OPPOSITE	1970 MODEL
MANUFACTURER	ROLEX
MODEL	'TEXANO' 5100
CALIBRE	BETA 21
MOVEMENT	QUARTZ
PRODUCTION	SOLD COMMERCIALLY
MATERIAL	WHITE GOLD
STRAP	INTEGRATED

ROLEX AND THE CEH

All eyes were on the Beta 21 upon its remarkable debut at the Basel trade fair, especially where it had been used by the big names. Of the approximately 6,000 Beta 21 movements manufactured, 1,500 units came from the 'big four' renowned watchmaking companies: LeCoultre, Longines, Patek Philippe and Rolex. The remainder had been produced by Omega and Ébauches SA. Unsurprisingly, there was particular hubbub around the model featuring the Beta 21 being released by the prestigious Rolex company. The firm with the famous crown logo masterfully adopted this exceptional movement and convincingly incorporated it into the legendary reference 5100. The watch was the very embodiment of innovative watchmaking when it was released, and undoubtedly remains the most cutting-edge watch to feature in the Rolex catalogue.

INNOVATIONS FROM ROLEX

The generously proportioned (40mm) reference 5100, which houses a Beta 21 movement, was not just a pioneering quartz wristwatch, it was also the first Rolex to be fitted with a sapphire crystal and feature the quickset function that permitted the date to be changed rapidly. It was produced in limited quantities and came in two 18-carat yellow gold versions (one of which even featured indices encrusted with diamonds) that delighted the Basel public. A tiny number of white gold models were also released and soon became highly sought-after as they were as rare as hens' teeth. Lacking the screw-down crown that was the very essence of Rolex in its heyday, the watch was notable both for its price (the highest in the Rolex catalogue) and its integrated strap (a trend fashionable at the time of its release). It was later to be eclipsed by Gérald Genta's visionary creations, the Audemars Piguet Royal Oak models and Patek Philippe's Nautilus. Some collectors have even suggested that this watch designer was actually behind the exceptional reference 5100, as these three watches are so similar to one another. The reference 5100 was met with wild enthusiasm upon its release and all the units found a buyer before it was officially on the market.

A DESIRE FOR INDEPENDENCE AND EVOLUTION

Despite its apparent success, the reference 5100 was not manufactured for long, and for obvious reasons: while the Beta 21 movement boasted attractive accuracy and efficiency, it could not escape the fatal flaw of not being a Rolex creation. To maintain its image and its independence, the brand therefore decided to break its ties with the CEH and design quartz movements of its own: the 5035 (Datejust) and the 5055 (Day-Date). Above all, however, the reference 5100 had to cease production. The rarity of this watch and the unique contribution it made to the history of watchmaking have made it a favourite among watch enthusiasts, who over time have named it the 'Texano'. No one is quite sure why – maybe everything is bigger in Texas, including Rolexes.

ROLEX
QUARTZ
16

THE ASTRON AND THE INDUSTRIAL PRODUCTION OF QUARTZ

FACT SHEET N°4

The Beta 21 was the brainchild of research carried out by the CEH, the creator of the first prototype quartz watch. Seiko stole a march on Longines' announcement and successfully brought the first quartz watch to market, inspiring other firms as it did so.

THE END OF THE BETA 21 PROJECT

Some 6,000 Beta 21 movements were produced in 1970 before rapidly being replaced by Omega's Beta 22 (see page 50). By 1972, both had been superseded, as most manufacturers (such as Seiko, with the Astron) had drawn inspiration from the CEH's Beta 1 project and were now opting for stepping motors. Although initially abandoned because of its poor battery life (blamed on its frequency dividers), Beta 1 also featured a stepping motor, the later industrial standard. It was ultimately to be Girard-Perregaux, working with Motorola, that would definitively resolve the problem of battery life, with an improved integrated circuit to reduce energy consumption that was never manufactured. The latter movement represented a considerable step forward with a 524-kHz quartz resonator. Piaget (Complication SA) launched this in parallel with the calibre 7P in 1976 (see page 56). Despite this progress, brands now followed the Seiko model and worked in-house; the CEH turned its focus towards research and, in 1984, merged with the Fondation Suisse pour la Recherche en Microtechnique (FSRM) and the Laboratoire Suisse de Recherches Horlogères (LSRH) to become the Centre Suisse d'Électronique et de Microtechnique (CSEM).

THE FAILURE OF THE ULTRA-QUARTZ PROJECT

Longines called a press conference in Geneva in advance of the 1970 Basel trade fair to unveil its quartz wristwatch of the future, the famed Ultra-Quartz (see page 66). Having been in partnership with the Bernard Golay SA engineering company since 1964 (see page 70), it had a headstart of several months on Seiko and all the Swiss brands. Although praised for its cybernetic electronic movement, the watch was to prove a commercial failure. With Longines taking care of the mechanical elements and Golay responsible for the electronics, and the quartz resonators commissioned from Ébauches SA, production was too splintered, technical flaws proliferated and the partners descended into mutual recriminations. By the time it was completed in 1971, the movement had been outstripped by quartz versions that were cheaper and more efficient.

SEIKO'S INDUSTRIAL MASTERY

In 1969, Seiko made a momentous choice: the brand adopted a stepping motor for its Astron model (see page 64). Having first perfected the technology, it brought out around a hundred gold models of its Astron 35SQ, the first quartz wristwatch to be sold commercially, preceding the more extensive sales of the Beta 21. Seiko's aim remained large-scale production, and it followed Longines' approach with Golay, later outsourcing skills by recruiting the specialist American company Intersil for its integrated circuits and drawing on the Japanese academic community. However, it struck out on its own by returning the production of the electronic modules to its own factories and, in so doing, assured itself of direct control of manufacturing. It put right the shortcomings of the original calibre and integrated manufacture of the components of its quartz watch movement via its subsidiaries Suwa (now Seiko Epson) and Daini-Seikosha. The original calibre was moved to a 16-kHz crystal in 1970 before achieving 32kHz four years later. The technology was then integrated into prototypes with digital displays. Seiko's domination of the electronic watch market was devastating. Despite Swiss resistance, the brand sold 1.7 million watches in 1975, 25 million in 1980 and more than 100 million in 1990.

A GLOBAL FIRST

New Japanese Watch Ready

TOKYO, Dec. 28 (UPI) K. Hattori & Co., Japan's leading watch maker, said this week-end it would begin marketing it's new « Seiko Quartz-Astron. » which it says is the world's first electronic wrist watch with a crystal oscillator.

ANNOUNCEMENT IN THE *NEW YORK TIMES* ON 29 DECEMBER 1969

The launch of the Seiko Astron was the first time a quartz wristwatch was brought to market.

CONCEPTION

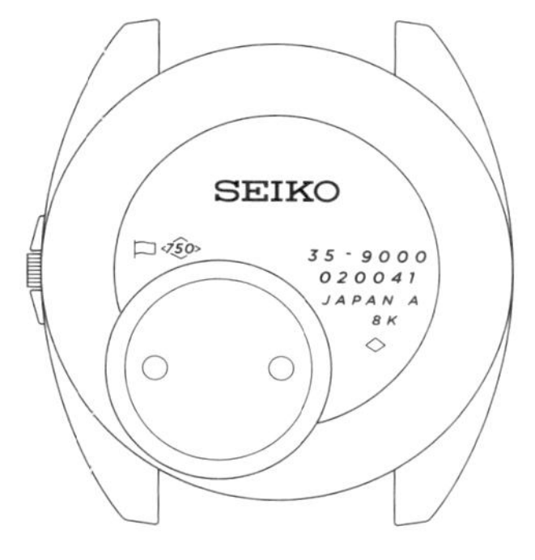

CASE
(BACK VIEW)

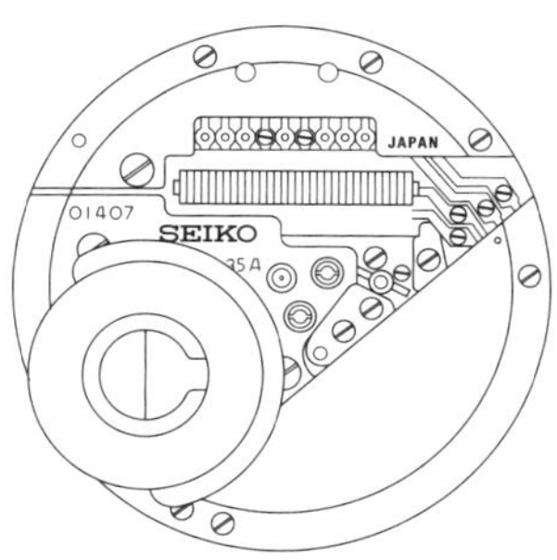

MOVEMENT
(BACK VIEW OF MAIN PLATE)

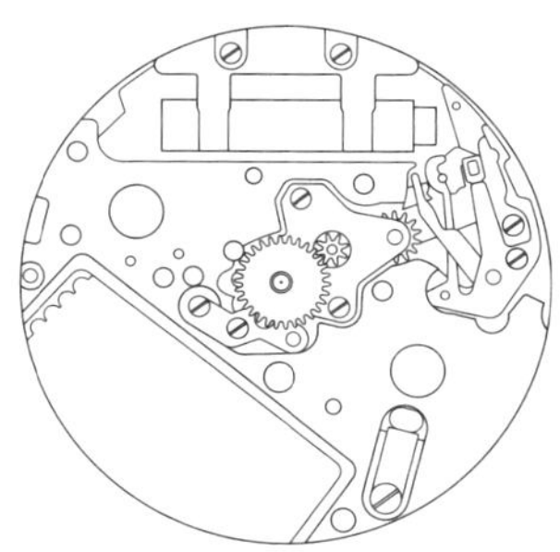

MOVEMENT
(FRONT VIEW OF MAIN PLATE)

STEPPING MOTOR & TRADITIONAL SHAPE

Unlike the Beta 21, the Seiko Astron employed a stepping motor. The movement was integrated into a traditional round watch case.

ASTRON

SEIKO – 1969

The Seiko Quartz Astron, which launched the calibre 35SQ, was revealed to the general public over the Christmas holidays in 1969. This was the first time that a quartz wristwatch had been brought to market.

SEE OPPOSITE	1969 MODEL
MANUFACTURER	SEIKO
MODEL	QUARTZ ASTRON
CALIBRE	35SQ
MOVEMENT	QUARTZ
PRODUCTION	SOLD COMMERCIALLY
MATERIAL	YELLOW GOLD
STRAP	N/A

MARKET LAUNCH OF THE QUARTZ WATCH

JULY 1967	1ST QUARTZ WATCH PROTOTYPE: CEH 1020 BETA 1
AUGUST 1969	FUTURE COMMERCIAL PRODUCTION OF A QUARTZ WATCH ANNOUNCED: THE LONGINES ULTRA-QUARTZ
CHRISTMAS 1969	1ST GLOBAL SALES OF A QUARTZ WATCH : THE SEIKO ASTRON
1970	COMMERCIAL PRODUCTION OF THE BETA 21

SEIKO AND ELECTRONICS

In 1959, Suwa-Seikosha (now Seiko-Epson) and a subsidiary of the K. Hattori & Co. group (the modern Seiko Watch Corporation) set about developing a quartz movement powered by a 1.5 V battery. Its aim – to mass produce the first quartz watch – was clear, but this would be a play in several acts, and the first of these came in 1963 with the unveiling of the Crystal Chronometer, a quartz desk clock. Seiko scored some successes in the 1964 Neuchâtel Observatory competition, notably second place in the Quartz Chronometer category, and the prizes continued to rain down over the next few years. This was not enough for the company, however, and it turned its attention to miniaturization. The watchmakers at Suwa then decided to make use of a stepping motor while Shoji Hattori, the president of K. Hattori, put a stop to a diapason (tuning-fork) watch project that was being conducted in parallel. The point of all this was to be in a position to bring a quartz watch to market in 1969 and, under the leadership of Tsuneya Nakamura, the research and development team created 20 models that year, including the Astron. Shoji Hattori, whose dream it had been to lend the watch an extraterrestrial feel, unveiled it on Christmas Eve, accompanied by an unambiguous slogan: 'Someday, all watches will be made this way.'

THE CALIBRE 35

The calibre 35 (35A/35SQ, the Astron movement) took its inspiration from prototypes tested in Neuchâtel in 1967 and featured a stepping motor (see page 42). Unlike the Beta movements, it was not thermocompensated, but its trump card was its shape, which enabled its discreet incorporation into round watches. It was manufactured by Suwa-Seikosha and featured an 8,192-Hz quartz crystal and a hybrid circuit built in-house. Despite Longines' earlier announcement, Seiko was the first company in the world to market a quartz watch successfully, and 100 units were sold in the first months. The design, the work of Kazunari Sasaki, looked to an aesthetic reminiscent of classic watches and high-end finishes. The barrel-shaped case was made of 18-carat gold and the dial had a textured finish. The price, which was thought to be quite high, was 450,000 Japanese yen (about $1,250). More than 1,500 units were sold the following year.

AND ITS EVOLUTION

The calibre 35 remained in limited production until 1971. Although the architecture of the movement remained the same, several improvements were undertaken before it was mass-produced. Following the success of the first models, the catalogue was expanded with a version featuring a date complication (the calibre 3502/35SQC) even as Daini-Seikosha was unveiling the calibre 3600. Neither was signed off for large-scale production, however, and the real revolution came only at the end of 1971 with the advent of the calibre 38, which used new components to power the quartz crystal at 16,384Hz. The calibre 38 thus realized Seiko's ambition to bring quartz into the age of mass production – a major turning-point in the history of watchmaking.

SEIKO
Quartz-Astron

ULTRA-QUARTZ

LONGINES – 1971

Longines made history in 1969 by announcing the future launch of the first quartz watch – the Ultra-Quartz – but the process of bringing the model to market took longer than anticipated.

MANUFACTURER	LONGINES
1. SEE OPPOSITE	
YEAR	1970 MODEL
MODEL	ULTRA-QUARTZ
CALIBRE	6512
MOVEMENT	QUARTZ
PRODUCTION	PROTOTYPE
MATERIAL	STEEL
STRAP	N/A
2. SEE OVERLEAF	
YEAR	1971 MODEL
MODEL	ULTRA-QUARTZ
CALIBRE	6512
MOVEMENT	QUARTZ
PRODUCTION	SOLD COMMERCIALLY
MATERIAL	YELLOW GOLD
STRAP	INTEGRATED

THE MARKET LAUNCH OF A QUARTZ WATCH IS ANNOUNCED

Since 1964, Longines had been making a name for itself by setting accuracy records at the Neuchâtel Observatory with its first quartz clock. This technology was then applied to the Chronocinégines, a revolutionary piece of equipment that gave us the famous photo-finish. A strategic alliance with Bernard Golay SA in the 1960s brought Longines to the cutting edge of quartz miniaturization, with research and development shared between Longines (mechanical components) and Golay (electronics). The quartz resonators were sourced from Ébauches SA's Oscilloquartz department. They were combined to create the Micro Quartz calibre 800 chronometer. The miniaturization process went further with the integration of quartz into a pocket chronometer in 1966. Three years later in Geneva, Longines finally announced the future market launch of the Ultra-Quartz, the first quartz wristwatch. Despite its involvement in the Beta 21 project, Longines was betting firmly on the Ultra-Quartz.

RECIPROCATION AND THE ABSENCE OF AN INTEGRATED CIRCUIT

Taking its inspiration from mathematician Norbert Wiener, the father of cybernetics, Longines dubbed the calibre 6512 a 'Cybernetic' movement. However, the Ultra-Quartz was in fact based on the interaction of two oscillators that worked as follows: a 9,350-Hz quartz crystal played the role of primary timekeeper while a vibration motor turned more slowly at 170Hz, moving the wheel train like a tuning fork. Each oscillator acted in reciprocation with the other, ensuring precise regulation of timekeeping. While the CEH made rapid strides in the field of integrated circuits, Longines and Golay did not have the technical capability required for such progress and so elected to assemble the nearly 40 miniature analog components manually. This fiddly process proved to be particularly expensive and energy-hungry.

DIFFICULT PRODUCTION

There was an obvious reason for these tricky flaws – the lack of coordination between Longines and Golay in the design of the movement. Under these conditions it was impossible to manufacture the model industrially without rejigging the calibre and redeveloping an appropriate electronic circuit. Despite the magnitude of these challenges, mass production was attempted in August 1971 but unsurprisingly tripped up over numerous technical problems that delayed the market launch by several months. There was further bad news here, too – the watch was technically outdated and overpriced in comparison to competing calibres and did not meet with anything like the success anticipated. In 1971, Longines joined Ébauches SA in the Société Suisse pour l'Industrie Horlogère (which later produced quartz movements) but rarely made use of the products manufactured by its parent company, preferring those made by Golay – only the latter's bankruptcy in 1975 finally persuaded Longines to source its supplies from Ébauches SA. The board finally began to develop movements of its own in 1977 in response to the rise of quartz on the global watchmaking scene.

LONGINES
10
T SWISS MADE T

LONGINES

CALIBRE 6512 'CYBERNETIC'

Here, nearly 40 miniature analog electronic components have been assembled by hand.
The complexity of manufacture partially explains the delay of almost two years between the announcement of the watch and its difficult market launch.

LONGINES
ULTRA-QUARTZ
SWISS
MADE
19

MICRO QUARTZ

GOLAY – 1972

Bernard Golay SA played a major role in developing and miniaturizing quartz technology. Besides its collaboration with Longines, the company also dipped a toe into mechanism design, although the success it hoped for never materialized.

SEE OPPOSITE	1972 MODEL
MANUFACTURER	GOLAY
MODEL	MICRO QUARTZ
CALIBRE	FB 7723
MOVEMENT	QUARTZ
PRODUCTION	PROTOTYPE
MATERIAL	STEEL
STRAP	N/A

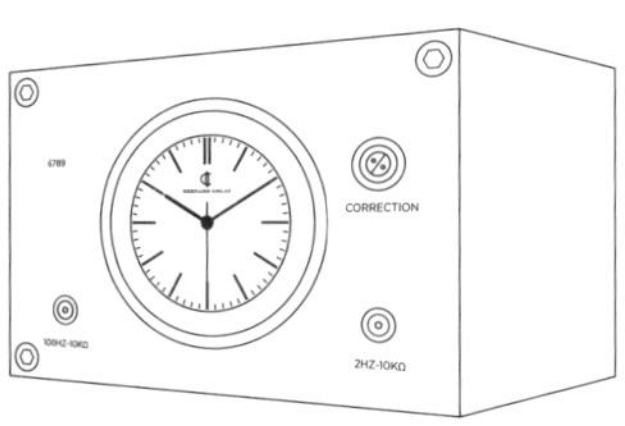

GOLAY CHRONOMETER
MICRO QUARTZ

The Micro Quartz Desk Chronometer was a commercial success. Its accuracy appealed to industrialists and athletes alike, prompting Golay to develop a wristwatch.

BERNARD GOLAY SA

Bernard Golay was a skilled watchmaker who made a name for himself in the 1950s as a specialist in the design of ultra-thin movements. He attracted particular attention for his contribution to the development of Frédéric Piguet's prestigious calibre 99 P. After a decade in operation, the Lausanne company switched its focus to electronic technical instruments, starting with marine chronometers, and through which it created its own distribution network. Inspired by a trip through India and Ceylon (modern-day Sri Lanka) during this lively period, Bernard Golay established an Indo-Swiss factory (called Hegde And Golay Private Limited) to make electronic components in the Indian city of Bangalore. This was part of an ambitious plan to expand his business empire, in the course of which he acquired Cicorel, an innovative firm specializing in the manufacture of printed circuits that was based in Renens, Switzerland.

THE MICRO QUARTZ CHRONOMETER

In 1964, the company succeeded in creating the Micro Quartz, the smallest electronic quartz ship's chronometer ever made. The circuits were printed, and the mechanical components manufactured and assembled, in Longines' facility in Saint-Imier, Switzerland. The whole thing worked so well that this small device took a well-deserved first place in the Neuchâtel Observatory competition in the Marine Chronometer category; its score of 0.15 generally left its competitors' performances in the dust. This instrument's smaller successor, the L800, featured an oscillator vibrating at 12,000Hz and was to prove its worth to scientists, industrialists and athletes alike, who all used it for different purposes. Once launched commercially, its affordable price, remarkable accuracy and wide range of uses ensured its success was all the greater. Miniaturization of the Golay-Longines design was achieved in 1966 with the creation of an experimental pocket chronometer, the L400. The name Micro Quartz was such hot commercial property that Bernard Golay also gave it to a quartz wristwatch with functions rather different from the initial chronometer.

THE MICRO QUARTZ WATCH

In parallel with development of the Ultra-Quartz for Longines (see page 66), Golay's researchers had been developing an innovative movement that combined quartz with a spiral balance wheel. Sales brochures of the time described it as 'a quartz watch with a heart'. Primarily intended for Mirexal, one of the company's clients, the marketing of this watch was aimed at underpinning Golay's expansion in India. The solution it came up with had a double advantage: it was easy to manufacture and reliable operation was guaranteed. The new mechanism was dubbed the calibre FB 7723 for the date version, and calibre FB 7743 for the day-date version. Despite the ingenious nature of the movement, success was to elude it and high development costs, design flaws and long marketing lead times would eventually catapult the company into bankruptcy in 1975, bringing to an end a long watchmaking history – as well as serving as a reminder that innovation, however much it brims with promise, is not always synonymous with commercial prosperity.

Guilde
des
Orfèvres
QUARTZ
14
11
SWISS
MADE

GP350

GIRARD-PERREGAUX – 1972

Girard-Perregaux made quartz watch history by establishing the frequency of 32,768Hz, which is now a universal standard used by quartz movement manufacturers across the globe.

1. SEE OPPOSITE

MANUFACTURER	GIRARD-PERREGAUX
MODEL	9444 'TRON'
YEAR	1972
CALIBRE	GP350
MOVEMENT	QUARTZ
PRODUCTION	SOLD COMMERCIALLY
MATERIAL	STEEL
STRAP	N/A

2. SEE OVERLEAF, LEFT

MANUFACTURER	FAVRE LEUBA
MODEL	QUARTZ RAIDER
YEAR	1972
CALIBRE	GP352
MOVEMENT	QUARTZ
PRODUCTION	SOLD COMMERCIALLY
MATERIAL	STEEL
STRAP	INTEGRATED

3. SEE OVERLEAF, RIGHT

MANUFACTURER	JAEGER-LECOULTRE
MODEL	MASTER QUARTZ
YEAR	1972
CALIBRE	GP352
MOVEMENT	QUARTZ
PRODUCTION	SOLD COMMERCIALLY
MATERIAL	STEEL
STRAP	INTEGRATED

SOLO DEVELOPMENT

In the 1960s, Girard-Perregaux was one of the few manufacturers to boast a research and development department of its own, which allowed it to commit its full resources to the emergence of electronics, the greatest revolution in modern watchmaking history. While the majority of Swiss companies had teamed up and farmed out their research to the CEH from 1962, Girard-Perregaux boldly ploughed its own furrow while also equipping itself with the means to realize its ambitions, investing in new facilities, acquiring cutting-edge machinery and enthusiastically training its workforce.
In 1966, the firm recruited Georges Vuffray, a creative young electronics engineer, and established a three-point plan to build a quartz master clock, a quartz desk clock and a wristwatch.

32,768HZ: THE CREATION OF A UNIVERSAL STANDARD

A minor revolution began in 1970. This was the year that Girard-Perregaux stepped up its efforts and achieved the remarkable feat of presenting a quartz wristwatch prototype (the Elcron) featuring a 8,192-Hz quartz crystal oscillator at the Basel trade fair. It managed to unveil this considerable innovation as a solo effort at the time when watches incorporating the CEH's Beta 21 were appearing (see page 42). However, it was the launch of the second generation of Girard-Perregaux watches in 1972 that was to turn everything upside down. With a quartz oscillating at 32,768Hz and achieving an accuracy heralded as approximately 0.164 seconds per day, the new calibre GP350 so outperformed its competitors that the frequency became the universal standard and remains at the heart of manufacturing practices to this day.

THE CALIBRE GP350 – WITH AN INTEGRATED MOTOROLA CIRCUIT

The GP350 movement featured a cutting-edge integrated circuit (designed by Motorola) that crammed the equivalent of 300 transistors onto a tiny surface area of 5mm^2. Its power consumption was reduced to a mere 4 μA, guaranteeing particularly effective battery life, and its mean variation rate was less than one minute per year.
To put this technological marvel to the test, Girard-Perregaux took it to the Neuchâtel Observatory and the results were unambiguous: for the first time, a quartz wristwatch passed the institution's static and dynamic tests with flying colours.
After 38 days of analysis, the watches were officially certified by the observatory, demonstrating their unfailing accuracy. The firm was also able to manufacture and retail this innovation at a competitive price, so the watch was a resounding commercial success. More than 20,000 movements were produced as a result, some of which incorporated the reference 9444. Some of them also featured a representation of a printed circuit on the dial, earning them the name 'Tron'. A refined version of the calibre (the GP352) would later be installed in top brands such as Jaeger-LeCoultre (Master Quartz model, see page 75) and Favre Leuba (Quartz Raider model, see page 74).

GIRARD-PERREGAUX
5
QUARTZ
SWISS

FAVRE-LEUBA
GENÈVE
12
QUARTZ RAIDER
32768 Hz
SWISS MADE

MASTER-QUARTZ
SWISS MADE

MARINE

OMEGA – 1974

In 1974, Omega launched its Megaquartz 2400 Marine Chronometer, which delivered a tiny mean daily variation rate of 0.002 seconds. This appeared in parallel with the Megaquartz 32 line that, while less accurate, threw open the door to production on a large scale.

SEE OPPOSITE	1974 MODEL
MANUFACTURER	OMEGA
MODEL	MARINE
CALIBRE	1300 MEGAQUARTZ 32
MOVEMENT	QUARTZ
PRODUCTION	SOLD COMMERCIALLY
MATERIAL	STEEL
STRAP	INTEGRATED

OMEGA
CONSTELLATION
MARINE CHRONOMETER

This watch fitted with the calibre 1511 (a variant of the 1510) achieved legendary status in 1974 as the first and only wristwatch to be certified as a marine chronometer by the Neuchâtel Observatory.

THE MARINE

In 1932, Omega created the most waterproof watch of its time, the aptly named Marine. Secure in a patent case featuring a cork seal, this model effortlessly resisted all incursions of water and dust, emerging unscathed even when tested at a depth of 73m (239ft) in Lake Geneva near the company's headquarters. Five years later, it was to remain watertight even when immersed to 135m (443ft). Forty-two years later, as the watchmaking world (including Omega) was beginning to shift in the direction of quartz, the brand unveiled a new model, the Marine Chronometer, featuring the calibre 1511 (dubbed the Megaquartz 2400, see page 90) on which Omega had been working for four years. This rectangular watch, the upshot of some 15 years of research, was submitted to 63 days of testing before becoming the only wristwatch to be certified as a marine chronometer. It featured a high-frequency quartz crystal and a mean daily variation rate of 0.002 seconds – a tiny fraction of time equating to less than a second a month. It was released in a run of nearly 1,000 units and was sold at a price more than six times that of a Speedmaster, although this did not stop famous mariners such as Jacques Cousteau and Éric Tabarly from falling for its charms.

MEGAQUARTZ 32

Capitalizing on its achievement, Omega simultaneously unveiled the calibre 1300 Megaquartz 32, which was presented as the 'little brother' of the prestigious calibre 1511 Megaquartz 2400 that powered the Marine Chronometer so accurately. Its performance was less impressive than its elder sibling, but its accuracy was nonetheless exceptional. More importantly still, it paved the way for easier access to watches via a distribution network on a scale far larger than that of the Marine Chronometer. The new calibre 1300 was fitted to various timepieces in the brand's collections, in particular the Constellation and Seamaster, with the latter (named Marine, with no chronometer certification) featuring an eye-catching round case with crisp angles, set off by an integrated strap that lent a touch of modernity.

BRAND NEW FUNCTIONS

The Megaquartz 32 (the name of which was a reference to its oscillation rate of 32kHz) had some remarkable features. The eye was immediately drawn by two pushers, like those found on a chronograph, the uppermost of which was used to set the second hand and the lower to quickset the date. Each rapid press of the upper pusher advanced the central second hand by one second to set the exact time, while a long push would immobilize it completely. The brand justified these features as offering the possibility for the wearer to reset the time when changing time zones and, more prosaically, to adjust the date (especially in months of 28 or 30 days) – all without affecting the calibre's accuracy of 5 seconds per month.

OMEGA
MEGAQUARTZ 32 KHz
JEU
23
Genève
QUARTZ

MUST

CARTIER – 1977

In launching its Must range of watches in 1977 (including the famous Tank), Cartier made luxury watchmaking accessible to a far greater audience – a democratization greatly facilitated by its adoption of quartz movements.

SEE OPPOSITE	1977 MODEL
MANUFACTURER	CARTIER
MODEL	MUST TANK
CALIBRE	CARTIER-EBEL
MOVEMENT	QUARTZ
PRODUCTION	SOLD COMMERCIALLY
MATERIAL	VERMEIL (GOLD-PLATED SILVER)
STRAP	N/A

THE TANK

In 1904, with the help of Edmond Jaeger, Louis Cartier crafted the first wristwatch in history for the aviator Alberto Santos-Dumont. From 1906, he set about carving out his niche as a 'watchmaker of shapes', playing with gold, the main plate, the railway track dial (see page 236) and the cabochon sapphire. His research first produced the Tonneau watch, followed six years later by the Tortue. The iconic Tank arrived in 1917. Its name – a contrast with its elegance – was inspired by the Renault FT-17 light tank, with the lugs on the case (the parts linking it to the strap) reminiscent of the tracks on an armoured vehicle. The success of this model spans the ages, and although initially worn by an elite echelon of society, it was opened up to a wider public from 1977 – thanks to the magic of quartz.

A CARTIER FOR EVERYONE

Faced with the irresistible rise of quartz watches on the market, in 1973 Cartier decided it was time to react. The arrival of Alain Dominique Perrin as president of the group two years later was a clear illustration of this new approach. Initially recruited as a sales rep to promote Robert Hocq's Silver Match Licence Cartier lighters, he went on to revolutionize the luxury industry with the Must de Cartier line, which extended the range of the brand. To complement its high-end jewellery, the company turned its hand to leather goods, fountain pens, perfumes and affordable watches (including the Tank, which cost less than $500). The Tank Must Collection was launched in 1977 and caused quite a stir – designed as an homage to the original model, it featured a number of dial options (including some with lacquer), in shades from blue to black to wine red. This was a novelty for buyers and brand alike, for which it was also the first large-scale production run of watches. Although it initially sold only 3,000 watches a year, by the end of the 1970s it had racked up sales of more than 160,000. Even more surprising – but no less revealing – was the fact that this was also the first time that Cartier had consistently used a non-precious metal for its watches; for example, the Tank Must was made of vermeil, a type of gold-plated silver. The watch, which rapidly became a must-have item, found favour with the great and the good among watch enthusiasts, including in particular the fashion designer Yves Saint Laurent, who was immortalized with his Must by the famous photographer Irving Penn.

TIMELESS MUST

While some Must watches were fitted with mechanical workings in 1977, most featured a quartz movement. This was produced in the workshops of the Ebel watchmaking firm (see page 80), which specialized in quartz for its own creations and those made by other prestigious firms. Although technologically basic, the movement was notable for its jewels and ornamentation, features generally reserved for mechanical movements, and also for its spacer ring, which was red to match its corporate colours. Cartier revisited the Must collection in 2021, showcasing watches with dials lacquered in red, blue and green. The original steel design with its quartz movement now features gold trim and a mechanical movement – a return to form for an absolute 'Must' in watchmaking.

must de
Cartier
SWISS

SPORT CLASSIC

EBEL – 1977

The Ebel brand, founded by Eugène Blum and Alice Lévy, has carved out a niche for itself by creating quartz calibres for use in-house and by other prestigious firms. Its Sport Classic models (with their 'Wave' straps) have been particularly popular and established the brand's reputation in the 1980s.

SEE OPPOSITE	1983 MODEL
MANUFACTURER	EBEL
MODEL	SPORT CLASSIC
CALIBRE	EBEL
MOVEMENT	QUARTZ
PRODUCTION	SOLD COMMERCIALLY
MATERIAL	GOLD AND STEEL
STRAP	GOLD AND STEEL

EUGÈNE BLUM AND LÉVY: PARTNERS IN LIFE AND IN WATCHMAKING

On 15 July 1911, Eugène Blum and Alice Lévy marked a milestone in their marriage by registering the Ebel brand (the name came from Eugène Blum et Lévy) with the chamber of commerce in the Swiss watchmaking bastion of La Chaux-de-Fonds. They unveiled their first wristwatches the following year and went on to win a gold medal at the 1914 Swiss National Exhibition for their patented ring watches, which featured a hidden setting system. As a result of this achievement, Ebel became one of the main suppliers of watches to other labels, which rapidly became the firm's principal line of business. Ebel continued to innovate in the 1930s, adopting the Western Electric system to control the accuracy of its watches, and received another endorsement in 1939 when it became the official supplier to the UK's Royal Air Force. Paradoxically, the firm achieved popularity with the general public only after three decades of success elsewhere, under the enlightened management of Pierre-Alain Blum, the third generation of the family to lead the company.

THE SPIRIT OF THE NEW WAVE

Ebel made a name for itself thanks to its unique style, including the elegant wristwatches produced for the Sport Classic collection in 1977. Thanks to partnerships in the 1980s, these exclusively quartz versions found their way onto the wrists of tennis stars including Yannick Noah, Andre Agassi and Boris Becker, and raised the profile of the collection within the industry. More than anything, however, they embodied Ebel's philosophy: 'Beauty marries function.' The cases were hexagonal or rectangular with rounded corners and featured a distinctive integrated strap dubbed the 'Wave', which effortlessly combined elegance and sportiness. It was particularly praised for the way its flexibility and finesse made it feel like a second skin. Other lines were launched in the wake of this success and found favour far beyond the world of tennis, with the Beluga being worn by the supermodel Claudia Schiffer. Ebel then went on to take a more active role in sponsoring sport and culture, which reached a peak at La Chaux-de-Fonds in 1986 with the brand's acquisition of the Villa Schwob (also known as the Villa Turque), which had been designed 70 years earlier by the influential architect Le Corbusier. The building was renovated in 2011 and rechristened the Maison Ebel; it remains the cultural heart of the brand.

A MECHANICAL INTEREST

Ebel did not rest on its laurels with the quartz calibres it produced and which made the brand's name. Always looking to surprise, it released a mechanical automatic chronograph movement in the mid-1980s – and wisely so, as at the height of the quartz era Pierre-Alain Blum had sensed a new interest in mechanical watches in the luxury sector. He had therefore approached Zenith, which created its first automatic chronograph movement; it was dubbed El Primero. The Ebel CEO used this movement to create the brand's calibre 134, which was slipped in among the quartz watches in the brand's range. This was a decision that says much about the brand's passion for innovation and excellence in watchmaking.

EBEL
SWISS

COLOUR TIME

CHROMACHRON – 1981

The 1980s saw the appearance of the Colour Time Chromachron, a watch that was deliberately inexact. Lacking any hands, it offered a subtle, relaxed display of the time that took the industry and the world quite unawares.

SEE OPPOSITE	1985 MODEL
MANUFACTURER	CHROMACHRON
MODEL	COLOUR TIME
CALIBRE	ISA 268
MOVEMENT	QUARTZ
PRODUCTION	SOLD COMMERCIALLY
MATERIAL	STEEL
STRAP	LEATHER

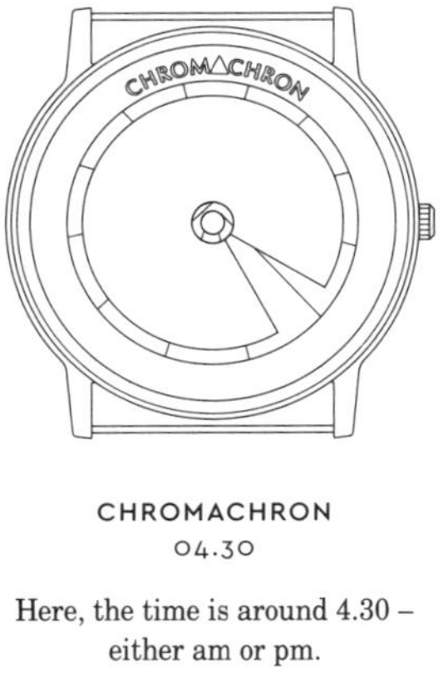

CHROMACHRON
04.30

Here, the time is around 4.30 – either am or pm.

THE END OF THE 'DICTATORSHIP OF THE EXACT TIME'

Tian Harlan, a German artist born in Berlin in 1939, threw himself into inventing a new method of telling the time in the 1970s. What he came up with was the Chromachron system, a particularly ambitious response to what its creator called the 'dictatorship of the exact time'. To achieve this, the Chromachron system spurned the use of numbers and hands. Instead, Harlan replaced these with colours whose shades subtly indicated the passing of time. This was a controversial approach (and the subject of much debate) but one which nonetheless served a clear and understandable ambition: to revolutionize our concept of the passage of time and to reduce the anxiety that accompanies it. And while the Chromachron system might pose questions, it also had its attractions. In 1972, to mark the Munich Olympic Games, it was incorporated in a column that lit up Berlin. Although the official patent was not filed in Germany for another two years, distribution of the mechanical Chromachron watches was already in full swing.

AN ANTI-STRESS WATCH

The original nature and philosophy of the Chromachron system required some explanation to the general public. One advertisement showed the new system, in wristwatch form, on board the first commercial Concorde flight bound for New York in 1976 with the slogan 'The most relaxed watch on the fastest plane to America'. Though something of a paradox, it was intended to illustrate Harlan's thinking – the watch was designed for people, 'not for machines or those who function like machines'. Not long after this formidable publicity campaign, a massive Chromachron clock was installed in Baden-Baden, Germany, although the watches themselves did not really take off until 1981, when their creator left Germany for Switzerland and founded Chromachron AG. Around a hundred models were then sold, thanks to the use of inexpensive quartz movements. But who cares about quality? For once, precision was not a fundamental issue.

THE CHROMACHRON SYSTEM

The Chromachron offered a new vision of the passing of time by doing away with the traditional means of measuring it. The hands were replaced with a black disc that rotates at a rate of one shaded segment per hour, with each hour represented by a colour. The minutes are indicated by the borders between the colours, dividing the dial into five-minute segments. As a result, it was impossible to tell the exact time – only our perception of the colour variations, indeed, our emotions and state of mind, were left to guide us in our relationship with time, and it was here that the particular charm of Chromachron watches was to be found. The colours the system used (which were fixed in a patent filed in 1980) were not chosen at random – each one was meticulously selected to match the time of day to which it corresponded, with a bright yellow for noon and ever darker shades as the sun went down. The 1980s saw these deliberately inexact watches proudly worn by celebrities such as Ringo Starr, Max Bill and Charles Aznavour, for whom punctuality was perhaps not a priority.

CHROMACHRON
SWISS MADE

ROCKWATCH

TISSOT – 1985

The fascinating RockWatch appeared without warning and in all its originality in 1985. A bold design, the world's first wristwatch with a natural stone case went on to be a resounding international success.

SEE OPPOSITE	1987 MODEL
MANUFACTURER	TISSOT
MODEL	ROCKWATCH R150
CALIBRE	CAL. ETA
MOVEMENT	QUARTZ
PRODUCTION	SOLD COMMERCIALLY
MATERIAL	STONE AND STEEL
STRAP	STONE

'A GOOD JOKE'

Tissot felt the full impact of the quartz crisis that was unleashed during the 1970s, when the industry was invaded by new Japanese technologies, to the extent that in 1976 the company decided to cease production of *ébauche* movements (see page 236) altogether. It was a shock development, it has to be said; fewer than 15,000 watches were sold in 1984, compared to nearly a million a little over a decade earlier. However, as a member of the network of brands that comprised the Société Suisse de Microélectronique et d'Horlogerie (SMH) headed by Nicolas Hayek, the future founder of the Swatch Group, Tissot was poised for a renaissance. Inspired by the success of Swatch (see page 190), Ernst Thomke (see page 235) had made a surprising proposal during the course of one well-lubricated evening, suggesting a watch made of stone. 'When I suggested the idea of marketing a watch of stone, their reaction was, "It's a good joke. Okay, if you insist; we'll sell 3,000 of them." I replied, "At least 10,000, otherwise I'm taking it to another brand." I think they thought I had gone completely mad.'

AMERICA AS A TEST BED

The initial investment was enormous, with between 5 and 6 million Swiss francs being used to purchase machinery capable of working stone. A further 20 million was allocated for marketing. Fortunately for Tissot's finances, the 1985 launch of the RockWatch on the American market, which it had neglected for a decade, was a resounding success. Priced at around $200, the watch was sculpted from Swiss Alpine granite and featured red and yellow hands that evoked the colour-coding of hiking trails. It was so successful that the brand had to take swift action, informing the press that staff were now working overtime to meet demand. Buoyed up by these achievements, the RockWatch was officially launched on the Swiss market in March 1986 and, when production ceased in 1994, more than 800,000 had been sold. This catapulted Tissot into the top flight of the SMH.

A WATCHMAKING FOSSIL

The RockWatch, with its quartz movement, was available in various sizes and initially featured a leather strap; each watch was unique due to the different veins running through the stone. Tissot celebrated the uniqueness of each model in its advertising: 'A watch like a stone sculpture. Each one is unique.' The brand subsequently expanded its range, using various natural materials such as jade, sodalite and aventurine, as well as corals. The idea was taken a step further in 1988 with the PearlWatch, which was entirely faced in mother-of-pearl. The WoodWatch, made of wood, followed a year later. The series would later give way to LCD and Digi-Ana models (see page 162). The RockWatch was truly a watchmaking fossil but one that left a lasting impression on the minds of customers, especially in America.

TISSOT
SWISS MADE

AW 10

BRAUN – 1989

Designed by Dieter Rams (with the aid of Dietrich Lubs), Braun's AW10 watch was a contemporary design icon. Its widespread popularity was facilitated by the use of quartz.

SEE OPPOSITE	1989 MODEL
MANUFACTURER	BRAUN
MODEL	AW10 I
CALIBRE	QUARTZ RONDA
MOVEMENT	QUARTZ
PRODUCTION	SOLD COMMERCIALLY
MATERIAL	STEEL
STRAP	LEATHER

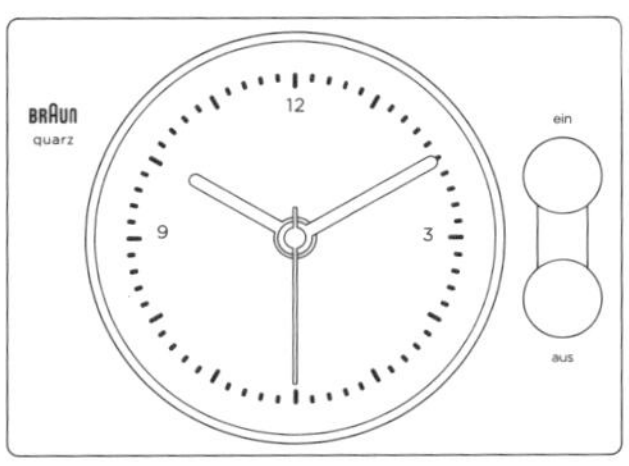

BRAUN
AB20 TRAVEL CLOCK

In 1975, this alarm clock was notable for its purity and simplicity, but it was its orange-yellow second hand that was especially eye-catching and that would go on to become a trademark feature of Rams and Lubs designs.

BRAUN AND DIETER RAMS

Founded by the German engineer Max Braun in 1921, the brand named for him placed particular emphasis on the design of its products. Braun's vision really began to bear fruit in 1955 when he began a long-term partnership with Dieter Rams. After six years of work, during which he made a name for himself with designs such as the SK4 radio/phonograph combo, Braun took over management of the design department, a post he was to hold for 40 years. Acknowledged as the father of 'good design', Rams set out the ten basic principles that informed his approach: a good design should be innovative, useful, aesthetic, understandable, unobtrusive, honest, long-lasting, thorough, environmentally friendly and minimalist. In the 1970s, he worked with Dietrich Lubs to instil a dynamic into the brand with an innovative range of watches.

FROM CLOCKS TO DIGITAL WATCHES

Braun's watchmaking journey began with a chance encounter on a plane between Max Braun and one of his Swiss counterparts, a specialist in the production of watch movements. Braun then embarked on his adventure. Under Rams's leadership, assisted by Lubs, the design department began work on Phase 1, an analogue clock. Its success paved the way for Phase 2 and then Phase 3, followed by the DN18 and DN42 digital clocks. In 1975, the AB20 alarm clock signalled its presence with an orange-yellow second hand, a signature feature of Rams and Lubs designs. Two years later, Braun launched its first wristwatches with a digital LCD display (see page 157). An anachronistic choice, two generations of DW (Digital Watch) followed – first the DW20, a circular model with an integrated strap that was manufactured for just a year due to malfunctions, and then the rectangular DW30 with its leather strap and an improved module. It stayed in the catalogue until 1981.

THE ANALOGUE WATCH

According to Lubs, the desire to get an analogue watch off the ground first took shape at the end of the 1970s, when he noticed that Braun was giving favoured customers a plastic Japanese watch featuring its logo. Feeling that these less than robust timepieces did not do justice to the top-flight reputation of the brand, he mentioned this to Rams and they set about creating an analogue watch (AW) that embraced the principle of less is more. The AW10, which first saw the light of day in 1989, was thin (8mm) and an ideal size (33.5mm), with a steel case reinforced with a black fibreglass bezel to protect the crown. It was powered by a Swiss quartz movement and featured an orange-yellow second hand; its Akzidenz-Grotesk font only enhanced its minimalist aesthetic. It was followed by the AW50, a more elegant version with a grey dial stripped of Arabic numerals and a date window subtly highlighted in red. The range has been expanded right up to the present day to include models incorporating automatic movements. Before this, only quartz watches had been able to offer top-flight design at attractive prices, having undergone stringent quality control coordinated from Braun's company headquarters in Kronberg.

BRAUN
quartz
Made in Germany

HIGH FREQUENCY AND THERMOCOMPENSATION

FACT SHEET N°5

Like the mechanical watch before it, the quartz watch exploited the principle of quantified vibration, but instead of a balance, it used a quartz crystal. Its only vulnerability was the pronounced sensitivity of the oscillation frequency to its environment.

FREQUENCIES

In a mechanical movement, one beat equates to one oscillation of the balance wheel. Each tick-tock therefore corresponds to a 'return journey' of two vibrations. It is the number of these that determines the frequency, which is expressed in Hertz (Hz) or beats per hour (bph). The most common rate for the movements of modern mechanical wristwatches is 4Hz, or 28,800bph.

In an electronic watch, the vibration arises from a piece of carved quartz that resonates as a result of piezoelectricity, a principle established by Pierre and Jacques Curie in 1880. In essence, when acted on by an electric current and placed under stress, a quartz crystal will generate an electric field and begin to vibrate. The universal standard is a vibration rate of 32,768Hz (32kHz), 8,000 times faster than a spiral balance wheel in a modern mechanical watch.

THE BIRTH AND EVOLUTION OF HIGH FREQUENCY

The first electromechanical watches of the 1950s featured a balance wheel oscillating at a frequency approaching 3Hz (see page 16). Progress was made in 1960 with the Bulova Accutron, whose tuning fork vibrated at 360Hz (see page 34), and the Beta 21 movement launched in 1970, which came equipped with a quartz crystal vibrating at 8,192Hz (8kHz) – see page 42. The standard frequency for quartz watches was finally established by Girard-Perregaux the following year with its calibre GP350, whose frequency of 32,768Hz (32kHz) maintained accuracy with a mean variation rate of around 0.164 seconds per day (see page 72).

Of the Swiss quartz pioneers, Omega unveiled its calibre 1510 with the Megaquartz 2400 of 1974 (see page 90). The movement achieved a frequency of 2.4MHz (with a tiny lenticular quartz crystal oscillating at 2,359,206 times a second) and recorded a mean variation rate of +/- one second per month. A variation of this calibre (cal. 1511), fitted with a thick case, passed the static marine chronometer tests at the Neuchâtel Observatory, a distinction hitherto reserved for large-format timepieces. Japanese company Citizen also set about exploring high-frequency movements with its calibre 8650 Crystron 4MHz which, to put the others in perspective, recorded an accuracy and mean rate variation of +/- three seconds per year. Without adequate protection of the quartz crystal from its environment (for example in the form of thermocompensation or a specific case), very high frequency movements offered no guarantee of accuracy. This was why Omega, which was well aware of its limitations, also subjected its model to tests for shock-resistance, magnetism and humidity.

FREQUENCY TOLERANCE

While a quartz movement is inherently more accurate than a mechanical movement, quartz's great sensitivity makes it fickle: temperature and humidity can significantly affect its smooth running, while heat, magnetism, vibration and radiation can disrupt the oscillation frequency recorded by a watch because it has been calculated at an average temperature of 25°C (77°F). To mitigate expansion caused by temperature variations, high-quality quartz watches incorporated a thermocompensation system. One such model was the Rolex Oysterquartz, launched in 1977 (see page 94), whose oscillator was stabilized over a wide range of temperatures to ensure constant accuracy. According to the Contrôle Officiel Suisse des Chronomètres (COSC), a quartz movement was required to feature thermocompensation and a robust case.

THE MECHANISM OF AN ANALOGUE QUARTZ WATCH

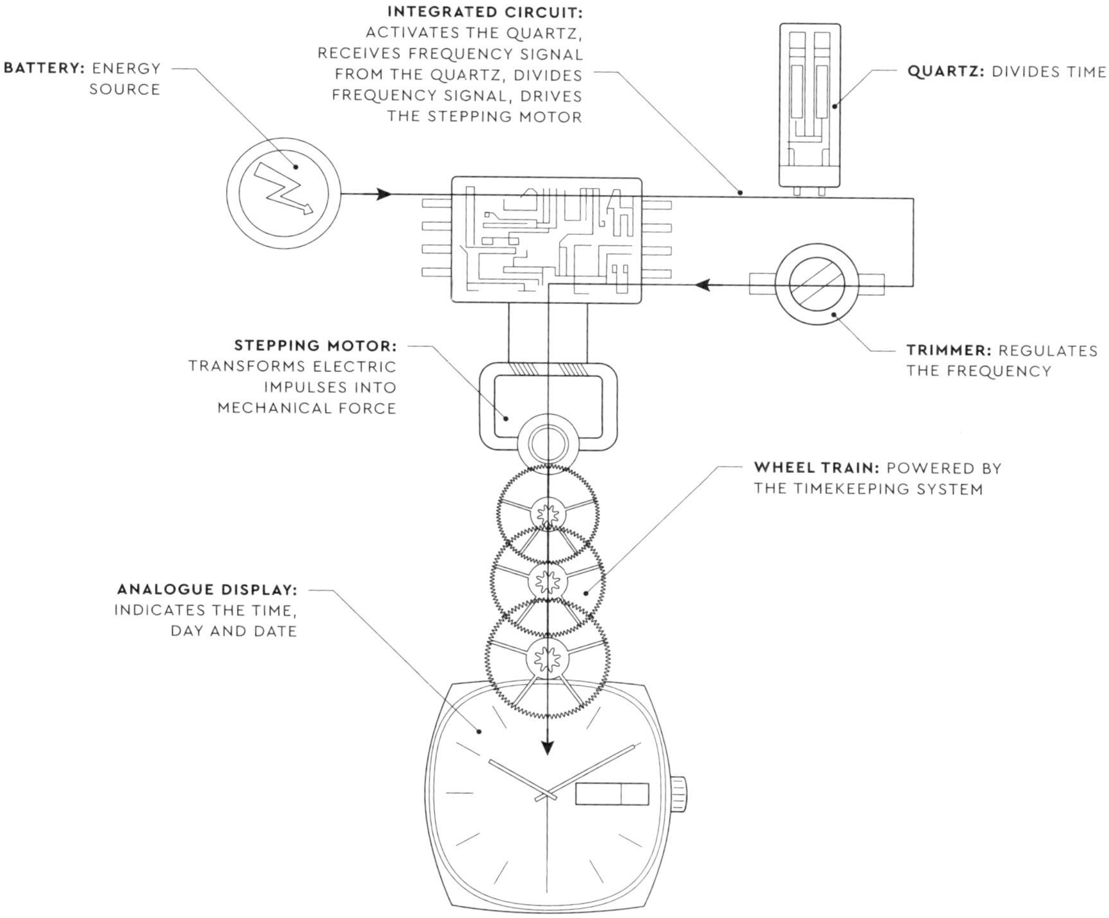

THERMAL BEHAVIOUR OF QUARTZ

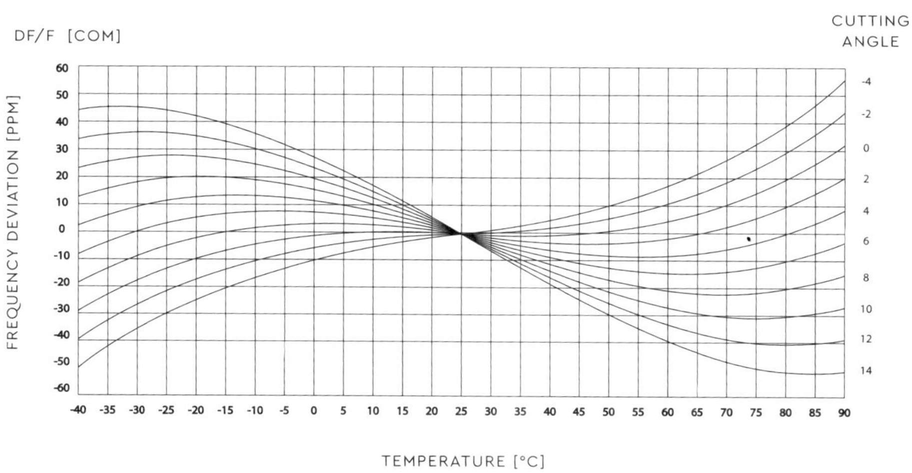

MEGAQUARTZ 2400

OMEGA – 1974

After 15 years of research, Omega unveiled the first wristwatch to be certified as a marine chronometer in 1974. Its accuracy of +/- one second per month was thanks to its high-frequency (2.4MHz) calibre.

SEE OPPOSITE	1974 MODEL
MANUFACTURER	OMEGA
MODEL	CONSTELLATION
CALIBRE	1510 MEGAQUARTZ 2400
MOVEMENT	QUARTZ
PRODUCTION	SOLD COMMERCIALLY
MATERIAL	STEEL
STRAP	INTEGRATED

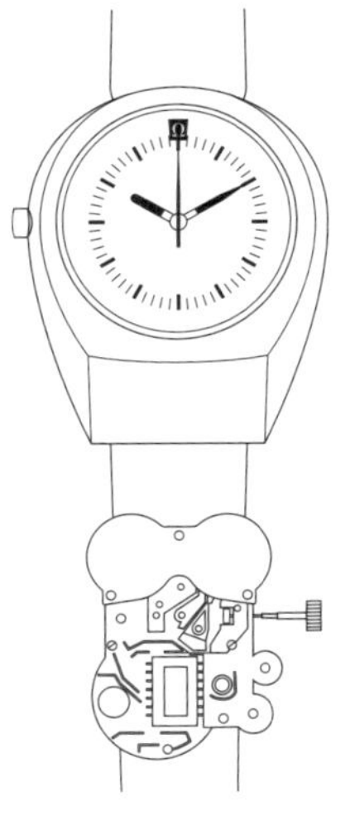

OMEGA
'ELEPHANT' PROTOTYPE OF THE CALIBRE 1500

This prototype, unveiled in Basel in 1970, derived its name from its size and the two batteries located side by side that resembled an elephant's ears.

FRANTIC PACE

The calibre 1500, developed in close collaboration with the Institut Battelle in Geneva, whose contract with the Société Suisse pour l'Industrie Horlogère (SSIH) was initially signed in 1955 and was taken over by Omega in 1969, proved to be a minor revolution in watchmaking. The result of 15 years of meticulous research and christened the Megaquartz 2400, it offered unparalleled accuracy of +/- one second per month. Behind this feat lay the ingenious design of its high-frequency movement, which featured a tiny, disc-shaped lenticular quartz crystal enclosed in a capsule. The calibre oscillated at an almost unimaginable speed of 2,359,296 beats per second, or 2.4MHz. On 25 February 1974, one of its variants, the calibre 1511, won the approval of the Neuchâtel Observatory – the first and only time the institution had certified a wristwatch as a marine chronometer.

MARINE CHRONOMETERS

Marine chronometers ruled the waves in the pre-digital era as they were essential for navigation at sea. However, their accuracy came at a price – they were big and bulky, although their size was justified by the extreme accuracy of their movements. As early as 1970, Omega set out to change this situation by miniaturizing the calibre on which mariners could rely, and the first prototype was revealed in Basel. Dubbed the 'Elephant' for its size and the two batteries located side by side that were reminiscent of an elephant's ears, it was refined, rebuilt and then truly perfected with the calibre 1510 in 1972, although it was the 1511–1516 version that established its legendary status two years later. After 63 days of rigorous testing, the watch in which it had been installed not only met the standards set by the observatory, but greatly exceeded them, with a mean daily variation rate of no more than +/- two-thousandths of a second, or 0.73 seconds per year. As these official trials were static only, Omega supplemented them with tests for resistance to shock, magnetism and humidity. And so was born the first and only watch to obtain this prestigious certification.

A WHOLE HOST OF VARIANTS

In achieving a beat frequency of 2.4MHz, the Megaquartz 2400 scaled new heights. When it was launched, it was quite simply the most accurate non-thermocompensated movement ever made. Omega was all too aware of the sensitivity of the quartz crystal that made this performance possible, and protected the calibre against shock and temperature variations with a pyramid-shaped steel case designed by the Italian company Fontana. It was also unique in being the first watch that made it possible to adjust the hour without affecting the minutes and seconds. This movement was also the first to feature a TSA (time second adjustment) pusher, which allowed extremely precise synchronization with a reference time piece. The first Megaquartz 2400 version was part of the prestigious Constellation range, certain models of which featured a dial made of blue aventurine, a natural mineral that was particularly popular in watchmaking. The calibre later received official certification in the guise of the Omega Marine Chronometer, housed in a steel case with a gold bezel (see page 236) and the movement number engraved on the front of the case.

Constellation
OMEGA
MEGAQUARTZ
f 2,4 MHz
5
SWISS MADE

4.2 MHZ

OMEGA – 1977

Even as it was developing its 2.4Hz calibre, Omega was attempting to produce an even higher-frequency (4.2MHz) movement. This never went into production in the form of a wristwatch, although several now rare prototypes were built.

SEE OPPOSITE	1977 MODEL
MANUFACTURER	OMEGA
MODEL	PROTOTYPE
CALIBRE	1522 4.2MHZ
MOVEMENT	QUARTZ
PRODUCTION	PROTOTYPE
MATERIAL	STEEL
STRAP	LEATHER

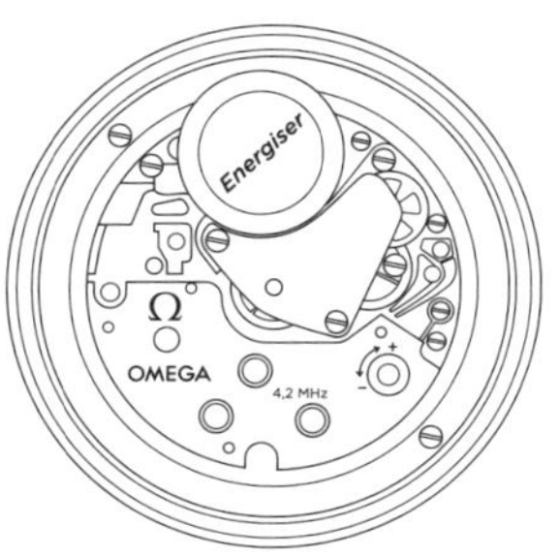

OMEGA
4.2MHZ PROTOTYPE

Although it featured an architecture similar to the calibre 1342, which vibrated at 32kHz, the calibre 1522 had a very high frequency beat of 4.2MHz.

THE VEGA MOVEMENT

During the 1970s, all kinds of experiments with a range of different frequencies were carried out on quartz. Although Omega had grabbed the headlines with the audacious 2.4MHz calibre that it proudly incorporated into its Marine Chronometer (see page 76), the Japanese company Citizen harboured ambitions to offer some competition in the form of its intriguing 4-MHz Crystron calibre. The Swiss company was more than ready for a race for high frequency and enthusiastically introduced the calibre 1525, a sophisticated movement known as the 'Vega', into imposing marine chronometers – although whether this innovation was relevant to the more small-scale world of wristwatches was another question.

A 4.2-MHZ PROTOTYPE

Around 15 years ago, on an internet forum dedicated to watch-collecting, a community of enthusiasts made an intriguing discovery when they unearthed a prototype of a quartz watch developed by Omega governed by a crystal vibrating at a frequency of 4.2MHz. However, the attribution of this model to Omega raised a number of questions. The prototype was housed in a square Seamaster case of the type once reserved for tuning-fork watches. It also curiously featured the word 'Automatic' on its dial and the calibre was unsigned. After some enquiries, Omega confirmed the authenticity of the timepiece and a handful of models then came to light. One version did not feature the word 'Automatic' but had a calibre signed 'cal. 1522', while another, illustrated here, proudly bore the word 'Quartz' along with a calibre signature. The 4.2MHz movement developed by Omega for this wristwatch shares several features with the calibre 1342, another of the brand's movements, which vibrated at a standard rate of 32kHz.

PRODUCTION INTERRUPTED

The production of high-frequency Megaquartz 2400 movements was fairly limited and amounted to no more than around 10,000 units. The comparatively high prices demanded for these models limited the market considerably. The principal obstacle for further developments was the complexity and high cost of designing the cases that were essential for ensuring the accuracy of the quartz crystal, and this was mainly what discouraged Omega from continuing to manufacture a watch running at the very high frequency of 4.2MHz. The rare examples that may be encountered are elegant but very fragile, and have been discovered thanks to the company's former employees. Choosing to stop the development was entirely understandable for a brand as demanding as Omega. These prototypes are relics of a time when the quest for accuracy was at its height, but their rarity has nonetheless made them a watchmaking holy grail sought after by electric watch enthusiasts.

OMEGA
26
Seamaster
QUARTZ
SWISS MADE

OYSTERQUARTZ

ROLEX – 1977

After the Beta 21, Rolex decided to plough its own watchmaking furrow and design a movement in-house. The Oysterquartz, which was in production for 25 years, featured this calibre, which oscillated at a regular 32KHz whatever the temperature thanks to the thermocompensation integrated into its mechanism.

MANUFACTURER	ROLEX

1. SEE OPPOSITE

MODEL	18019
YEAR	1987
CALIBRE	5055
MOVEMENT	QUARTZ
PRODUCTION	SOLD COMMERCIALLY
MATERIAL	WHITE GOLD
STRAP	INTEGRATED

2. SEE OVERLEAF, LEFT

MODEL	1700
YEAR	1987
CALIBRE	5035
MOVEMENT	QUARTZ
PRODUCTION	SOLD COMMERCIALLY
MATERIAL	STEEL
STRAP	INTEGRATED

3. SEE OVERLEAF, RIGHT

MODEL	17013
YEAR	1978
CALIBRE	5035
MOVEMENT	QUARTZ
PRODUCTION	SOLD COMMERCIALLY
MATERIAL	GOLD AND STEEL
STRAP	INTEGRATED

THERMOCOMPENSATED QUARTZ

Like so many others, Rolex's first quartz watch, the 5100, was powered by the Beta 21 (see page 42). Despite its success, however, the determinedly independent brand with its trademark crown believed that it was not in its own interest to market watches with movements identical to those of its competitors. In 1972, Rolex's collaboration with the CEH came to an end when it began to develop a quartz movement of its own.
In 1977, after five years of development and testing, Rolex unveiled the calibre 5035 for the Oysterquartz Datejust and the calibre 5055 for the Oysterquartz Day-Date. These calibres, which featured functions such as quickset for rapid date-changing and a hack system to adjust the second hand, vibrated at the standard frequency of 32kHz (see page 88), but their real unique selling point was the analogue thermocompensation that protected the quartz movement from environmental variation. The theoretical frequency of a watch was determined at a reference temperature of 25°C (77°F), and any variation in temperature would affect its accuracy. Rolex ensured a constant frequency for its movement by stabilizing the oscillator across a wide range of temperatures, and the company's in-house quartz calibres were hailed as technological and aesthetic marvels. They also stood out for the lavish attention paid to decorating the movements.

'SUPERLATIVE CHRONOMETER OFFICIALLY CERTIFIED'

It is interesting to note that the first examples of the 5035 movement used in the Datejust were not subjected to certification by the Contrôle Officiel Suisse des Chronomètres (COSC) and, as a result, the dials of the Oysterquartz Datejust models manufactured during this period do not bear the inscription 'Superlative Chronometer Officially Certified'. The calibre 5035 was sent to the COSC in 1979 and obtained the relevant certification (thanks to a minor modification to the cut of the quartz crystal) and the dials bore this inscription from that time onwards. Collectors refer to calibre 5035 watches that are not COSC-certified as Mark I and the later ones as Mark II. The calibre 5055 used in the Day-Date was certified by COSC from the outset, and all dials in the Oysterquartz Day-Date series proudly proclaim 'Superlative Chronometer Officially Certified'.

TWENTY-SEVEN YEARS OF PRODUCTION

Oysterquartz were manufactured for nearly 27 years as part of the Datejust and Day-Date series. Much like the mechanical watches, the Oysterquartz featured a 36-mm Oyster case with a screw-down crown and was available in various materials. Unlike the reference 5100, however, the case had a more angular shape than the classic version with its rounded corners, and also featured an integrated strap. Rolex requested COSC certification of its quartz movements for the last time in 2001, even though Oysterquartz models were retained in the brand's catalogue until 2003. Despite the long production run, it has been estimated that fewer than 25,000 units were manufactured and this relative rarity means that Oysterquartzes are much prized by collectors.

TUESDAY
ROLEX
OYSTERQUARTZ
DAY-DATE
SUPERLATIVE CHRONOMETER
OFFICIALLY CERTIFIED
SWISS MADE

ROLEX
OYSTERQUARTZ
DATEJUST
SUPERLATIVE CHRONOMETER
OFFICIALLY CERTIFIED
SWISS MADE

ROLEX
DATEJUST
OYSTERQUARTZ

27
SWISSONIC
100

1

OMEGA
30
ELECTRONIC
f 300

2

OMEGA
LUN 20

3

TACHYMETRE
OMEGA
Speedmaster
AUTOMATIC

4

ZENITH
automatic
28800

5

TISSOT
2250

6

THE COMPETITION TO QUARTZ

Despite the burgeoning popularity of quartz watches in the 1970s, some manufacturers put up resistance and tried out other technologies to offer some competition.

RESISTANCE FROM THE TUNING FORK

The tuning-fork calibre invented by Max Hetzel in the 1950s refused to lie down in the face of quartz. This revolutionary technology, which surpassed mechanical watches in accuracy, was first brought to market by Bulova in 1960. Balance wheels were out: the resonator was now a metal tuning fork vibrating at around 360Hz (see page 34). The calibre 214, the first movement to feature this system, was on the market for seven years before it evolved into the calibre 218, creating a technology that was still winning consumer confidence 20 years after its launch.

It was so popular that a licence for its use was granted to Ébauches SA in 1968, and the company incorporated it into the calibre 9162 Mosaba for the Swissonic 100 series **(1)**, which slotted in between the Swissonic 10 (the preserve of Dynotron electric movements, see page 30) and the Swissonnic 1000, which was reserved for the new quartz watches. Although its frequency was slightly lower than the Accutron's, the Mosaba maintained its position as the benchmark tuning-fork movement. In much the same way, two Omega ranges came to the fore in the 1970s: the widely distributed F300 **(2)**, which was based on the highly reliable calibre ESA Mosaba 9162, and the Megasonic 720Hz **(3)**, which had been designed by Max Hetzel himself and ran at twice the frequency. Although it was not widely available, it featured smoothly sweeping hands unmatched by the 32-kHz quartz movements that used a stepping motor.

ACCUQUARTZ & AUTOQUARTZ

The new Accuquartz, which was based on the calibre 224, was launched by Bulova in 1971. It featured a tuning fork vibrating at 341.3Hz that powered all its mechanical components and was deftly regulated by a 32-kHz quartz crystal that guaranteed accuracy. This extremely affordable calibre was widely adopted and incorporated into more than 30 models (see page 46). However, its story did not end there. Some 20 years later, Omega resurrected this supposedly obsolete technology in the Autoquartz. Similarly, while the Speedmaster remained hand-wound, the Speedmaster Reduced was an automatic model springing from the expertise of the Swiss *ébauche* manufacturer Dubois Dépraz. Although never produced, Omega took its audacity a step further for the Japanese market, designing an electronic model powered by a battery recharged by a central rotor **(4)**. Some projects never made it into production but the prototypes have become highly sought after.

AUTOMATIC HIGH FREQUENCY

The menacing shadow of quartz watches had been looming large over Swiss watchmaking since 1969, so much so that some companies took a stand against it. The champion they chose was the high-frequency mechanical movement (see page 88), known for its exceptional watchmaking accuracy. Zenith made a name for itself that same year by unveiling not one but two high-frequency automatic watches: the Zenith Defy 4Hz **(5)**, running at 28,800bph, and the El Primero 5Hz, a pioneering automatic chronograph vibrating at 36,000bph. The Zenith brand did not take to the field alone. Certina also entered the fray with its DS 288 series but, despite their determination, any victory achieved by watches adopting this technology would be Pyrrhic. Vindication would come only later.

PLASTIC MECHANICAL MOVEMENTS

Manufacturers didn't stop there, however, and pushed their imaginations to the limit to stem the rise of quartz watches. This was the case with Tissot, which unveiled the Astrolon, also known as the Idea 2001, in 1971. This thinly concealed nod to Stanley Kubrick's film *2001: A Space Odyssey* was an all-plastic design with a unique mechanical movement, the calibre 2250 Systal, referring to Tissot's system of auto-lubrication **(6)**. But the design was just too cutting-edge and the launch was an unmitigated disaster, frightening off distributors who found themselves in the middle of the quartz watch war. Nonetheless, 40 years on, Swatch would breathe new life into the notion of a plastic mechanical watch with its Sistem51.

SEIKO
395
Energiser
MADE IN USA

JAPANESE SUPREMACY

CHAPTER 3

JAPANESE SUPREMACY

INDEPENDENCE AND ACCURACY

Having arisen from Switzerland's technological heritage of the second half of the 19th century, Japanese watchmaking shook itself free of Swiss influence with a single objective: to design ever more accurate watches.

BREAKING FREE FROM THE SWISS YOKE

The first watches reached the Japanese archipelago during the 1860s, and watchmaking remained under the control of Swiss merchants based in Yokohama until the end of the 19th century. In response to the specific requirements of the Japanese market, these traders imported Swiss watches that were then supplied to Japanese businessmen who took care of distribution and sales. This market became more and more lucrative as the country industrialized, with 145,000 watches being sold in 1900 (the total had been scarcely 47,000 in 1880). These political and commercial circumstances gradually persuaded bold Japanese merchants to free themselves from the domination of the Swiss and begin to produce of watches of their own – and so the Seiko watchmaking factory (see page 104) was founded by the watchmaking merchant Kintaro Hattori in Tokyo in 1892. Its first watch, the Timekeeper, had been designed a few years previously by engineers trained in the Swiss town of Le Locle who were now using machinery sourced from Switzerland and the United States.

Hattori faced a major problem, however: the price of his watches was just too high compared to imported timepieces. Never short of ideas, he managed to talk the Japanese political classes into increasing customs tariffs so that Japanese products could compete. Importers took fright at this brutal protectionism and adopted an approach that came to be known as *chablonnage* (importing watches in the form of spare parts to evade taxation). This was not a technique designed to put the minds of Swiss watchmakers (Rolex included) at rest, as they feared that the major companies might relocate.

FROM NEUCHÂTEL TO YOKOHAMA

Swiss apprehension was confirmed with a boom in the business of Rodolphe Schmid, a watch importer born in Neuchâtel in 1871 who settled in Yokohama in 1894. Schmid was one of the largest foreign merchants in Japan and had moved a portion of his business to the country to avoid the consequences of customs protectionism. In 1908, he began importing component parts that were assembled in a small workshop in Yokohama. To support this business, his family opened a watch case factory in Neuchâtel the same year and a further decisive step was taken in 1913, it began to produce cases in Japan. Schmid's Japanese facility (which had since been relocated to Tokyo) went into overdrive. Five years later, when the Shokosha Watch Research Institute (founded by the jeweller Kamekichi Yamazaki) designed a pocket watch, Schmid teamed up with the Institute to found the company that would become Citizen (see page 108). The workforce increased from 30 employees in 1913 to 110 in 1920, and then to nearly 200 by 1927. Citizen was fast becoming the country's second-largest watchmaking factory and gearing up to compete with Seiko.

A QUEST FOR ACCURACY

Seiko unveiled its first wristwatch in 1924, firing the starting gun for a career based on innovation. More than 30 years later (in 1956), this took the form of an anti-shock system that revolutionized the watch industry, and which was followed (in 1959) by the Marvel automatic watch. The Grand Seiko, the result of an ambitious spec sheet, made an appearance a year after that and embodied the very essence of watchmaking excellence, combining accuracy, legibility and durability, and leaving its competitors in the dust. Its overnight success proved a shot in the arm for Seiko, a company that had been more and more distracted by its obsession with accuracy, even in the face of its nascent rivalry with Citizen, which had forged partnerships with foreign firms such as LIP for electric technology (see page 18) and Bulova for its tuning fork (see page 34). Having emerged victorious from chronometer testing in Japan, from 1964 onwards the Seiko team turned its attention towards foreign challenges and the famous Swiss observatory competitions. So much so that in 1968 a Grand Seiko movement won the mechanical watch prize at Geneva Observatory – recognition at last. As a final stroke, at its launch on 25 December 1969, the Astron became the first quartz watch to be sold commercially, promising performance unrivalled at the time. The whole world was sitting up and taking notice of the might of this Japanese firm – although this first model would turn out to be no more than a foretaste of the expertise it would demonstrate in the matters of accuracy in general and quartz in particular.

39SQC

DAINI-SEIKOSHA – 1972

The meteoric rise of Seiko watches at the end of the 1960s was orchestrated from two production facilities – Suwa and Daini. The calibre 39, the first quartz watch manufactured at Daini, was notable for its excellence and unique design.

SEE OPPOSITE	1972 MODEL
MANUFACTURER	DAINI-SEIKOSHA
MODEL	QUARTZ
CALIBRE	CALIBRE 39
MOVEMENT	QUARTZ
PRODUCTION	SOLD COMMERCIALLY
MATERIAL	STEEL
STRAP	LEATHER

DAINI-SEIKOSHA AND SUWA-SEIKOSHA

Two logos – Daini-Seikosha (left) and Suwa-Seikosha (right).

SUWA VS DAINI

Kintaro Hattori opened his watchmaker's workshop in Tokyo's dynamic Ginza district in 1881, and the profits allowed this ambitious horologist to begin importing (and selling) Swiss clocks. His business flourished, enabling him to acquire premises in which to establish a factory of his own in 1892, which was christened Seikosha (a portmanteau word combining *seiko*, which means 'exquisite' or 'tiny', and *sha*, 'house'). A second facility, dubbed Daini-Seikosha (literally, second Seikosha) was built in the Kameido district of Tokyo in 1937. The division of labour was initially straightforward, with Seikosha making clocks and Daini specializing in wristwatches, but World War II put in an unwelcome appearance and the Daini factory was obliged to evacuate to flee the bombing, moving out of the capital to Suwa in the Japanese Alps. During the war, the original factory in Kameido was completely destroyed and had to be rebuilt, leaving Seiko with two production facilities: Daini-Seikosha in Kameido, which retained the name Daini, and Daini-Seikosha in Suwa, which was later dubbed Suwa-Seikosha.

SIBLING RIVALRY

After the war, the Suwa site was dedicated to developing highly accurate wristwatches for men, a programme that gave rise to iconic models such as the Marvel, the Lord Marvel and the Crown. In 1959, just before the company was rechristened Suwa-Seikosha, Daini-Seikosha (in Suwa) acquired the Daiwa-Kogyo manufacturing company and it was this partnership that produced the Grand Seiko in 1960. The Daini team, which had initially concentrated its efforts on mechanical watches for women, gradually began to compete with the teams based in Suwa and, by the end of the 1960s, these two separate sites each created Seiko watches using their own methods and culture – there was now healthy competition between them.

THE DAINI QUARTZ MOVEMENT

The rivalry between the teams at Suwa and Daini played a major role in the development of Seiko's quartz watches. In 1969, the calibre 35, the first production quartz movement, was installed in the Astron, a model created by the Suwa team. A year later, Daini developed the calibre 36, the world's first calibre with a high performing CMOS (complementary metal-oxide semiconductor) integrated circuit, but which upon commercialization showed major flaws and was immediately retracted. Not to be outdone, Suwa immediately responded with the calibre 38, a technical improvement on all the preceding movements thanks to its integrated circuit and faster-oscillating quartz. Around 1971, Daini launched the calibre 39, a high-end quartz movement to rival Suwa's calibre 38. This incorporated an electromagnetic escapement rather than a stepping motor and also featured a flashing LED at the top right-hand side of the dial to indicate that it was running. It was powered by two batteries and launched as part of the 39SQ series, a line that boasted chunky rectangular cases reminiscent of the Beta 21 but clearly differing from the later Astron versions, which were fitted with calibre 38 movements. These quartz movements, with their unique design, were produced until 1976 and never resurrected. The idea of a flashing LED was also to be a feature unique in quartz watch history.

Quartz
SEIKO
V.F.A.
19

KING TWIN QUARTZ

SUWA-SEIKOSHA – 1978

The accuracy of Seiko watches improved in regular leaps and bounds over the course of the 1970s thanks to Twin Quartz technology. This made it possible to progress from a mean deviation rate that could be measured monthly to one that was best expressed annually.

SEE OPPOSITE	1978 MODEL
MANUFACTURER	SUWA-SEIKOSHA
MODEL	KING TWIN QUARTZ
CALIBRE	CALIBRE 9923
MOVEMENT	QUARTZ
PRODUCTION	SOLD COMMERCIALLY
MATERIAL	GOLD-PLATED
STRAP	INTEGRATED

ACCURACY CALCULATION

- 1974 — KING QUARTZ 48: +/- 10 SECONDS PER MONTH
- 1975 — GRAND QUARTZ 48: +/- 5 SECONDS PER MONTH
- 1976 — QUARTZ SUPERIOR 48: +/- 1 SECOND PER MONTH
- 1978 — KING TWIN QUARTZ: +/- 20 SECONDS PER YEAR
- 1978 — GRAND TWIN QUARTZ: +/- 10 SECONDS PER YEAR
- 1978 — SUPERIOR TWIN QUARTZ: +/- 5 SECONDS PER YEAR

THE VFA LABEL

The launch of the world's first production quartz watch in December 1969 was nothing short of a watchmaking revolution. But far from resting on its laurels, Seiko continued to invest in innovation, focusing first on miniaturization and accuracy. Now at the cutting edge of technology, the Japanese brand introduced the VFA (Very Fine Adjusted) label for its mechanical watches with the intention of cementing the undisputed accuracy of its timepieces in people's minds. Seiko unveiled its calibre 35 the following year, doubling the frequency to 16kHz, although the oscillator was still sensitive to temperature variations. Quartz, initially conceived as a simple scientific project, had transformed into a technology for large-scale, high-end production.

ACCURACY CALCULATED ANNUALLY

The brand's aim was now clear: it wished to attach its name to a VFA quartz movement for all temperatures. Suwa-Seikosha unveiled the calibre 38, its first quartz calibre under the VFA banner, in 1971 and its initial frequency of 16kHz was increased to 32kHz in 1974. Suwa then released its calibre 48 to compete with the calibre 39 manufactured by Daini, its rival subsidiary (see page 104). These movements were built into various models, including the King Quartz (+/- ten seconds per month), the Grand Quartz (+/- five seconds per month) and the Quartz Superior (+/- one second per month). The calibre 48 watches were produced in 1978, just as thermocompensated Twin Quartz movements, regulated by two crystals, were arriving on the market. This was the exact moment that Seiko stopped measuring its accuracy by the month and started to calculate it by the year.

TWIN QUARTZ TECHNOLOGY

A quartz crystal oscillator fulfils the same function as a free-sprung balance wheel in a mechanical watch, although the beat rate of the former may be as much as 32kHz, as opposed to about 4Hz for a mechanical watch. Unsurprisingly there is a vast difference in accuracy between the two technologies, but any variation in temperature (either up or down) may alter the oscillation rate of a quartz crystal. A range of different technologies had been developed to reduce the effect of the temperature variations to which quartz may be exposed (see page 88), but none seemed to match the approach of the Twin Quartz; the technology was more efficient than that of its competitors in terms of both design and energy consumption. The watchmakers at Seiko had had the cunning idea of arranging two crystal oscillators side-by-side, the first was used to detect temperature variations so that it could compensate for any wobble in frequency from the other. This technology was integrated into a range of variants, including the King Twin Quartz (+/- 20 seconds per year), the Grand Twin Quartz (+/- 10 seconds per year) and the Superior Twin Quartz (+/- 5 seconds per year).

SEIKO
TWIN QUARTZ
DIM 9

0100

CITIZEN – 2019

Fifty years after marketing its first quartz watch model, Citizen – whose research in the field had never let up – finally made it to the top. The company now held the much-prized record for the most accurate watch.

SEE OPPOSITE	2019 MODEL
MANUFACTURER	CITIZEN
MODEL	AQ6010
CALIBRE	0100
MOVEMENT	QUARTZ ECO DRIVE
PRODUCTION	SOLD COMMERCIALLY
MATERIAL	WHITE GOLD
STRAP	LEATHER

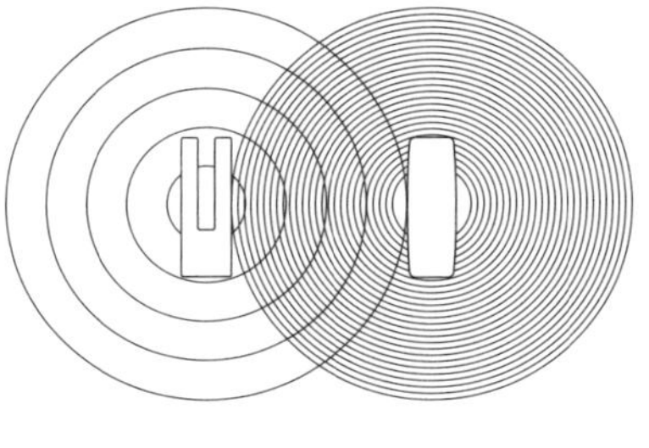

CUTTING QUARTZ

On the left, a traditional quartz cut in the shape of a tuning fork vibrating at 32,768Hz; on the right, an AT-cut quartz crystal vibrating at 8,388,608Hz.

FROM ELECTRIC TO TUNING FORK

In 1966, slightly later than its Western competitors, Citizen unveiled the X-8, the first electromechanical watch to be manufactured in Japan. While its fixed-coil movement (see page 16) did not make much of an impression and left little trace in watchmaking history, the watch nonetheless stood out for its use of a titanium case. A year later, Citizen went a step further by incorporating a transistor (see page 16) into an electronic quartz clock. The interest the firm was showing in electrical power was also apparent in its acquisition of a licence from Bulova for its tuning-fork calibre 218, which was incorporated into the Hisonic series in 1971 at a time when some competitors were already looking to quartz for their wristwatches.

FROM HIGH-FREQUENCY TO SOLAR

Wishing to make its presence felt on the quartz market, the brand unveiled the Quartz Crystron in the mid-1970s. The watch was fitted with a very high-frequency quartz crystal vibrating at 4MHz (see page 88) and claimed an accuracy of +/- three seconds per year (a performance that should be taken with a pinch of salt as it lacked a thermocompensation system). This was not the principal innovation introduced by Citizen during this prolific decade of new releases, however. That accolade is reserved for its development of the Crystron Solar Cell, an analogue watch fitted with small solar panels that ran on light, anticipating the brand's Eco-Drive technology.

THE MOST ACCURATE WATCH

In 2019, 50 years after bringing its first quartz watch to market, Citizen set a technological record with its calibre 0100. This is considered to be the most accurate watch movement ever made, with an approximate mean variation rate of only one second per year. To achieve such a performance, the movement used an AT-cut quartz crystal oscillator vibrating at the ultra-high frequency of 8.4MHz (in fact, 8,388,608Hz). It had been known that the cut of a quartz crystal can influence its vibration and its resistance to temperature variations since 1934. The usual cut used in watchmaking was in the shape of a tuning fork – until the engineers at Citizen hit upon the idea of using an AT-cut quartz crystal oscillator and optimizing every aspect relating to energy consumption so that it could be built into a watch. And with good reason – up to this point, such a system had been reserved for much larger devices such as computers.

CITIZEN

JAPANESE SUPREMACY

THE 7A28

The Seiko 7A28 was launched in 1983 with a mission as noble as it was ambitious: to provide the same durability as a traditional mechanical chronograph combined with the revolutionary accuracy of quartz technology.

A QUARTZ CHRONOGRAPH WITH HANDS IN THE DIGITAL AGE

When Seiko unveiled its 7A28 movement in 1983, quartz had become the norm and many companies were also turning towards displaying the time digitally, with a particular focus on LCD technology (see page 157). Most quartz watches used disposable plastic movements that were destined to be thrown away when they stopped working, and digital watches are difficult to service. For its first analogue quartz chronograph movement, Seiko chose an approach that set it apart from the rest of the market. The calibre was constructed entirely from metal, featured 15 rubies to prevent friction (see page 236) and was decorated like a mechanical movement (see page 124). As far as its performance was concerned, the brochures Seiko distributed when it was presented to the public boasted a timing accuracy of '5/100ths of a second'. As the more mathematically inclined know, this means it was capable of measuring time to one-twentieth of a second, as these two fractions are equal. It should also be noted that some models featured a more modest accuracy of one-tenth of a second on their dials. Overall the accuracy of the Seiko 7A28 was about 15 seconds per month at a normal temperature (see page 88).

ONE CROWN, THREE PUSHERS

Unlike a classic chronograph, the 7A28 did not have two push-buttons and a crown located at 3 o'clock. Instead, it featured three push-buttons complemented by a setting crown at 8 o'clock. As with other chronographs, the start/stop button was at 2 o'clock and the reset button at 4 o'clock.

Pressing the button at 2 o'clock started the stopwatch; the hand on the right-hand subdial rotated to record the tenths of a second while the central hand on the subdial at 6 o'clock moved in increments of one second. A second press at 2 o'clock stopped the stopwatch, and then pressing the push-button at 4 o'clock returned the hands to their original positions.

The third push-button, located at 10 o'clock, operated a split function, a variant on the stopwatch function that made it possible to measure two events starting at the same time but finishing at different points. Such a function was generally reserved for high-end mechanical chronographs.

A ROBUST MOVEMENT

From the moment of its release, the 7A28 was designed for long-term use thanks to a power cell offering battery life of two years. The movement also featured a low-battery indicator that caused the second hand to jump every two seconds when the power was running low. The four stepping motors tucked away behind metal plates contained no plastic components and could be repaired indefinitely – and still can be today, if you can find the parts required. Similarly, the 7A28 could be recalibrated when the battery was changed. If the hands of the chronograph ever became misaligned, it was possible to reset them to zero in a few steps:

- pull the crown out to the first click,
- hold each push-button down until the hands return to the zero position,
- push the crown back in.

The 7A28 was particularly popular for its robust movement and ease of maintenance, and was used in a host of Seiko models as well as in watches from other brands. Many of these are still going strong, despite the passage of time and the sometimes harsh treatment meted out by their owners. Launched in 1973, the Seiko 7A28 had a noble and ambitious vocation: to offer the same level of durability as a traditional mechanical chronograph, combined with the revolutionary precision of quartz technology.

GREY GHOST

SEIKO - 1983

The 'Grey Ghost' version of the 7A28 chronograph is notable for its particularly understated design. The lines of this model provide a sharp contrast to those of other, more disruptive designs, but it is a rare and sought-after variant nonetheless.

SEE OPPOSITE	1983 MODEL
MANUFACTURER	SEIKO
MODEL	7A28-7079 'GREY GHOST'
CALIBRE	7A28
MOVEMENT	QUARTZ
PRODUCTION	SOLD COMMERCIALLY
MATERIAL	STEEL
STRAP	INTEGRATED

JDM VS EXPORT

Some of the many 7A28 models produced by Seiko were reserved for the Japanese market from their release; these are known as JDM (Japanese Domestic Market) models. They can be identified by a distinctive inscription on the dial that reads 'Seiko Chronograph Quartz' (see page 127), whereas the dials on models exported to other markets read 'Seiko Quartz Chronograph'. Some of these export models also bore the legend 'Sports 100'. The watches intended for the rest of the world can be distinguished from their domestic cousins by the inscriptions 'Min.' on the minute counter and '1/10s.' on the second counter, which would seem to suggest that the 7A28-7079 model was intended for the international market. It has nonetheless always been a rarity and difficult to find, hence its nickname, the 'Grey Ghost'.

THE 'GREY GHOST'

The vast range of 7A28 variants includes several bold designs that emphasize anything but purity of line or colour scheme. But in the 7A28-7079, Seiko created a watch with minimalist charm worthy of a racing driver's on-board chronograph. The dial is finished in matte grey with three sunburst sub-registers, a subtle contrast that lights up the whole watch. Legibility is guaranteed by precise railway tracks (see page 236) in jet black that are never intrusive, paired with white lumed indices that set off the elegance of the dial. The 40-mm *tonneau* (barrel) case featured a meticulously sand-blasted finish. The whole package is rounded off with a shiny, bevelled bezel (see page 236) that adds a touch of sophistication. This watch was Seiko's first foray into a sporty chic aesthetic that was underlined by the presence of an integrated strap.

INTEGRATED STRAP AND DAGGER HANDS

Unlike other 7A28 straps, the 'Grey Ghost' bracelet comprises five bands of links and is completely integrated into the watch. Its sand-blasted finish blends harmoniously into the case and its staircase-patterned hinges are effortlessly incorporated into the overall look. Another attractive feature of the 7A28-7079 model are its hands, shaped like the blade of a knife or dagger tapering elegantly to a point with a carbon finish that enhances legibility in an eye-catching fashion.

SEIKO
QUARTZ
20 MIN. 10
1/10S.

YACHT TIMER

SEIKO – 1983

The 7A28 quartz chronograph movement built into the Yacht Timer model was Seiko's entrance ticket to the prestigious world of yacht-race timekeeping, a mark of recognition that did not stop this iconic model from evolving over the years.

SEE OPPOSITE	1983 MODEL
MANUFACTURER	SEIKO
MODEL	YACHT TIMER 7A28-7090
CALIBRE	7A28
MOVEMENT	QUARTZ
PRODUCTION	SOLD COMMERCIALLY
MATERIAL	STEEL
STRAP	TROPIC

SEIKO
YACHT TIMER 6M

The Seiko Yacht Timer 6M models that appeared in the 1990s featured discs on their dials that were a nod to the first regatta watches developed by Aquastar.

FROM THE OLYMPICS TO SAILING

Seiko was an official partner of the 1964 Tokyo Olympic Games, an event unprecedented in the history of global watchmaking as it was the first time the Japanese had assumed responsibility for timekeeping, relegating the Swiss to second place. This humiliation was so painful that Longines, Omega and the Federation of the Swiss Watch Industry teamed up in 1972 to found the Société Suisse de Chronométrage Sportif SA (known as Swiss Timing) to compete with the Japanese brand. These efforts were in vain, however, and 20 years later, Seiko was still able to net the contract for the Olympic Games in Barcelona – and for good reason, as its sporting expertise had been constantly improving. Though there had been no end to the rivalry, the Japanese company now had a place at the table for many different events, from athletics to football to sailing.

QUARTZ REGATTA WATCHES

The regatta chronograph launched by Aquastar in 1961 and popularized by Yema in 1967 was a watchmaking innovation that revolutionized competition sailing. It was used for the five-minute mark, the five minutes before the start of a yacht race in which the skippers jockey to find the best possible position for their vessels. Despite the patents filed by Aquastar and Yema, these specialized chronographs did not require any major modifications to their movements. Much like the Valjoux mechanical movements previously used, the 7A28 proved perfectly suited to the task. The Yacht Timer 7A28-7090, which appeared in catalogues in 1983 at a price of 35,000 Japanese yen, instantly stood out for its case design. While the button at 4 o'clock remained short, those at 10 o'clock and 2 o'clock were longer than usual and there was a minutes sub-register at 9 o'clock divided into 30 minutes, with 6 sections of 5 minutes alternately coloured pale and royal blue, with a striking yellow indicator hand. The outer perimeter of the dial featured a railway track displaying a countdown in seconds from 60 to 0.

FROM DANCING HANDS TO DISCS

The 7A28-7090 Yacht Timer disappeared from shop windows in 1985 and production was halted, but the legacy of this regatta watch lives on in its calibre 8M movement. The watches that followed had various modes that could be activated via the crown, such as time (the normal time) and timer (a countdown). When the latter was selected, the hands would spring into life and defy conventional watch logic by running backwards. In addition, the countdown could be set in one-minute intervals from one to thirty minutes and even featured pre-programmed settings of five, ten and fifteen minutes. Collectors were particularly fond of these models, affectionately naming them 'Dancing Hands' watches. Seiko went further down this road with the calibre 6M of the 1990s which, in a cheeky nod to the first models developed by Aquastar, featured Yacht Timer-style coloured discs.

SEIKO
YACHT TIMER
QUARTZ

ROYAL AIR FORCE

SEIKO – 1984

After years of sourcing mechanical chronographs in the West, the UK's Ministry of Defence turned to Japan and ordered enough robust calibre 7A28s from Seiko to equip the entire Royal Air Force.

SEE OPPOSITE	1984 MODEL
MANUFACTURER	SEIKO
MODEL	7A28-7020 RAF
CALIBRE	7A28
MOVEMENT	QUARTZ
PRODUCTION	MILITARY
MATERIAL	STEEL
STRAP	N/A

SEIKO
MILITARY INSCRIPTIONS

Specifications for military watches ensure that the NATO stock number, manufacturing attribution details and issue reference number are stamped on the caseback, as well as the MOD broad arrow that indicates UK government property.

THE MOD IN THE QUARTZ ERA

The chronographs used by the Royal Air Force (RAF), the UK's aerial defence force, are subject to Def Stan (defence standardization) specifications, with the first iteration of this norm requiring the use of chronographs with a single pusher. The Lemania calibre 2200 was more or less the only watch to satisfy this requirement and was therefore standard issue for UK pilots for a number of years. The country's Ministry of Defence (MOD) modified its Def Stan spec sheet in 1970 with a view to reducing costs, and opened up tenders to other manufacturers. Chronographs with two pushers were now permitted, with the calibre Valjoux 7733 an obvious choice. The principal suppliers of RAF watches for the next 12 years were mainly brands from Switzerland (Newmark), America (Hamilton) and the domestic market (CWC and Precista), but things changed in the 1980s, when the quartz watches developed by Seiko offered such good value for money that it was awarded the MOD's business.

RESPECTED SPECIFICATIONS

Despite the concession on the number of pushers, Def Stan specifications remained demanding, requiring a matte black dial with two or three sub-registers, lumed hour indices and white, lumed hands. In addition, specially designed lugs were welded to the case to accommodate the famed NATO military strap. The 7A28-7120 model was a perfect fit for these prerequisites, with a case that was probably the most stripped-down of all the 7A28s, a sand-blasted matte finish and welded lugs. To meet the UK's specifications, Seiko also marked the dial with a 'P' in a circle, referring to the chemical symbol for promethium, the luminescent substance used to illuminate the hour indices and hands. To comply with military watch standards, the NATO stock number, manufacturing attribution details and issue reference number were stamped on the caseback, along with the MOD broad arrow that indicates something is the property of the UK government.

AN OBVIOUS CHOICE

It came as no surprise that the UK's MOD looked to Japan for its new chronograph in 1984. When the decision was taken, Seiko had been producing excellent quartz watches for 15 years, and the 7A28 model was a perfect fit for military watch specifications. It measured time to one-twentieth of a second and featured a split function that made it possible to time two events that started simultaneously but finished at different points, a capability of particular use during a military operation. Other advantages included its long battery life and the ease with which the metal movement could be repaired (see page 111). A total of 11,307 units of the model were issued to all ranks of the RAF over the course of six years of deployment, making it one of the most popular within the armed forces. The MOD again put its faith in Seiko in the 1990s, choosing its 7T27-7A20 model.

12
30
20 MIN. 10
0
8 2
1/10 S.
6 4
45 15
SEC.
30

JAMES BOND

SEIKO - 1985

From the moment in 1973 when he was cast as 007 in the film *Live and Let Die*, Roger Moore maintained his loyalty to Seiko watches - notably so in *A View to a Kill*, for which he wore an analogue chronograph from the Japanese brand that sparked debate among experts.

SEE OPPOSITE	1985 MODEL
MANUFACTURER	SEIKO
MODEL	7A28-7020
CALIBRE	7A28
MOVEMENT	QUARTZ
PRODUCTION	SOLD COMMERCIALLY
MATERIAL	STEEL
STRAP	N/A

A VIEW TO A KILL

In the course of a perilous mission to the Siberian coast, James Bond recovers a top-secret microchip from the abandoned body of agent 003. With the Russian army (also hunting for this valuable technology) on his heels, 007 gets caught up in a breakneck ski chase but uses his trademark skills to shake off his pursuers. He takes refuge on board a mini-submarine (camouflaged as an iceberg) under the command of Kimberley Jones, a top field agent for MI6 (the UK's overseas intelligence agency)...but despite all this, it was the watch on Roger Moore's wrist at the end of the exciting pre-titles sequence of *A View to a Kill* (1985) that drew the attention of watch connoisseurs – an elegant Seiko chronograph.

JAMES BOND WITH A 7A28-7020?

At first sight, Bond's watch seemed to be a reference 7A28-7020. However, while resembling the 'Grey Ghost' model (see page 112), it featured a case with curved lugs and had no integrated strap. The design was more reminiscent of the models selected by the MOD (see page 116), of which some models with pale dials had been supplied to the British army. The notion that Roger Moore's James Bond would wear a 7A28-7020 was also challenged by some aficionados of the world's most famous secret agent. Using high-resolution images from the film, they established that 007's watch had a day/date display, which was not the case for the model mentioned above. The watch worn by the British actor was still undoubtedly a Seiko, however, being a variant of the 7A28 – a 7A38-7060 model (see page 120), to be more precise.

ROGER MOORE'S SEIKOS

Roger Moore wore Seiko watches from the moment he donned agent 007's tuxedo, favouring in particular the LCD models to which he remained loyal for his entire career as a spy on the silver screen. His outings with digital watches began with *Live and Let Die* (1973), in which he also wore an LED Pulsar (see page 144), and include *Moonraker* (1979) and *For Your Eyes Only* (1981), in which he is briefly glimpsed wearing a Golden Tuna dive watch (see page 132). He continued the tradition in *Octopussy* (1983) in which Q, always ready with cutting-edge technologies, issues him with the famous LCD TV Watch (see page 214). In his last appearance as Bond in *A View to a Kill* (1985), the actor went back to using an analogue watch, choosing a 7A28-7020 chronograph...or rather, the 7A38-7060, the Day-Date version.

TACHYMETER
SEIKO
QUARTZ
Chronograph
MIN.
1/10S.

7A38

SEIKO – 1984

Seiko brought out a number of different versions of its analogue chronograph during the 1980s, with several 7A movements making an appearance; the 7A38 was enhanced with a day/date complication.

SEE OPPOSITE	1985 MODEL
MANUFACTURER	SEIKO
MODEL	7A38
CALIBRE	7A
MOVEMENT	QUARTZ
PRODUCTION	SOLD COMMERCIALLY
MATERIAL	TITANIUM
STRAP	INTEGRATED

SEIKO
'SEIKO OAK'

The integrated strap was reminiscent of Gérald Genta's design for Audemars Piguet, although the ornamental bezel had 12 sides rather than 8.

A DAY/DATE COMPLICATION

In the wake of the resounding success achieved by the 7A28 in 1983, Seiko unveiled the 7A38 with its improved movement the following year. True to its essential nature as a chronograph, it featured three sub-registers, recording minutes, seconds and the nearest tenth (in actual fact, twentieth) of a second. This third sub-register now also featured an additional day and date function and, to cap it all, the two displays could be set independently and easily by operating the crown. Much like the 7A28, this movement was then installed in a wide range of models, including some that were available only on the Japanese market. These are easily identified by the inscription 'Seiko Chronograph Quartz' on the dial, without 'Min.' and '1/10s.' (see page 112).

A HOST OF VERSIONS

While Seiko produced models closely related to the 7A28 (such as the reference 7A38-7060 worn by the iconic James Bond, which was very similar to the 7A28-7020 – see page 118), the brand also installed its movement in a host of variants, some of which were exclusively destined for certain markets.
The most striking of these was probably the reference 7A38-7020. Marketed as the Sports 100 and affectionately rechristened the 'Seiko Oak', the watch was soon much sought after, and it is easy to see why: with its integrated strap, the layout was a clear nod to Gérald Genta's design for Audemars Piguet, although the ornamental bezel had 12 sides instead of 8 in this case.

7A VARIANTS

The legendary 7A28 chronograph was created in 1982 and first marketed a year later. It was available in a number of versions, all categorized with the prefix 7A, including the 7A07, nicknamed the 'Bullhead'. This combined push-buttons at 10 o'clock and 1 o'clock with sub-registers at 12 o'clock and 6 o'clock, lending the overall configuration a distinctive bull's head appearance. The 7A34 featured a date window at 12 o'clock, as did its pocket watch counterpart the 7A7, while the 7A36, with the date at 3 o'clock, dispensed with the famous 1/10s. sub-register. The 7A48 and the 7A54 (the pocket watch version) were notable for their poetic ability to display the phases of the moon for those who took the time to pay attention to such details. This illustrious series of 7A movements was retired in the 1990s to make way for the 7T range.

SEIKO
CHRONOGRAPH
QUARTZ
TACHYMETER
TUE
16

7T

SEIKO – 1992

The highly respected 7A range of Seiko chronographs was retired in the 1990s to make way for its successors. The new line, known as 7T, achieved the technological marvel of being able to measure time to one-hundredth of a second.

SEE OPPOSITE	1997 MODEL
MANUFACTURER	SEIKO
MODEL	7T
CALIBRE	7T
MOVEMENT	QUARTZ
PRODUCTION	SOLD COMMERCIALLY
MATERIAL	STEEL
STRAP	INTEGRATED

SEIKO
OLYMPIC

This rare chronograph, which was never sold in the United States, was unveiled to coincide with the 1992 Barcelona Olympic Games. It was capable of measuring time to one-hundredth of a second.

THE 1992 BARCELONA OLYMPICS

Twenty-eight years after making its mark as the official timekeeper of the 1964 Summer Olympics in Tokyo (see page 114), Seiko returned in style to take up timing duties for the 25th outing of the world's largest athletics event. More than 300 engineers and timing specialists were deployed on site for the 1992 Summer Olympics in Barcelona, in anticipation of which the creative minds of the brand's researchers had pushed the analogue chronograph to its very limits. The upshot was new technological capabilities twinned with a powerful advertising campaign for the Olympic 1/100 chronograph, also known as the reference 7T59-7A20.

PRECISION TO 1/100 OF A SECOND

The advent of this new watch calibre was heralded with a bold and astonishing claim from the brand's top brass. They had wanted to show the world that the impossible was possible, and that they had achieved it in style. Indeed, to this day, the calibre 7T59 remains the only analogue quartz chronograph that is capable of accuracy to 1/100 of a second while also featuring day, date and GMT complications (see page 236). It was sold at prices that could exceed $1,000 (equivalent to about $3,500 today) and its high-end status was due, at least in part, to quartz technology.

SHORT PRODUCTION RUNS AND SCARCE VARIANTS

The lifespan of the calibre 7T59 was short and glorious in equal measure – it was unveiled just before the start of the Olympic Games and taken off the shelves soon after the closing ceremony. It was also never sold in the United States. However, as was often the case with Seiko, the movement gave rise to a number of different variants. A rare version of this highly accurate chronograph, able to measure time to the nearest hundredth of a second but lacking day, date and GMT complications, was released as the calibre 7T52, while another version, the 7T82, featured a retrograde minute complication and a battery power level indicator. Modern high-end Seiko chronographs have generally turned their backs on traditional quartz, although electronic modules have not been abandoned entirely – one has been pressed into service by a traditional mechanical movement in the Spring Drive calibre 9R and is used to regulate the watch without an external source of energy: a motor spring drives the wheel train while a rotor generates an electric discharge that activates the electronic circuit and the quartz crystal oscillator – the perfect blend of tradition and modernity.

SEIKO
TACHYMETER
1/100 Chronograph

DESIGN BY GIUGIARO

FACT SHEET N°6

Giorgetto Giugiaro and his company Italdesign created a series of revolutionary designs for Seiko watches, including two cult chronographs fitted with the 7A28 movement.

THE ITALDESIGN STUDIO

Even within the vast constellation of Italian designers, Giorgetto Giugiaro is a star. Coming from a long line of artists and having trained at Turin's Academy of Fine Arts, he skilfully divides his time between the worlds of motoring and everyday objects, effortlessly merging the luxurious and the practical. After learning his craft at Fiat and the prestigious coachbuilding firms Bertone and Ghia, in 1968 Giugiaro joined engineer Aldo Mantovani in founding a firm that they called Italdesign. Giugiaro demonstrated huge versatility in his creative output from the outset, in everything from the shape of the first Volkswagen Golf to supercars for Bugatti and Maserati. His skills were not confined to cars, and encompassed camera design for Nikon, bottles for Shiseido, and he even invented a pasta shape for Voiello. The sky was the limit for Italdesign, and the company entered the world of watchmaking when Seiko called on its talents.

SPEEDMASTER & ALIEN

It all began in 1983 with the launch of four chronographs in the new Speedmaster series (two digital and two analogue models). The design of the digital SSBA series was conspicuously bold – one of the watches was fitted with a nylon strap that was ideal for fixing it to a dashboard, transforming it into a dashboard instrument, while another featured an angled dial to make it easier to read while driving; this latter model became a favourite of the legendary Formula 1 driver Ayrton Senna. The two analogue versions shared the same 7A28 module (see page 111) and featured asymmetrical designs. The reference 7A28-6000 had a case offset from the strap so that it would not be covered by a shirtsleeve, while the reference 7A28-7000 had a unique arrangement of push-buttons that meant they were always within reach, whichever way the watch was turned. Although analogue, these two 7A28 models represented the watch of the future as imagined in the 1980s. If you need proof of this, they were worn in the film *Aliens*, James Cameron's comeback opus. Ripley, the heroine, proudly wears the 7A28-7000 model in silver while Lance Bishop, her android companion, has been issued with the 7A28-6000. The two chronographs have become iconic and have, of course, been rechristened the 'Seiko Ripley' and 'Seiko Bishop'.

THE SECOND WAVE

The collaboration between Seiko and Giugiaro did not stop at these four chronographs. Others followed, although some were reserved for the Japanese market, such as the 7A28-7050, a model with a case that could rotate through 360 degrees thanks to an ingenious array of ball bearings. The brand teamed up with the designer once again in 1986 to design dive watches. The fruits of this second period of collaboration included two SBBN models with offset cases, one in blue (see page 129) and the other in gold. The same year saw Seiko and Giugiaro launch the SBBJ, their most daring design, which was nicknamed the 'Steering Wheel' – not only did it look like one, it had a strap that could be fixed to a dashboard.

HERITAGE

Seiko unveiled its Macchina Sportiva range in 1996, more than 20 years later. Never content to rest on its laurels, Giugiaro's studio continued to draw inspiration from the world of motoring that its founder knew so well. Giugiaro sold 90.1 per cent of his stake in Italdesign in 2010, before giving up the rest of his shares in 2015. However, his departure did not put an end to the collaboration and reissues between the Japanese brand and the Italian studio. The 'Bishop' reappeared in 2013 and was marketed in celebration of the 30th anniversary of the 7A28. Seiko revived the 'Ripley' model in nine different colour options two years later and the dive watch resurfaced in 2017, alongside the launch of a new GPS solar watch. Ayrton Senna's LCD SSBA model was brought up-to-date in 2018. Both the original and reissued Seikos designed with Giugiaro continue to arouse the passion of quartz watch collectors to this day.

SEIKO 7A28-7000 'RIPLEY'

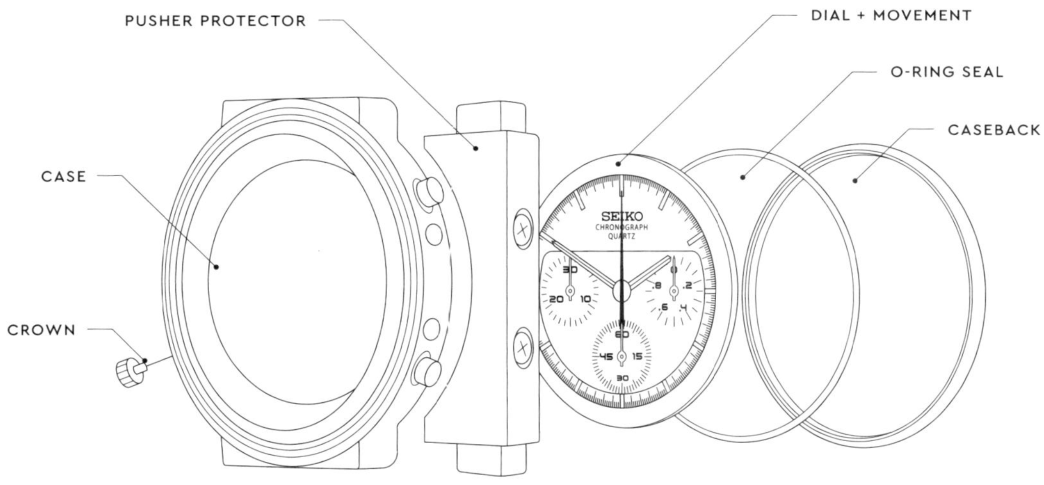

Although faintly reminiscent of the LIP Mach 2000 designed by Roger Tallon, the Seiko 7A28-7000 featured a unique arrangement of push-buttons, ensuring they were always within reach and could be accessed whatever the angle of the watch.

SPEEDMASTER RANGE

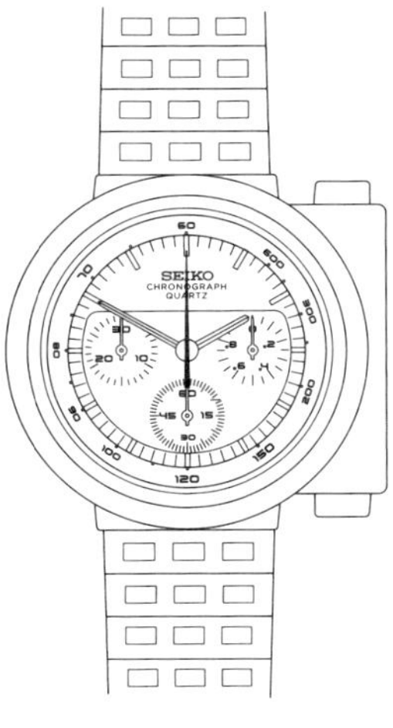

7A28-7000

This model was nicknamed the 'Ripley' in reference to the heroine of the film *Aliens.*

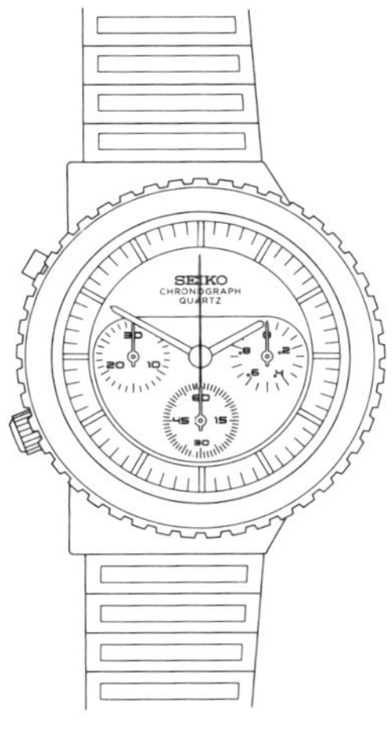

7A28-6000

This model was nicknamed 'Bishop' in reference to the android in the film *Aliens.*

SSBA022

This LCD display model was popularized by the legendary racing driver Ayrton Senna in the 1980s.

SSBA028

Unlike its stablemates, this LCD 'fieldwatch' with its nylon strap has yet to be reissued by the Japanese brand.

SEIKO

7A28-5000 'STEERING WHEEL'

This model, still featuring the robust 7A28 movement, is reminiscent in shape of a steering wheel and can be attached by its strap to a car dashboard as a supplementary instrument.

SEIKO

7A28-7000 'RIPLEY'

Full disclosure: the real 'Ripley' model is actually grey, but this black 7A28-7000 model made for the Japanese market is a killer design.

SEIKO

7A28-7050 'ROTATING'

This model was produced exclusively for the Japanese market and features a case that can rotate through 360 degrees thanks to an ingenious array of ball bearings.

SEIKO
SBBN 'SCUBA DIVER BLUE'

Two dive watches, another key business segment for Seiko, put in an appearance during the designer's creative ferment of the mid-1980s, including this blue model. They were reissued 30 years later.

JAPANESE SUPREMACY

SEIKO DIVE WATCHES

In 1978, Seiko introduced a quartz movement in a professional model intended for saturation diving. After many years of innovation, the Japanese firm's dive watch became the global standard in 1996.

1960–1968: RESEARCHING WATERTIGHTNESS

In the 1960s, Japan witnessed an explosion in watersports and nautical activities, prompting Seiko to develop a number of notable waterproof models, including the Dolphin Water Protected, the Seahorse, the Silverwave (inspired by Ervin Piquerez's Super-Compressor) and the robust Sportsmatic series. Despite these many releases, Seiko's reputation for water resistance remained a little shaky. This was before the adoption of the millimetre and probably due to its use of a unit of measurement known as the *ligne* (see page 236), which was considered to be imprecise.

Rather than just giving up, Seiko pulled out all the stops in 1965 with a new dive watch, the 62MAS. This was waterproof to a depth of 150m (492ft) and allowed the Japanese brand to restore its reputation. Much like the Rolex Submariner in Hans Wilsdorf's communications strategy 12 years before, the 62MAS was displayed in shop windows in an aquarium, a marketing coup that prompted Seiko to go a step further with its next models. The company made further improvements to its designs and, by 1986, had succeeded in making some watches watertight to a depth of 300m (984ft): the first of these was the 6215-7000, followed by the 6159-7000, featuring a Hi-Beat automatic movement with a high-frequency pulse (see page 132). However, not everyone was happy with this performance. That same year, Seiko received a letter from a professional diver who complained the 6159 was 'unusable'!

1968: 'AN UNUSABLE DIVE WATCH!'

With his pride wounded, Taro Tanaka, the head designer, read the letter carefully and discovered that the watch of a certain Mr Oshima had exploded during decompression in a hyperbaric chamber on a saturation dive. Seven years of research followed, in which Seiko engineers made crucial adjustments to meet the needs of professional divers, with the aim of designing a watch that would be waterproof to 600m (1,968ft). The result was the Seiko 6159-70, affectionately named 'Tuna' for its resemblance to a can of fish. The watch was the result of meticulous engineering, boasting some 20 patents, and its monobloc titanium case, enhanced by an innovative external shroud, revolutionized the sector. It eliminated the need for a decompression valve with an L-shaped, helium-proof gasket and its inset polyurethane strap ensured a perfect fit and was resistant to extremes of temperature – all elements that made the 'Tuna' a step-change in underwater watchmaking norms. Seiko made further innovations in 1978 with two quartz variants: the 7549-7010, which was the first quartz watch to be water-resistant to a depth of 300m (984ft), and the 7549-7009, nicknamed the 'Golden Tuna', which (like its mechanical counterpart) could be used at depths up to 600m (1,968ft). This version, immediately identifiable by its gold bezel, marked a turning-point in the history of quartz dive watches (see page 132).

1975: SEIKO EXPERTISE

Although saturation diving is carried out only by experts, sales of 'Tuna' watches – including both Hi-Beat and quartz movements – exceeded 16,000 units in 8 years. Capitalizing on this success, Seiko made this niche market a cornerstone of its output. The new 'Tunas' of the 1980s were waterproofed to a depth of 1,000m (3,280ft) and the Quartz Diver's, which was first guaranteed to 150m (492ft) and then 200m (656ft), became the best-selling quartz dive watch (see page 134). The innovations did not stop there; in 1990, Seiko revolutionized the market with the Scuba Master, the world's first computerized dive watch. It was fitted with water sensors and depth gauges and could also measure the length of a dive. This was followed in 1992 by the analogue Kinetic Diver's 200m, which opened up new horizons as it was powered by physical movement (see page 136). In a further surprising development, Seiko imposed new standards on the International Organization for Standardization (ISO) for underwater watchmaking, so much so that the ISO 6425 certification was introduced in 1996 under the brand's influence. Seiko dive watches were now to be taken seriously. Guaranteeing underwater reliability and accuracy, they were anything but unusable!

GOLDEN TUNA

SEIKO – 1986

Seiko responded to a 1975 complaint from an experienced diver by launching its legendary 'Tuna', followed three years later by several quartz versions of the same watch. Seiko pushed the envelope once again in 1986 with the quartz 'Golden Tuna', which was waterproof to a depth of 1,000m (3,280ft).

SEE OPPOSITE	1986 MODEL
MANUFACTURER	SEIKO
MODEL	'GOLDEN TUNA 1000M'
CALIBRE	7C46
MOVEMENT	QUARTZ
PRODUCTION	SOLD COMMERCIALLY
MATERIAL	TITANIUM
STRAP	POLYURETHANE

'TUNA' TIMELINE

- 1975 — 6159-7010 AUTOMATIC HI-BEAT 600M 'GRANDFATHER TUNA'
- 1978 — 7549-7010 QUARTZ 300M 'TUNA'
- 1978 — 7549-7009 QUARTZ 600M 'GOLDEN TUNA'
- 1986 — 7C46-7009 QUARTZ 1,000M 'GOLDEN TUNA 1000M'

CONSTRUCTIVE CRITICISM

Seiko fully immersed itself in the world of dive watches in 1965 with the 62MAS, which was waterproof to a depth of 150m (492ft).This was followed three years later by a major step forward in the form of a monobloc case that pushed this figure to 300m (984ft).This was first achieved by the 6215, followed by the 6159-7000 with its high-frequency automatic movement (see page 99). A crucial incident took place when Yo Oshima, an experienced diver, claimed that his Seiko was 'unusable' and had failed to fulfil its promises. The development team was determined to get to the bottom of this mystery and joined Oshima on board his diving boat to shed some light on the matter. The investigators ascertained that the mixture of air, helium and hydrogen in hyperbaric decompression chambers affected the seals of the case, causing the crystal to explode under pressure. Instead of adopting Rolex's idea of a helium release valve, Seiko chose to take its inspiration from the barnacle, a small crustacean, and the result was the 6159-7010, a mechanical model with an innovative titanium case that was watertight to 600m (1,968ft). The watch featured an L-shaped, helium-proof gasket that protected the crown and bezel, and also made it easier to clean.

GOLDEN TUNA

Seiko unveiled two quartz models in 1978, starting with the 7549-7010 (nicknamed the 'Tuna'), the first quartz watch to be guaranteed to a depth of 300m (984ft), closely followed by the 7549-7009 'Golden Tuna', which was identifiable by its golden bezel and (like its mechanical counterpart) could be used to depths of 600m (1,968ft). In the winter of 1982, Seiko decided to subject the 'Golden Tuna' to a test dive under real-world conditions, sinking it to a depth of 300m (984ft) with the aid of JAMSTEC (the Japan Agency for Marine-Earth Science and Technology). This was a great success, swelling Japan's metaphorical chest with pride; it meant that the 'Golden Tuna' could be considered the world's best dive watch. It was subjected to a test at a greater depth the following year when it was attached to the robotic arm of the Shinkai 2000, a new underwater exploration submersible, and sunk more than 1,000m (3,280ft) below sea level, exceeding its claimed guaranteed depth of 600m (1,968ft). Three years after this achievement (in 1986), Seiko launched the new 7C46 'Golden Tuna' model, which was waterproof to a depth of 1,000m (3,280ft).

CONSTANT EVOLUTION

Seiko's professional dive watch has been affectionately dubbed the 'Tuna' thanks to a shape that is more than a little reminiscent of a can of tuna and, though the name is completely unofficial, the brand has not been slow to capitalize on this over the years, even bringing out advertisements where the watch morphs into a tin can. The distinctive design of the 'Tuna', along with its great success, naturally encouraged Seiko to upgrade it over the decades. The first generation, which featured an automatic movement, was rapidly replaced by quartz versions. A Kinetic version (see page 136) appeared by the 1990s, followed by a reversion to new, high-performance automatic mechanical models. The now iconic design has been reused for a wide range of dive watches since the 2010s.

SEIKO
QUARTZ
TUE 25
PROFESSIONAL
DIVER'S 1000m

QUARTZ DIVER'S

SEIKO – 1978

The Quartz Diver's 7548 was a veritable pioneer among Seiko's consumer dive watches. Its waterproofing rating was increased from 150m (492ft) to 200m (656ft) over the course of the 1980s. Today it is remembered for its timeless styling.

SEE OPPOSITE	1978 MODEL
MANUFACTURER	SEIKO
MODEL	QUARTZ DIVER'S 150M
CALIBRE	7548
MOVEMENT	QUARTZ
PRODUCTION	SOLD COMMERCIALLY
MATERIAL	STEEL
STRAP	POLYURETHANE

SEIKO
62MAS

The Japanese brand's first dive watch was reissued in 2023.

A CONSUMER DIVE WATCH

Seiko heralded the dawn of a new era in 1965 as it launched its first dive watch, the 62MAS. A decade later, the brand took the idea a considerable step further by creating the 'Tuna', a model specifically designed for professional divers (see page 132), followed three years later by several quartz versions. Seiko broadened its horizons again when it introduced the 7548, an amateur dive watch that was every bit as remarkable as its elder sibling. While less sophisticated in design than the 'Tuna', it will be remembered for the positioning of the crown at 4 o'clock and its 'Pepsi' bezel, so called because it shared a colour scheme with the famous American soft drink. The watch has stood the test of time to the point of becoming an icon of the brand, a pioneer among consumer quartz dive watches that remained on sale until 1986, co-existing for a long time with the equally popular automatic 6309 version (dubbed the 'Turtle' because of its shape). Waterproof to a depth of 150m (492ft), it completed the holy trinity of Seiko quartz dive watches, alongside the 7549-7010 'Tuna' and 7549-7009 'Golden Tuna', which were waterproof to 300m (984ft) and 600m (1,968ft) respectively – a sacrosanct trio that affirmed Seiko's foundational position in submarine watchmaking.

HIGH-QUALITY QUARTZ

Although it featured a quartz movement, the Quartz Diver's eschewed any sophistication. The mechanism powering the 7548 was made entirely of metal and shared several characteristics with the movement of the automatic 6309 dive watch, beginning with what would have been its mainspring, where a printed quartz circuit powered by a battery was now housed. It was anything but a disposable movement and was designed to be serviced and repaired – a gamble that paid off, as the 7548 is unanimously considered to be one of Seiko's best quartz movements. It was fitted with five rubies to minimize friction, boasted a battery life of two years, and there was even an alert when the battery was running low. If properly serviced, it could vie with the professional models (the 'Tuna' and 'Golden Tuna') for accuracy, with a monthly mean variation rate of no more than around five seconds.

FROM 150 TO 200 METRES

After the achievements of the 'Golden Tuna' in the 1980s, which remained waterproof to a depth of 1,000m (3,280ft), Seiko decided to release a new version of its 'Pepsi' bezel dive watch. This time, however, it was to be certified to a depth of 200m (656ft), outdoing the 150m (492ft) of the preceding version. The Quartz Diver's would go on to become the world's best-selling quartz dive watch. The iconic two-coloured 'Pepsi' bezel became so popular that it began to be used in other references intended for diving, such as the 7N36 and the 5H26. This styling is still used for the automatic SKX 200m models and, for millions of fans and collectors, it remains associated with one of the best-value watches ever sold.

TUE 11
DIVER'S 150m

KINETIC DIVER'S

SEIKO – 1988

The quartz Kinetic watch, which came to market in 1988 under the name AGS, converted the motion of the wearer's wrist into energy that was stored in a battery with a longer life than traditional batteries.

SEE OPPOSITE	2000 MODEL
MANUFACTURER	SEIKO
MODEL	SKA371 'BFK'
CALIBRE	5M62
MOVEMENT	QUARTZ KINETIC
PRODUCTION	SOLD COMMERCIALLY
MATERIAL	STEEL
STRAP	N/A

THE ISO 6425 STANDARD

The watch must:

- be water-resistant to a depth of at least 100m (328ft);
- be resistant to corrosion;
- be legible at a distance of 25cm (10in) in total darkness;
- be resistant to temperature variations;
- have some means of telling if it has stopped;
- have a rotating, unidirectional bezel;
- be shock-resistant;
- include a strap that is securely attached to the watch;
- not be liable to condensation;
- have a low battery life alert if it is electronic.

TECHNOLOGY PATENTED IN 1986

The name of this watch was derived from the Greek word *kinesis*, meaning 'movement'. It was first used by Seiko at the 1986 Basel trade fair, where the brand unveiled a first prototype provisionally named AGM (Automatic Generating Movement). When these innovative timepieces – which dispensed with button batteries entirely – finally arrived on the market in 1988, they had been renamed AGS (Automatic Generating System, see page 213). Capturing kinetic energy and turning it into electricity was a remarkable technological breakthrough for the time. This ingenious integrated electricity generation system, which was activated by movements of the wrist, addressed two historic challenges facing the watchmaking industry: accuracy and battery life. It was an impressive solution; the watches were capable of running for four years with no battery replacement, almost rendering the question of battery life irrelevant. As for precision, any losses in accuracy were mitigated by this power stability. This innovation was ultimately dubbed Kinetic in 1992 and was a resounding success, with millions of watches fitted with the movement sold around the world.

CHARACTERISTICS

The calibre 5M62 Kinetic movement was the beating heart of a number of Seiko analogue quartz watches. Thanks to some cunning engineering, the electricity that powers the watches was generated by the natural movements of the wearer and then stored in a rechargeable battery. Unlike watches with a conventional button battery, there was no periodic replacement to interrupt the watch's operation. However, that was not all that was special about such a movement. For one thing, it could be rapidly restarted – even if the watch had stopped for a long period of time, it could be returned to operation with just a few movements. All the wearer had to do was swing it from side to side to recharge the battery and prolong its life. The calibre also featured a low battery alert: when the second hand began to tick at two-second intervals, the watch was about to stop.

BIG FREAKIN' KINETIC

The calibre 5M62 was also at the heart of the Seiko SKA371, a dive watch that caused a big stir in the 2000s and was known colloquially as the 'BFK' (for 'Big Freakin' Kinetic') because of its imposing 14mm-thick case. For many fans it was the ultimate version of the electronic analogue dive watch as far as performance was concerned. Indeed it ticked all the boxes for the ISO 6425 standard first established in 1982 and subsequently taken over by Seiko in 1996 (and since updated). It was waterproof to 200m (656ft), featured a rotating bezel to safely measure dive time, and guaranteed perfect legibility, even in the dark. It also had a push-button positioned at 2 o'clock so the wearer could easily check the power reserve, a feature the ISO standard required of all electronic models.

SEIKO
KINETIC
DIVER'S 200m
14
JAPAN
50
40
30
20
10

10 LAP
set / light
start / lap
12:53 51
mode
SEP 3
stop
H20 100m
view

THE DIGITAL WATCH

CHAPTER 4

SWISSONIC

JAZ DERBY – 1975

A digital watch displays the time using numbers rather than hands. They may use either light-emitting diodes (LED), liquid crystals (LCD) or, as with the Swissonic model, rotating mechanical cylinders.

SEE OPPOSITE	1975 MODEL
MANUFACTURER	JAZ DERBY
MODEL	SWISSONIC
CALIBRE	ESA 9176
MOVEMENT	ELECTROMECHANICAL, TRANSISTOR
PRODUCTION	SOLD COMMERCIALLY
MATERIAL	STEEL, CHROME
STRAP	STEEL

AUDEMARS PIGUET
'JUMPING HOUR'

Audemars Piguet unveiled its first digital display wristwatch in 1921. The number indicating the hour was displayed in a window at 12 o'clock, to be replaced as each successive hour passed, while the progress of the minutes was displayed in a window at 6 o'clock.

DIGITAL: AN OLD STORY

Digital displays go back to the 19th century, long before the age of quartz. The first known example was a pocket watch made by French watchmaker Blondeau for the king of France in the 1830s. This device used a mechanical system known as 'jumping hour' whereby the hour is displayed in Arabic numerals in a large window and jumps directly from one number to the next, replacing the hand that usually indicates the hour. The minutes are printed on a disc, driven by the minute wheel, which completes a rotation every 60 minutes. This system did not appear on wristwatches until decades later (at the turn of the 1920s) with the first of these, designed by Audemars Piguet, being fitted with a calibre 10 GHSM movement. The idea was picked up by Cartier with the Tank, then by Vacheron Constantin and Rolex (with one of the Brancard models).

ELECTROMECHANICAL JUMPING MINUTE

In 1967, Ébauches SA (ESA) released the calibre 9150 Dynotron, using a fixed-coil, balance-driven system (see page 30) that eliminated all mechanical contact by means of an integrated magnet. As the balance wheel passed the coils, it generated a current that was amplified by a transistor (see page 16), a major innovation for the time. Ten years later, as quartz was growing in influence, further innovation was required to maintain public interest in electromechanical technology. Several variants, some of which had moving mechanical displays, were brought onto the market, including the calibre 9159 for Gruen, the 9156 for Certina and the 9176 for Derby. The latter had an entirely digital display for both hours and minutes, and was nicknamed the 'Jump Minute' rather than the 'Jump Hour'. This calibre, which was used only for Derby watches (a subsidiary of ESA) and watches made by the French brand Jaz, allowed watches to function rather like old radio alarm clocks, with the numerals displayed on rotating drums.

DERBY SWISSONIC

The Derby Swissonic was first brought to market in the mid-1970s, and two versions were made, in chromed steel and plated gold, with either a leather or a metal strap. The jumping hour functioned via a tiny spring attached to the drum. Unfortunately, this innovative design was plagued by malfunctions from its release; the spring was so delicate it was the cause of half the faults. The fragile movement contained numerous plastic components and few Derbys are still working these days. Although a highly intriguing idea, the watch was to be rapidly outstripped by two new booming technologies, LED (see page 143) and LCD (see page 157).

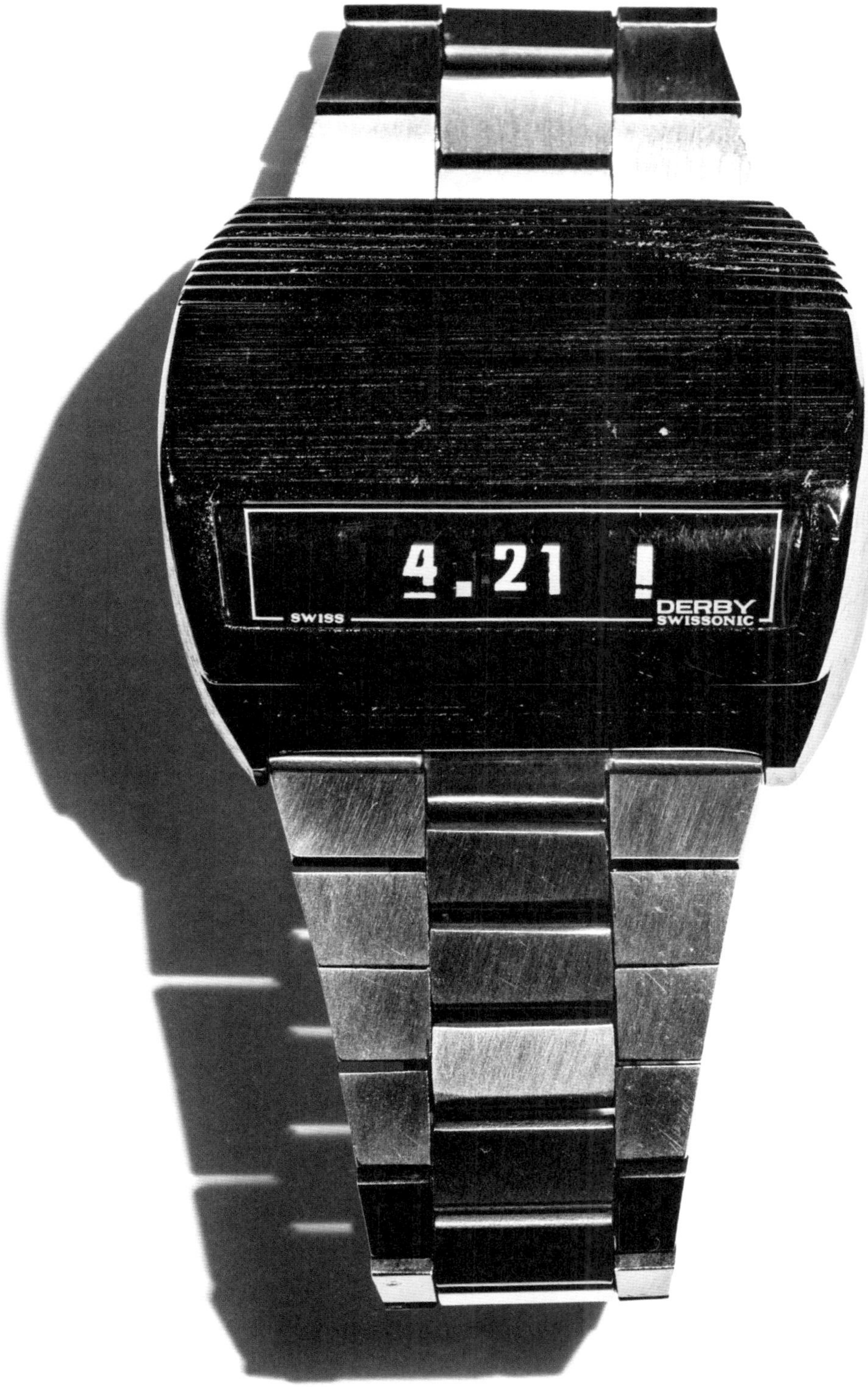
4.21
SWISS
DERBY
SWISSONIC

THE DIGITAL WATCH

LED

LED watches are named after the electronic devices (light-emitting diodes) they use to display the time in digital format.

LIGHT-EMITTING DIODES

LEDs were the result of research carried out on semiconductors during the 1960s. Scientists were well aware of the potential of the technology and spent the next ten years miniaturizing the components, leading to LEDs that were small enough to fit into wristwatches. LEDs enabled the first electronic display of time in a digital format in what experts hailed as the greatest advance in timekeeping technology since the sundial. The first digital watches were in fact mechanical or electromechanical. The displays of the new LED watches were initially predominantly red, thanks to the aluminium-gallium used, while green, which was slightly less common, was achieved using gallium nitride.

'A NEW ERA IN THE SCIENCE OF MEASURING TIME'

The Hamilton company (see page 144) unveiled the first LED wristwatch at the turn of the 1970s. It was also the first watch to be entirely electronic (with no moving parts) and to display the time in a digital format. It was named the Pulsar in reference to a star discovered at the time of its launch that emitted precisely timed radio waves. The name also bore connotations of the world of space travel and its associated technology. The story goes that the idea for this watch was suggested to Hamilton by Stanley Kubrick, for whom the brand had designed a model for the film *2001: A Space Odyssey* in 1968. The Pulsar was released commercially in 1972, in a range of versions (in steel, gold-plated and gold) that could cost more than $2,000, as much as a Chevrolet car. The *New York Times* hailed the launch of the watch as 'a new era in the science of measuring time'. Despite the high price, the first 400 units produced immediately found buyers, although the circuits manufactured by Electro-Data turned out to be so unreliable that this first series was withdrawn from the market.

FROM THE CUTTING EDGE TO MASS PRODUCTION

Pulsar's success stimulated demand and other LED models rapidly flooded onto the market. Hamilton launched its Calculator model for Christmas 1975, charging $3,950 for the gold version and $500 for the steel option (see page 144) – prices that were still very high, but which pushed the competition into lowering theirs. Bulova began selling its Computron at prices starting from $99 at the beginning of the following year. Even fiercer competition came in 1976, at the Chicago Consumer Electronics Show, when Texas Instruments finally made LED technology available to all by launching plastic models costing $20. Most manufacturers in Switzerland considered such watches to be no more than a fashion, although others, such as Omega, Zenith (see page 154) and Girard-Perregaux (see page 152), were a little more open-minded and took an interest nonetheless. Japanese producers were slow to enter the market, producing only a few LED models, although there was a reason for this: they were concentrating on LCD technology (see page 157).

ENERGY-HUNGRY TECHNOLOGY AND DECLINE

The batteries of the 1970s were not as powerful as modern cells, yet the first LED watches required a great deal of power and were considered particularly energy-hungry. To save energy, the time display would only light up when a button was pressed, so the watches provided just a brief glimpse of the time. Although initially appealing because of its novelty, LED technology (and its faults) eventually bored consumers to the extent that it was gradually ditched by manufacturers in favour of the liquid crystals of LCD, a technology that was fast-growing. The legendary Pulsar brand created by Hamilton was bought up by Seiko and registered as a new trademark under which the Japanese brand produced analogue watches alongside its LCD models.

PULSAR CALCULATOR

HAMILTON – 1975

The Pulsar was launched commercially by Hamilton in 1972 after two years of research. In response to the success of this watch, the brand began to bring out further models the following year and introduced the world's first electronic calculator watch in 1975.

SEE OPPOSITE	1975 MODEL
MANUFACTURER	HAMILTON
MODEL	PULSAR CALCULATOR 3822
CALIBRE	TIME COMPUTER INC.
MOVEMENT	LED
PRODUCTION	SOLD COMMERCIALLY
MATERIAL	STEEL
STRAP	STEEL

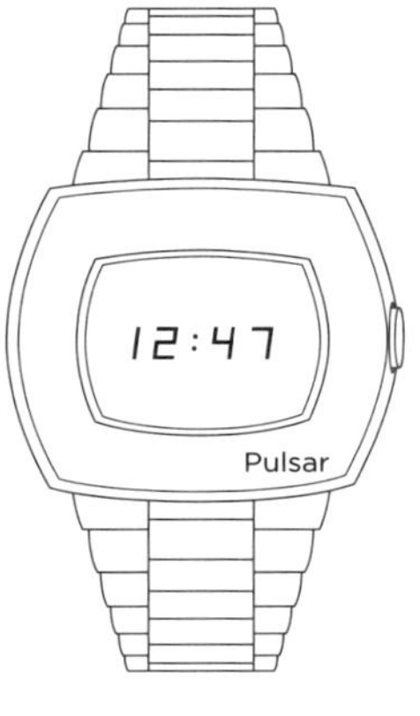

HAMILTON
PULSAR

The Pulsar was a pioneer; it was the first watch to have an LED digital display and not a single moving part in its movement, marking a revolutionary step forwards in watchmaking.

1972: MARKETING THE PULSAR

On 6 May 1970, the Hamilton Watch Company, based in the American city of Lancaster, Pennsylvania, unveiled the Pulsar to the world, the revolutionary prototype of the first entirely electronic watch. Born following many expensive years of research, it dispensed with both hands and dial and boasted a highly accurate display of the time. Primarily thanks to technology that Hamilton called 'solid state', the Pulsar was the first watch in history to have absolutely no moving parts in its mechanism. To design the watch, which had an LED digital display, the firm had teamed up with Electro-Data, with whom it had worked some 15 years previously to develop the electromechanical calibre 500, notably used in the Ventura model (see page 22). The circuits produced by Electro-Data turned out to be unreliable, however, and the first series (P1), which was launched in 1972, was taken off the market, signalling the end of the two companies' collaboration. Hamilton reorganized its operations at the end of the same year, creating Time Computer Inc., a division dedicated to the Pulsar. The second run (P2) was to become the first mass-produced digital watch.

1975: PULSAR TIME COMPUTER CALCULATOR

Several variants of the Pulsar were introduced by Time Computer Inc. One of these, released in 1973 (P3), had a date complication, followed in 1975 by a more compact model (P4). A digital calculator watch appeared in December that year – another global first for Hamilton and its already legendary Pulsar. The reference 1822, the first model to be released, was available in a limited run of 100 units in 18-carat gold at the astronomical price of $3,950, equating to some £17,000 today. The watch was sold with an elegant box and a stylus to operate the keypad. This particularly sophisticated device even caught the eye of Gerald Ford, the 38th president of the United States, who had been a fervent admirer of the Pulsar P3. But when he decided to treat himself to one for Christmas in 1975, his wife put her foot down with a firm 'no way'. The spring of 1976 saw the market launch of the reference 3822, a steel version, at the rather more reasonable price of $550. In 1977, the 901 electronic module was replaced with the 902, which could be activated to display the hours and minutes with a simple flick of the wrist.

LED CALCULATOR WATCHES

In the 1970s, when IT was still in its infancy, the Pulsar calculator watch was seen as a computer worn on the wrist and elicited such a reaction from the public that the competition jumped on the idea and three other major players in the sector joined the race. The first two of these, Compuchron and Uranus, sold products of far poorer quality than the Pulsar. Meanwhile, Hewlett-Packard produced the most sophisticated LED calculator watch of the time that was also the last of its line: 1977's HP-01 model.

11:13
7 8 9 A ÷ =
4 5 6 R X E
1 2 3 S – %
0 • Pulsar + C

MACH LED 2000

LIP – 1976

A year after its launch in 1975, the Mach 2000 model designed by Roger Tallon for the LIP brand committed fully to the electronic age. This change of tack was signalled from 1976 with the release of variants featuring an LED digital display.

SEE OPPOSITE	1976 MODEL
MANUFACTURER	LIP
MODEL	MACH 2000
CALIBRE	NOVUS
MOVEMENT	LED
PRODUCTION	SOLD COMMERCIALLY
MATERIAL	BLACK ANODIZED STEEL
STRAP	RUBBER

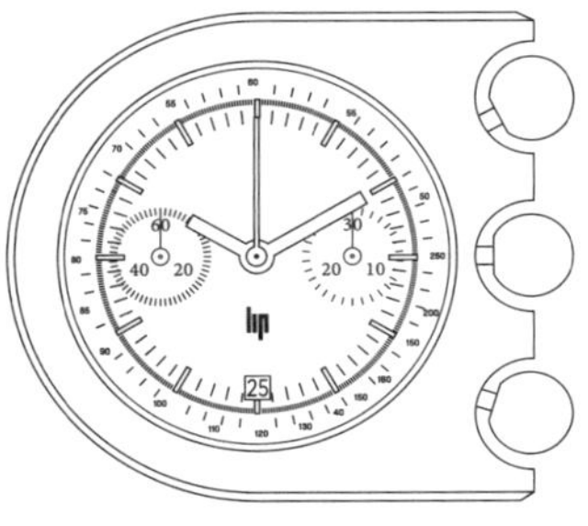

LIP
MACH 2000

With its asymmetrical styling and coloured buttons designed by Roger Tallon, the Mach 2000 summed up the boldly innovative spirit of the 1970s. Although initially mechanical, it rapidly evolved into electronic form.

THE INFLUENCE OF ROGER TALLON

By 1973, the electromechanical technology developed by LIP 15 years previously had become completely obsolete (see page 16), to the point that bankruptcy was looming for the company as its market share crumbled in the face of Japanese quartz watches. Even worse, it found itself embroiled in unprecedented company in-fighting. After a year of upheaval, Claude Neuschwander, a former advertising executive, took over the reins of the Besançon-based watchmaking company from Fred Lipmann. To balance the situation, he surrounded himself with the fashionable designers of the time, including Rudi Meyer, Marc Held, Michel Boyer, Isabelle Hebey, Michel Kinn and Jean Dinh Van, along with the renowned French industrial designer Roger Tallon, who was known for his obsession with combining form and function. In 1975, this dream team came up with the iconic Mach 2000, identifiable by its three circular, coloured buttons, two of which activated a chronograph function.

'NOW WE CAN TALK ABOUT THE FUTURE'

When first released, the LIP Mach 2000 was fitted with the Valjoux 7734, a prestigious mechanical calibre, but this renowned movement (which had powered any number of chronographs with two sub-registers) was replaced a year later when the watch entered the electronic era, a transition celebrated by LIP with the expressive advertising slogan, 'Now we can talk about the future'. The electronic Mach 2000s first appeared among the 150 models in the LIP collection in 1976, followed by LED variants. These had been designed in partnership with the German company Dugena, renowned for its expertise in quartz watches, and featured an LED module produced by Novus in the United States. Another novelty was an asymmetrical model in a black anodized alloy case. The original model's three coloured buttons had been reduced to a single pusher, a long press on which conjured up a digital time display.

QUARTZ AND DIODES

Despite this shift into electronics, the brand filed for bankruptcy again in 1976. Various buyers came and went and they all kept faith with the Mach 2000 – so much so that Roger Tallon was asked by LIP to reinvent the watch a second time, a collaboration that gave rise to a new series of 26 upgraded models powered by a France Ébauches quartz movement. The range realigned itself in 1996. Today, the original analogue model is still on sale, but with a quartz Ronda movement. As for digital displays, they are still to be found on a few novelty products such as the asymmetrical Roger Tallon LED model reissued in 2007 and the Diode model unveiled in 2018. The latter, however, no longer featured real LEDs. Instead it used more modern technology to imitate their visual effect.

1041
DUGENA

COMPUTRON

BULOVA – 1976

Bulova opted for LED technology in 1976, choosing a digital display for its Computron model, although this strategic decision did not close the door on the electronic watch market in which the firm had long been active.

SEE OPPOSITE	1976 MODEL
MANUFACTURER	BULOVA
MODEL	COMPUTRON
CALIBRE	COMPUTRON TIME CO.
MOVEMENT	LED
PRODUCTION	SOLD COMMERCIALLY
MATERIAL	GOLD-PLATED
STRAP	INTEGRATED

BULOVA TACKLES LED TECHNOLOGY

Bulova revolutionized watchmaking in 1960 when it unveiled the calibre 214 tuning-fork movement that propelled its ground-breaking Accutron model to the forefront of the international scene (see page 34). Sixteen years later the brand, which wished to maintain its reputation in the electric and electronic watch segment, set out on the new adventure of digital watches. Bulova then made a head-turning entry on the market by plumping for LED technology and, above all, selling a watch at $99, an unbeatable price. The watch featured a resolutely futuristic design and was available in chromed steel or gold-plated versions. As with the famous Pulsar (see page 144), the time display was not continuous, and the push-button had to be held down for some time to illuminate the screen and tell the time.

THE 'TRAPEZIUM'

The case of the Computron was bold and angular in shape, earning it the nickname the 'Trapezium'. The watch's creators located the LED display along the lower chamfer, breaking with traditional central positioning. Why was this? The explanation was simple: the wearer did not have to move their wrist to tell the time. This ingenious layout was reminiscent of the first motor racing watches that were angled to enable drivers to read the time rapidly. However, the Computron should not be categorized as a racing driver's watch. For a start, it does not have a chronograph function, and secondly the requirement to press and hold down the push-button to display the time disqualifies it from being ideal to use in motor racing.

A VICTORIOUS RETURN

The Computron was a game-changer when first released, but was rapidly forgotten with the advent of LCD (see page 157). After the acquisition of Bulova by Citizen, it made a remarkable comeback in 2019, however, and there were several versions on the menu, including a model in gold with vintage appeal, another in chromed steel with a blue digital display, and yet another in black with a rubber strap. The legendary trapezoidal case was still present and the angled screen was retained for optimal legibility. The LED screen was upgraded to be brighter and more reliable than its forerunner. Carl Rosen, the brand's historian, maintains that there is a simple explanation for this choice of retro technology: 'It's cool now because it was cool back in the day!'

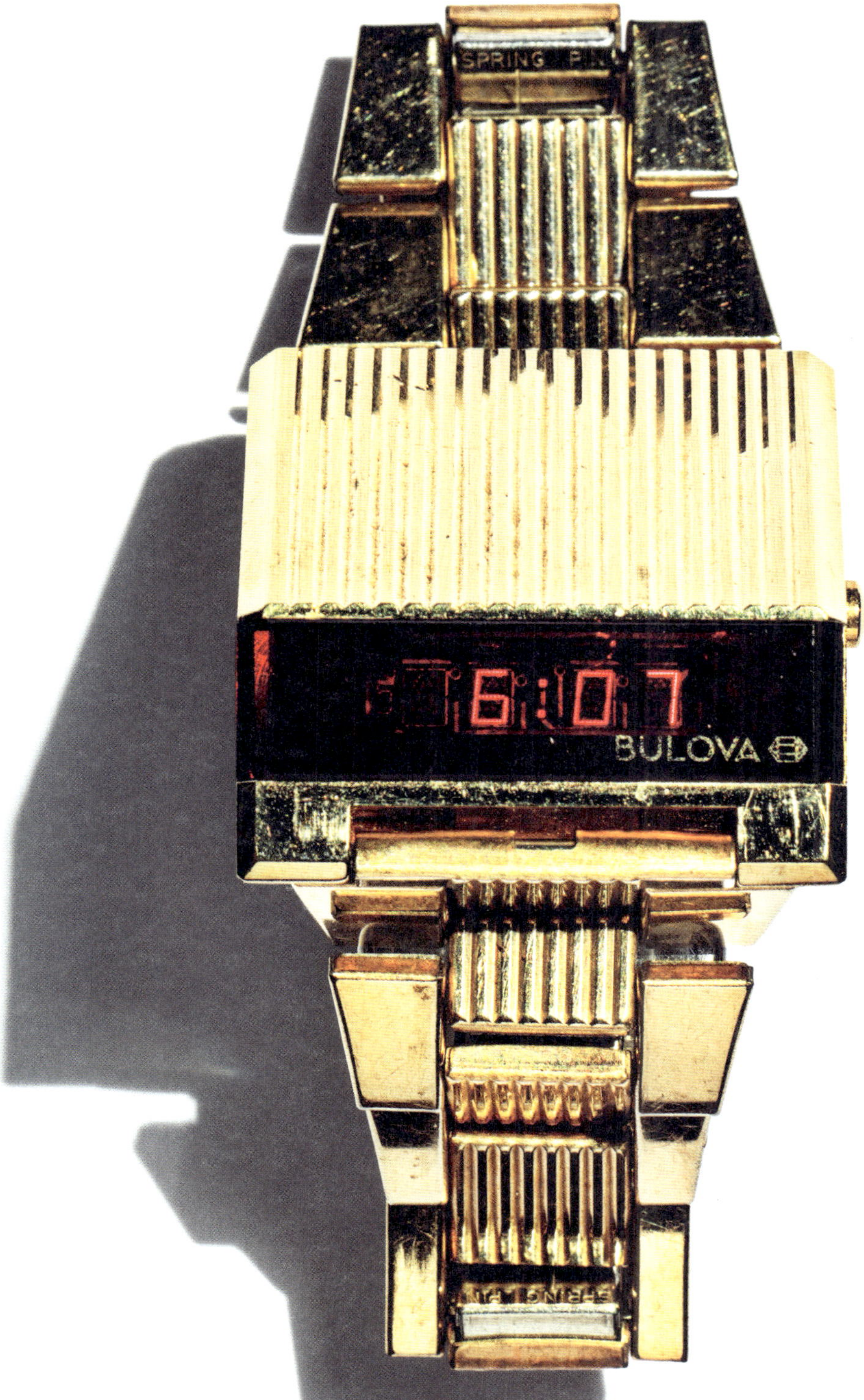
SPRING PIN
6:07
BULOVA

NIVADA
QUARTZONIC

The Nivada brand made a name for itself with its multifunctional mechanical chronographs. It adopted LED displays for some of its models in the mid-1970s.

FAVRE LEUBA

LED

Favre Leuba, one of the oldest Swiss watch manufacturers,
also took an interest in digital LED technology.

CASQUETTE

GIRARD-PERREGAUX – 1976

Four years after releasing the calibre 350, which was to become a benchmark in the world of quartz watches, Girard-Perregaux produced a further surprise by unveiling its first digital LED watch. This was affectionately christened the 'Casquette' (or 'cap') because of its shape.

SEE OPPOSITE	1976 MODEL
MANUFACTURER	GIRARD-PERREGAUX
MODEL	'CASQUETTE' 9931 DIGITAL QUARTZ
CALIBRE	GP395
MOVEMENT	LED
PRODUCTION	SOLD COMMERCIALLY
MATERIAL	STEEL
STRAP	INTEGRATED

DIGITAL QUARTZ

Girard-Perregaux entered the revolutionary quartz fray with a flourish when it introduced the calibre 350 at the turn of the 1970s (see page 72). This quartz movement created by in-house engineers was a real gamechanger in that it established 32,768Hz as the new global standard beat frequency. The brand also unveiled a digital creation of its own during this turbulent decade: the Digital Quartz, reference 9931/calibre 395, with a daringly tapered case featuring an angled screen that was supposed to resemble the shape of a racing car. However, the Digital Quartz was quickly nicknamed the 'Casquette', or 'cap', as it was shaped like this piece of headgear.

THE NEW FACE OF TIME

The Casquette made its debut in January 1976 with a number of different references, each with its own characteristics (standard or 24-hour display, date or day of the week) and available in different materials (steel, gold-plated and Makrolon, a shock-resistant polycarbonate that also protected against high temperatures). Sales brochures of the time described all these versions of the 'Casquette' as the 'new face of time' or the 'digital watch at a time of renewal'. Like all LED watches of the period, however, the Casquette only displayed the time when a button was pressed. The LED technology on which it was based was too energy-hungry for a permanent display. This did not prevent it from being a resounding success, selling nigh on 8,200 units even though production ceased in 1978.

CASQUETTE 2.0

Girard-Perregaux breathed new life into the spirit of this iconic model with a creation prosaically labelled 2.0 in 2022. The scratchproof ceramic case and titanium caseback of this modern reinterpretation immediately caught the eye, but Girard-Perregaux nonetheless decided to limit production of this new Casquette to 820 units, or a tenth of the total number sold of the original model. Just like its forebear, this model displayed hours, minutes, seconds, day and date via a tubular LED display. However, the new calibre GP3980 had a few other tricks up its sleeve: it could display the month and year, function as a chronograph, accommodate a second time zone and even show a secret date, adding a touch of mystery to this retro watch.

GP
4:12

FUTUR TIME

ZENITH – 1976

Zenith, who were experts in high-frequency automatic watches, took the world by surprise in 1976 with the unveiling of its quartz calibre 47 LED watch. The movement, a precursor of the ana-digi display, was driven by the brand's American management.

SEE OPPOSITE	1976 MODEL
MANUFACTURER	ZENITH
MODEL	FUTUR TIME COMMAND
CALIBRE	CALIBRE 47
MOVEMENT	LED
PRODUCTION	SOLD COMMERCIALLY
MATERIAL	STEEL
STRAP	INTEGRATED

A HIGH-FREQUENCY AUTOMATIC IN THE QUARTZ ERA

The tenth of January 1969 was an epic day in the world of watchmaking – it was the day that Zenith chose to unveil the El Primero calibre, its masterpiece, to the international press. Inside this movement beat the heart of some ground-breaking engineering – a high-frequency oscillator achieving a beat rate of 5Hz (36,000bph), equipping the watch with a timing capability of up to one-tenth of a second. At the same time, Zenith released the Defy, a high-frequency, non-chronograph automatic watch dubbed 'the vault of precision'. These two creations of undeniable quality would nonetheless soon be eclipsed by the spectacular advent of quartz watches.

THE END OF MECHANICAL CALIBRES

A new and unexpected development in the world of watchmaking arrived in 1972 when the Zenith Radio Corporation of Chicago took over control of the Zenith brand. After three short years, however, the new American management board was faced with the brutal reality that its investment was struggling to turn a profit, and so it took the radical decision to halt production of all mechanical calibres. No time was wasted and the machinery was dismantled and scrapped, including the *ébauches* for the El Primero calibre. Watching from the shadows of the workshop, however, Charles Vermot and his brother conducted a rearguard action and stashed away essential tooling in the dark corners of the factory, saving the last *ébauches* and the machines to manufacture them from oblivion. The new owners, entirely unaware of this act of rebellion, positioned themselves on the market in anticipation of the quartz revolution and orientated their distribution towards North America. The first quartz watches appeared very soon after, all powered by the calibre 47.

ANA-DIGI AND A RETURN TO MECHANICAL MOVEMENTS

Zenith reinvented itself once again in 1975, casting off several historical subsidiaries (such as Martel) and, with financial support from its American management board, threw itself headfirst into developing a quartz technology of its own. What it came up with was the calibre 47 LED Futur Time Command, a model with a bold ana-digi display and a single quartz movement that could power both the analogue hands and the digital display for the seconds and the calendar. Even at its launch, however, the calibre 47 LED was doomed to be overtaken by the arrival of LCD, and its display, which required a button to be pressed to show the seconds and the date, proved to be too power-hungry. Worse still, the integrated circuit was too complex and the stepping motor connected to the LED required the use of two batteries. In order to keep up with its competitors, Zenith eventually resorted to quartz movements made by Ébauches SA. In 1978, the Americans handed over the reins of Zenith to a Swiss consortium and production of high-frequency automatic calibres was resumed. Under the leadership of Pierre-Alain Blum, the president of Ebel (see page 80), a contract was signed with that manufacturer to supply the El Primero movement that had been saved by the Vermot brothers, and Rolex followed suit by calling on the services of the renowned chronograph. The flash-in-the-pan Futur Time Command was quietly removed from the catalogue.

QUARTZ
ZENITH

THE DIGITAL WATCH

LCD

Characterized by a screen of liquid crystals, LCD watches soon began to compete with their LED technology-based counterparts. By the end of the 1970s, they had cornered the world market.

DYNAMIC SCATTERING

Just as LED technology was enjoying an unprecedented boom in watchmaking (see page 143), the first watches using liquid crystals (LCD, or liquid crystal display) were also emerging. In 1968, a team led by George Heilmeier at American electronics giant the Radio Corporation of America (RCA), had taken an interest in this technology and, in particular, in a method involving the dynamic scattering of light. Two years later, several engineers from RCA teamed up with Optel Corporation with the aim of producing the first commercial electronic digital watch. As a result, four projects were presented at the 1972 Basel trade fair. Three of these employed the Optel display while the fourth was sourced from Texas Instruments (TI). The Microma company, recently acquired by the Intel Corporation, unveiled a project of its own the same year (see page 158).

The challenges that LCD was facing remained considerable. So much so that the LED Pulsar became the first electronic digital watch to be sold commercially (see page 144). The competing technology's headstart was to prove short-lived, however, as several technological advances made it easier to manufacture and market LCDs and a host of brands, using technologies from Optel, TI and Microma, threw themselves into watch production. The dynamic display turned out to be energy-hungry though, and the batteries had to be replaced every eight months. Even worse, the brightness dimmed as the batteries ran down, drastically reducing the appeal of such a watch.

FIELD EFFECT

To solve the problems facing dynamic scattering, the Ilixco company developed a technique dubbed 'the field effect', which in 1973 was incorporated into the Teletime, a watch produced by the Gruen brand. All the other brands rapidly followed suit and adopted the method, but approached it in different ways. Heuer skilfully combined an LCD display with LEDs in a chronograph, while other firms concentrated exclusively on LCD. Notable amongst the latter were Tissot (see page 162) in Switzerland and Seiko in Japan. The Japanese company even had the distinction of developing the first six-digit LCD display, which also included seconds (see page 166). Thanks to the field effect, LCD watches had become less energy-hungry and easier to manufacture than their LED cousins but, most importantly, they displayed the time continuously, which was more than enough to enable them to conquer the greater part of the global digital watch market in just a few years.

NOT JUST A SIMPLE TIME DISPLAY

Thanks to LCD technology, electronic watches could now provide more than just a read-out of the time. Seiko unveiled the first 100 per cent LCD chronograph in 1975, closely followed by a version with an alarm, and then a watch with multiple complications (see page 166). Switzerland's Omega launched the Chrono-Quartz in 1976, the first hybrid ana-digi chronograph (see page 160), combining analogue hands and an LCD screen (see page 161).

CALCULATOR, COMPUTER, G-SHOCK

Although LCD technology was taking some of its first faltering steps in the United States, no one could keep up with Japan. Thanks to partnerships with local companies specializing in electronics, Japanese manufacturers improved LCDs so rapidly that it was impossible for anyone even to get close in terms of competition. It was also around this time that Casio, a new Japanese player on the digital watch market, put in its first appearance. In 1974 and having specialized in calculators, a technology similar to that used in quartz watches, the brand presented its Casiotron to immediate and phenomenal success. All-out war then ensued between this tiny newcomer and the all-powerful Seiko, which took a direct swipe at its competitor's historical identity by launching the Calculator model in 1979. Casio responded in 1983 with the Databank (see page 174) and Melody watches that also included video games. In the Japan of the 1980s, these were no small innovations. Resolving not to be outdone, Seiko made a further innovation by inventing a wristwatch computer called the Data-2000 (see page 172). This was a huge blow but Casio, whose turnover had skyrocketed during the years of corporate hostilities, did not throw in the towel. The company was of the view that it should raise it sights and that an LCD watch should not just be content with being good value. It was from this idea that the G-Shock was born: a robust, waterproof watch with enhanced battery life (see page 176). This development cleared a path for the LCD watch to continue to reign supreme on the digital watch market more than 50 years after its arrival. Today, the highly coveted title of 'world's best-selling watch' is held by the Casio F-91W.

SPACESONIC

CATENA – 1977

Liquid crystal display (LCD) watches first appeared in the United States. Optel, Texas Instruments and Microma (acquired by Intel in 1972) played a major role in their development, first on American soil, then across the rest of the world.

SEE OPPOSITE	1977 MODEL
MANUFACTURER	CATENA
MODEL	SPACESONIC 'DARTH VADER'
CALIBRE	ESA 942711
MOVEMENT	LCD
PRODUCTION	SOLD COMMERCIALLY
MATERIAL	STEEL
STRAP	INTEGRATED

AVIA

This model from the Avia brand was one of the first watches with an LCD display to be sold commercially. It featured a module (developed by Optel) that made use of the dynamic scattering method.

MICROMA UNIVERSAL

The American-Swiss company Microma Universal was founded by Universal Genève in 1970 to produce electronic watch movements. From its base in the heart of Mountain View, California, the company carved out a niche for itself by creating printed circuits at the cutting edge of technology. The EWC-1000, a small integrated chip unveiled in 1971, was the absolute embodiment of this revolution, housing a whole world of technologies including an oscillator, a binary frequency divider, a pulse controller and even a compensator for the power of the motor. The following year, Microma unveiled the QTM-0001, an ingenious module designed to transform a mechanical movement into an analogue quartz.

ACQUISITION BY INTEL

On 14 July 1972, the American semi-conductor giant Intel (founded by Gordon Moore, a Silicon Valley pioneer) made the sensational announcement that it was buying Microma for $15 million, and Microma's offices were duly relocated from Mountain View to Cupertino, now the stamping ground of Apple (see page 232). The clear plan was to turn Microma into a watch brand in its own right – one that specialized in LCD displays. Just a few months after this acquisition, Intel joined forces with Hamlin to release the Microma 360 LCD. Despite interest from a number of brands, the high return rate (25 per cent) was an indication of the ongoing issues dynamic scattering displays were still experiencing. Microma reacted promptly the following year, replacing the dynamic scattering display with a more efficient field effect unit (see page 157). This was the beginning of a series of innovations from the company, with displays for seconds, date and chronometer functions enhancing a host of models in 1976, at which point Intel decided to part ways with Microma.

A 15-MILLION-DOLLAR MISTAKE

Intel's strategy focused on selling LCD watches to the general public. This proved a major challenge for the company, to the extent that Gordon Moore called the undertaking a '15-million-dollar mistake'. There was some justification for this, as selling watches is a universe of its own, far removed from the world of high technology. In addition to innovation, it also requires a very specific skill set and highly trained staff. Despite its best efforts, Intel eventually sold Microma in 1977 and the lucky purchaser was none other than ASUAG (see page 184), a Swiss holding company that already owned brands as prestigious as Longines and suppliers as essential as Ébauches SA (see page 24). The brand was retained under the name Microma Swiss and continued to sell affordable products, while Ébauches SA took advantage of Microma's technological advances and supplied a large number of brands with LCD modules. One striking example was the Catena brand's Spacesonic watch, which had been designed by André Le Marquand. The watch, which featured an ESA 942711 module, came out the same year as the first instalment of the *Star Wars* saga and was dubbed 'Darth Vader' for its resemblance to the Sith lord's helmet. Gordon Moore wore a Microma watch until the day he died in 2023, perhaps as a reminder not to invest in watches.

CHRONOGRAPH
SWISS MADE

CHRONO-QUARTZ

OMEGA – 1976

The Chrono-Quartz, which was unveiled to coincide with the 1976 Olympic Games in Montreal, made its name as the world's first digital and analogue chronograph. It became one of the finest exponents of the LCD technology that it featured with pride.

SEE OPPOSITE	1976 MODEL
MANUFACTURER	OMEGA
MODEL	CHRONO-QUARTZ MONTREAL
CALIBRE	1611 'ALBATROSS'
MOVEMENT	LCD ANALOGUE
PRODUCTION	SOLD COMMERCIALLY
MATERIAL	STEEL
STRAP	INTEGRATED

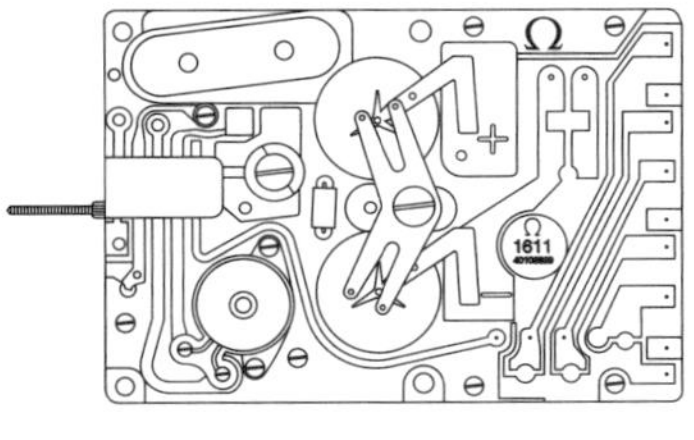

OMEGA
CAL. 1611 'ALBATROSS'

The shape of the battery clamp prompted Hans Widmer, head of R&D at SSIH, to christen the calibre the 'Albatross'. Once plans for the movement had been finalized, to a design by N Henry, final delivery of the watch was entrusted to Raymond Froidevaux.

DOUBLE-TIME DEVELOPMENT

Omega was at the cutting edge of the development of quartz technology in Switzerland, and boldly set itself apart from its competitors. The company first attracted attention in 1970 with its Electroquartz series, powered by the Beta 21 movement (dubbed the calibre 1300, see page 50), before bringing out the Megaquartz line four years later, featuring high-frequency calibres that oscillated at 2.4MHz and guaranteed an accuracy of +/- one second a month (see page 90). Omega was determined to hang on to this lead and the firm threw itself into producing watches with a digital display during the 1970s, and so the Time Computer, a watch with an LED display, was born. However, the brand rapidly pivoted towards LCD, a technology with a seemingly more promising future, and called upon Raymond Froidevaux to design an innovative watch combining an analogue display for timekeeping purposes and a digital screen for chronograph functions. Each of these would operate independently but was based on the same quartz resonator oscillating at a frequency of 32kHz – a global first for a revolutionary movement.

THE 'ALBATROSS' CALIBRE

This calibre, known as the reference 1611 'Albatross', took its name from the shape of the battery clamp, which was reminiscent of the majestic wings of that great bird. The chronograph's analog took its inspiration from the calibre 1302 (see page 50) but also featured a field effect LCD digital display (see page 157). The calibre 1611 was a particularly ingenious design that was easy to service thanks to its interchangeable components but, as it was reserved for the Chrono-Quartz, it was destined to be installed in only 15,000 units. Although several working versions appeared in 1975, Omega set itself the target of releasing the watch the following year, to coincide with the 1976 Olympic Games in Montreal, of which the brand was a sponsor.

AN OLYMPIC REVELATION IN MONTREAL

The retail version of the Albatross was unveiled during the 1976 Olympic Games, a sporting event whose main display board bore a striking resemblance to the watch itself. The case of the Chrono-Quartz was long and rectangular in design, 51mm in diameter and perfectly sized to house the calibre 1611. The chronograph's digital display, located on the left, was operated using three push-buttons, while the time display on the right was set using a crown on the same side. The caseback was decorated with a seahorse, symbolizing Omega's Seamaster range, and an Olympic crest to mark the occasion of the watch's launch. When the Albatross came out in 1976, it cost more than twice the reference 145.022 Speedmaster Professional, making it a particularly expensive model when compared with the brand's other chronographs. Despite its revolutionary design, the Chrono-Quartz's reign was to last for no more than a year. By 1977, Omega had launched the calibre 1620, whcih was incorporated into an entirely digital LCD chronograph. The Chrono-Quartz nonetheless still featured in the brand's catalogue for another two years before disappearing for good.

CHRONO-QUARTZ
start
stop
display
split
reset
lap
18
42
min.
hrs.
sec.
1/100s.
Seamaster
32 KHz
29
OMEGA

IDEA 2001 RESEARCH

TISSOT – 1976

Having previously focused on plastic mechanical watches rather than quartz, Tissot switched to producing watches with LCD displays in 1976, a strategy that aimed to compete with Asian manufacturers, especially from Japan.

SEE OPPOSITE	1976 MODEL
MANUFACTURER	TISSOT
MODEL	IDEA 2001 'RESEARCH'
CALIBRE	SSIH
MOVEMENT	LCD
PRODUCTION	SOLD COMMERCIALLY
MATERIAL	BLACK ANODIZED STEEL
STRAP	INTEGRATED

IDEA 2001

In 1971, well before Swatches exploded onto the scene in 1983 (see page 181), Tissot tore up the watchmaking rulebook with the Astrolon, a mechanical watch made almost entirely of plastic. This minor revolution, the fruit of two decades of research, was incorporated into the Idea 2001 range; the designation was a nod to Stanley Kubrick's film *2001: A Space Odyssey*, released three years previously. The name, evocative as it was of space travel and the future, concealed the far more down-to-earth objective of competing with the quartz movements that were appearing at every turn, starting with the Asian models that were flooding onto the market. This manual-wind watch with its calibre 2250 movement (dubbed the 'Sytal', a French acronym for *système total autolubrification* – 'fully self-lubricating system') was based on a simplified design that reduced production costs, but – more importantly – also anticipated by several decades the idea of a watch that was intended to be disposable in the event of a fault. It was, however, a resounding flop, mainly due to poor communications from the brand, retailers who were resistant to a plastic watch that could be taken apart but not repaired and, above all, the irresistible rise of quartz watches. In 1975, only 15,000 of the watches found buyers and Tissot was left with 500,000 units of unsold stock.

FROM PLASTIC MECHANICAL WATCHES TO DIGITAL

Although the Astrolon did not survive this fiasco, Tissot went on to produce limited quantities of an astonishing model known as the 'Research' for its Idea 2001 range. Very few examples of this watch, with its LCD display and coarse mesh strap remain, but its very existence is proof of the brand's change of tack from plastic mechanical watches to digital quartz. In 1975, for example, Tissot produced exclusively mechanical watches, manufacturing a total of 805,541 units. The following year, the company pivoted towards digital quartz in response to Japanese competition and sold 645,075 watches. A total of 47,972 of these were LED and 6,106 LCD. This was a further strategic error, as LED technology was to prove less reliable than LCD. Although sales were still hampered by such missteps, the brand responded in 1977 by selling 417,683 watches, of which 23,034 were LCD models and only 689 LED.

THE SUCCESS OF LCD

The year 1978 saw Tissot's first attempts to flood the European market with a host of different quartz digital watch variants in steel, gold-plated and black anodized steel, to stunning commercial success. It unveiled its analogue PRX model the same year, a quartz timepiece with a sophisticated design, featuring an elegant case, understated indices and an integrated strap that became quintessential characteristics. Tissot reinvented its iconic PRX in 2023 with the PRX Digital, combining the classic design of the PRX (and its integrated strap) with an LCD dial and, after a fashion, echoing the precepts of the 1978 range. This homage to a technology of yesteryear was part of a neo-vintage trend but nonetheless demonstrates the company's ability to evolve while remaining true to its roots. Tissot has become one of the few Swiss brands to stick with LCD technology.

T
research

START-STOP
DATE-SEC / RESET-LAP
12:36 59
Mo Tu We Th Fr Sa Su
3X CHRONO M
LIGHT
SPLIT
TISSOT
CHRONOGRAPH

START
DATE-SEC
STOP
RESET-LAP
12:36 59
Mo Tu We Th Fr Sa Su
3X CHRONO ◆ M
LIGHT
SPLIT
TISSOT
CHRONOGRAPH
QUARTZ

WORLD TIME ATLAS

SEIKO – 1979

In 1973, Seiko unveiled the very first quartz LCD watch to feature a six-digit display (hours, minutes and seconds). As this type of display became standard for every brand, the Japanese company strove to incorporate further complications into its digital watches in an effort to stand out.

SEE OPPOSITE	1979 MODEL
MANUFACTURER	SEIKO
MODEL	WORLD TIME 'ATLAS'
CALIBRE	A239
MOVEMENT	LCD
PRODUCTION	SOLD COMMERCIALLY
MATERIAL	STEEL
STRAP	INTEGRATED

SEIKO
LC V.F.A. 06LC

On 5 October 1973, Seiko sensationally unveiled the world's first quartz LCD watch with a six-digit display showing hours, minutes and seconds.

THE FIRST DIGITAL WATCH WITH A SIX-DIGIT DISPLAY

On 5 October 1973, Seiko unveiled (with some flourish) the rather oddly named LC V.F.A. 06LC, the world's first quartz LCD watch with a six-digit display. Looking both understated and futuristic in equal measure, the waterproof case of this revolutionary digital watch housed a calibre 0614 movement with a calendar function. This innovative module, born of cutting-edge engineering, had been developed in-house and was able to show hours, minutes and seconds continuously thanks to its field-effect liquid crystal display (see page 157). Better still, its screen could be lit up in the dark to provide excellent legibility at any time of the day or night. These were novelties that proved appealing, demonstrated by the fact that the model was a resounding success despite its prohibitive price of Yen 135,000 (around $850 nowadays). The six-digit display also rapidly became the undisputed standard for LCD watches for all the major brands.

LCD – WITH COMPLICATIONS

Wishing to stay at the cutting edge of this technology, Seiko knew it had to innovate. Only two years after launching its first six-digit digital LCD watch, the Japanese firm released the reference 0634, the first multifunctional digital chronograph and a marriage of quartz technology and field-effect display that laid the groundwork for integrating watchmaking complications into the world of LCD timekeeping. The first addition was the alarm function, an obvious choice that demonstrated the remarkable adaptability of such watches. Seiko went a step further in 1977 with the reference M158, which introduced the world time function, making it possible to view multiple time zones at a glance.

THE ATLAS

By 1979, the Seiko A239 World Timer, nicknamed the 'Atlas', was ready to be presented to the world. This was a watchmaking revolution with two faces, one displaying the time and date with impeccable accuracy, the other featuring a map of the world divided into time zones. The 'Atlas' soon became a symbol of sophistication and was appropriately marketed in a myriad of appealing versions, with some proudly bearing the legend 'World Time' (the 5020 and 502A) and others the title 'World Timer Alarm' (the 5000, 5009 and 5010), although this was discreetly engraved beneath the dial. The display, which could be blue, black or red, was housed in a stainless steel or gold case. Two styles of integrated straps (one in the classic style with centred links, the other jubilee-style) provided a choice to satisfy even the most demanding connoisseur. The revolutionary functionality the watch provided was reflected in its dazzling success, and it remained on sale until the end of the 1990s as the reference A7X8 (introduced in 1984).

SEIKO
D.S.T.
MODE
HOME TIME ALARM
WORLD TIME ALARM
DATE SELECT
HNL
LAX
DEN
CHI
NYC
SYD
TYO
HKG
BKK
H↔W
CCS
LON GMT
CAI
DXB
DEL
RIO
PAR·ROM
MOW
KHI
A.STOP
LIGHT
SET
WORLD TIME

BLUE THUNDER

CASIO – 1981

November 1974 saw a new player emerge in the world of LCD watches when Casio transferred the innovative technologies used in its calculators to timepieces. The company's reputation was largely cemented by the success of the film *Blue Thunder*, released in 1983.

SEE OPPOSITE	1983 MODEL
MANUFACTURER	CASIO
MODEL	A203 'BLUE THUNDER'
CALIBRE	MODULE 103
MOVEMENT	LCD
PRODUCTION	SOLD COMMERCIALLY
MATERIAL	STEEL
STRAP	INTEGRATED

CASIO
QW02 CASIOTRON

The Casiotron, Casio's first wristwatch, was launched in 1974. Its automatic calendar function revolutionized the market by eliminating the need to set the monthly calendar manually.

FROM PIPES TO CALCULATORS

In 1946, Tadao Kashio, his brother Toshio and their father Shigeru founded a firm in Mitaka (a western suburb of Tokyo) that they called Kashio Seisakujo. The company achieved considerable success with a rather original invention dubbed the Yubiwa pipe, an ingenious cigarette holder that allowed the user to smoke hands-free. Tadao and Toshio then joined forces with their two other brothers (Kazuo and Yukio) to found a second firm that they called Casio Computer Co. Led by their father, the company designed a new generation of calculators that performed so well that they were able to assign exclusive rights to its Casio 14-A model in its first year of existence. During the 1960s, Casio devoted itself to developing and producing calculating machinery (known as relay machines) for big corporations and research institutions.

1974: THE YEAR OF THE CASIOTRON

Casio did not stop at manufacturing calculators and cigarette holders. The family business entered the world of watchmaking in 1974, bringing with it its skills in calculator design, one of the most notable being a technology known as LSI. The first Casio watch, christened the QW02 Casiotron, could not only display hours, minutes and seconds with unswerving accuracy, but also featured a revolutionary calendar that automatically adjusted the months, putting an end to the annoying need to continually reset it. Casio immediately continued what was already a saga of innovation with an entirely automatic calendar watch that could even deal with 29 February in leap years. This was followed in 1976 by the X-1, a multifunction model with a chronometer and the world time complication (see page 236) – just one of the many products with which Casio carved a niche for itself with its technological expertise in the world of multifunction LCD watches.

MODULE 103

One of these creations, the module 103, unveiled in 1981 under a range of different reference numbers, stood out in particular. Featuring multiple functionalities (including a double LCD screen), it provided a unique user experience as it was possible to switch from a classic digital display to an analogue LCD display in the blink of an eye. Better still, its countdown feature displayed a striking animated graphic each time it was activated. This detail appealed to John Badham, director of the film *Blue Thunder* (1983), who happened to be looking for a watch for his movie that would be visually striking. It should be noted that the visual effect shown in the film is not an authentic function but rather a combination of settings accompanied by sound effects added in post-production. The appearance of this model in the film boosted the reputation of Casio LCD watches all round the world – so much so that it is now a real challenge to find a 'Blue Thunder' model in decent condition. However, Casio has rekindled interest by reissuing the iconic Casiotron, skilfully blending retro charm and modern technologies.

CASIO
ADJUST
LIGHT
LAP
RESET
ALARM
ON•OFF
1/100ST
ALARM
TIMER
SIGNAL
START
STOP
25
MODE
ANALOG
ALARM CHRONOGRAPH
JAPAN H

K.I.T.T. COMMLINK

AM RADIO – 1982

Michael Knight, hero of the 1980s television series *Knight Rider*, foils crimes by using his Commlink watch to communicate with K.I.T.T., his smart car. Despite its limited capabilities, this watch played a crucial role in popularizing LCD displays.

SEE OPPOSITE	2020 MODEL
MANUFACTURER	DOCTOR COLLECTOR
MODEL	K.I.T.T. COMMLINK
CALIBRE	MADE IN HONG KONG
MOVEMENT	LCD
PRODUCTION	SOLD COMMERCIALLY
MATERIAL	PLASTIC
STRAP	INTEGRATED

AM RADIO
STAR WARS

LCD watches with an AM radio were sold under a range of brands, particularly Bradley, which marketed a version decorated with *Star Wars* characters and other musical models that played the film's theme music.

THE SUCCESS OF *KNIGHT RIDER*

The *Knight Rider* television series emerged from the creative ferment of the 1980s with a winning blend of science fiction, action and suspense. The hero, Michael Knight, played by the charismatic David Hasselhoff, is a former cop who investigates crimes from behind the wheel of K.I.T.T., a talking car that possessed top-of-the-range artificial intelligence. The pair roam the United States, protecting the innocent, solving mysteries and doing battle with foes who are as Machiavellian as they are fiendish. In pursuit of these noble efforts, Michael Knight and K.I.T.T. conduct long-distance communications via a retro-futurist watch known as a Commlink, and it was this – and its LCD screen in particular – that became an object of fascination for viewers.

THE ORIGINAL COMMLINK

As 1980s viewers knew full well, using your watch to drive a car wasn't really a thing (especially back then) but this did not stop them from dreaming of owning a watch that, just like Michael Knight's, was capable of communicating over long distances. Such a watch, however, was already in existence – an AM radio model that was already being sold by a number of companies, including Bradley, Quasatron, Nelsonic, Advance, Gala and Armitron. These were not quite as sophisticated as the watch in the television series, but they were certainly radio watches with an LCD screen and earbuds, and it also seems likely that it was the Bradley model, released in 1982, that was used in the series. The watch had been marketed in partnership with Lucasfilm and was decorated with images of C-3PO and R2-D2, the two droids from the *Star Wars* films, so had to be extensively repurposed by the series' prop masters. The engage and transmit functions were particular features of radio communications in the series. Nowadays, the watch is marketed as a toy by a brand called Doctor Collector that specializes in products sold under licence.

LCD RADIO WATCHES

Whatever the brand, the genuine AM radio watch became an icon of the 1980s. It was much sought-after by a generation that, since 1979, had been lulled by the sound of the Walkman. As fashionable as they were, however, such watches could only pick up AM radio and suffered from poor reception and interference that limited their use. Things changed in 1985 when Sinclair brought out a digital LCD watch with an integrated FM tuner, but the technology was unfortunately not up to scratch and there were endless technical faults, to the extent that only 11,000 units were produced rather than the 500,000 anticipated. Nowadays, the Commlink is no more than a toy watch, but nonetheless is a reminder of the excitement elicited by LCD displays during this exuberant decade.

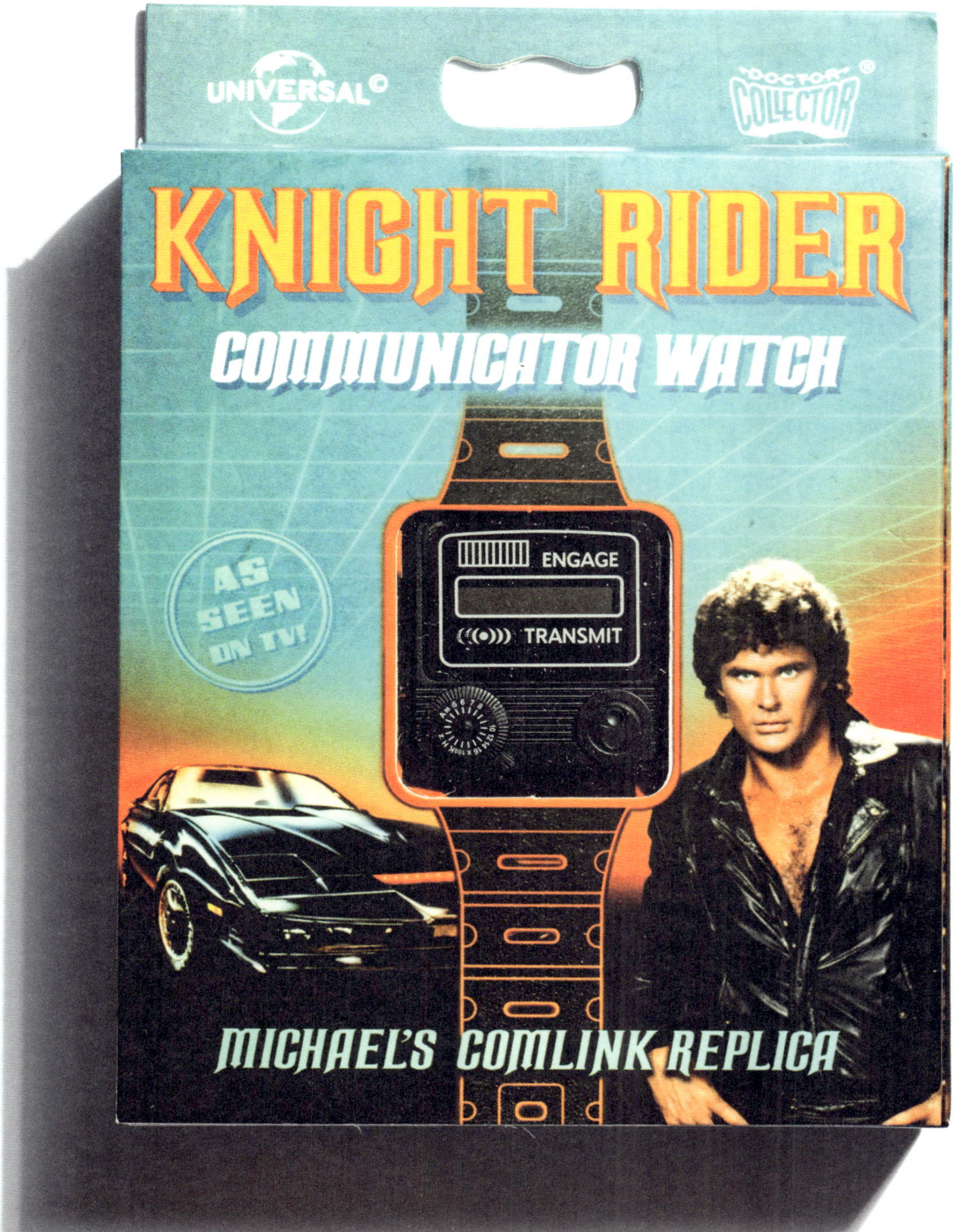
UNIVERSAL
DOCTOR COLLECTOR
KNIGHT RIDER
COMMUNICATOR WATCH
ENGAGE
TRANSMIT
AS SEEN ON TV!
MICHAEL'S COMLINK REPLICA

DATA-2000

SEIKO – 1983

In response to Casio's ascendancy in the industry, Seiko concentrated on creating ever more powerful LCD models. From 1982, the brand became a true pioneer in the smartwatch sector.

SEE OPPOSITE	1983 MODEL
MANUFACTURER	SEIKO
MODEL	DATA-2000
CALIBRE	CALIBRE UW01
MOVEMENT	LCD
PRODUCTION	SOLD COMMERCIALLY
MATERIAL	PLASTIC
STRAP	INTEGRATED

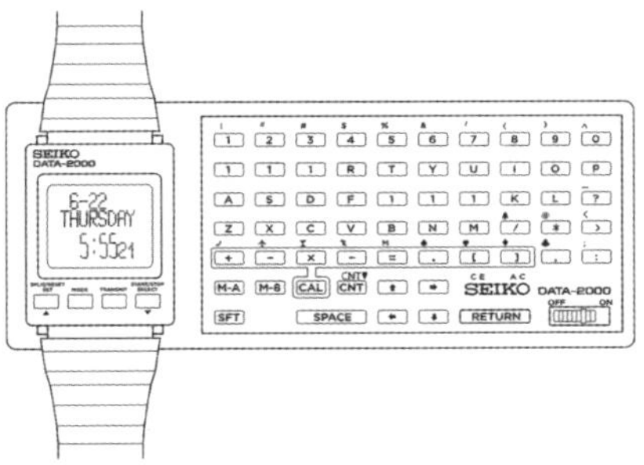

SEIKO
DATA-2000 KEYBOARD

The Data-2000 was supplied with an ergonomic keypad that could be ingeniously fixed to the wrist and allowed text to be entered directly onto the screen.

SMART WATCHES

Contrary to popular belief, smartwatches are anything but a recent invention. Engineers have been striving to add complications and smart functions to our wrists for more than a century. In the UK, the Plus Four Wristlet Route Indicator of 1927 included a map with directions from London to Bournemouth or Edinburgh and was also able to record the scores from a round of golf. Although having to scroll the map to use it was slightly annoying, the idea can only be applauded. The calculator watch first put in an appearance in a 1975 Pulsar model that used LED technology (see page 144), and the company (which was bought out by Seiko in 1978) caused a stir in 1982 when it created the NL C01 (with an LED display), the first real smartwatch. This pioneering timepiece was able to store 24 bits of information and connect to both a sublimation printer and a memory card slot. Most importantly, it heralded the dawn of an era of watches with programmable memories.

DATA-2000 AND RC-1000

The Data-2000 appeared on the market in 1983. Its name was an indicator of a storage capacity that was remarkable for its time – 2,000 bits, as opposed to the 24 achieved by its predecessors. Such extraordinary memory allowed it to do two very different things: make calculations using an app and record events in a diary. Seiko supplied the model with an ergonomic keypad that neatly attached to the wearer's wrist and made it easier to enter text onto the screen. Data was transmitted from the keypad to the watch via an electromagnetic system before being stored in the watch's memory. A variant known as the UC-200 was subsequently released, with a desktop dock that also featured the keypad. The RC-1000A, which came out a year later (in 1984), was the first watch to sync with a PC (either Apple or IBM), a new functionality that made it possible to download lists, address books and documents from the computer to the watch.

CONNECTED WATCHES

Although the watches mentioned above are without question smartwatches, the honour of being the first watch to be truly connected goes to the Receptor produced by Seiko in 1990. This was the first timepiece that could receive data without using a cable, display a short message of 16 characters and flash up the telephone number of an incoming call. Its memory also enabled it to retrieve the last eight messages received or phone numbers dialled. It sold for $275 but also required a monthly phone subscription of $12.50. Seiko attempted to relive the experience five years later with the Message Watch, a wrist-worn pager that could display sports results, stock market prices and the weather via FM signals transmitted by local radio stations. The company eventually gave up on the idea just when watches such as these began proliferating among other brands, albeit with mixed success – until the Apple Watch (see page 232) turned a new corner for connected watches, which by then had become ubiquitous.

SEIKO
DATA-2000
9-30
SATURDAY
1.11
1.1133
SPLIT/RESET
SET
MODE
TRANSMIT
START/STOP
SELECT

DATABANK

CASIO – 1985

Six years after releasing its first LCD watch, Casio caused a sensation by unveiling a calculator watch. This pushed the technological envelope of the time and, from 1984, it even featured a databank.

SEE OPPOSITE 1989 MODEL

MANUFACTURER	CASIO
MODEL	DBX-112
CALIBRE	MODULE 271
MOVEMENT	LCD
PRODUCTION	SOLD COMMERCIALLY
MATERIAL	STEEL
STRAP	INTEGRATED

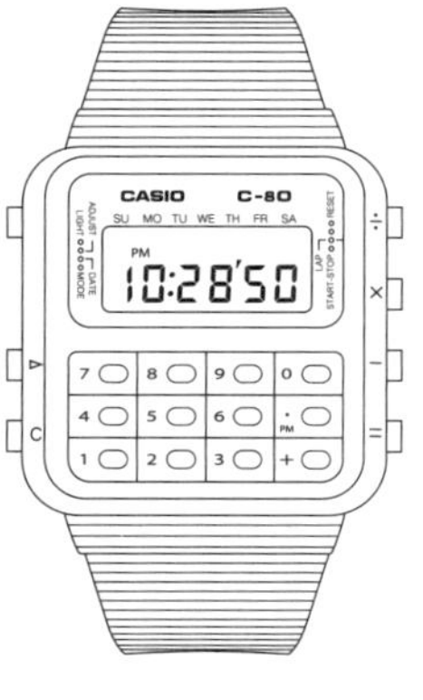

CASIO
C-80

Casio's first calculator watch was truly a milestone in the field and made it possible to carry out all four basic arithmetic operations (multiplication, division, addition, subtraction) on numbers up to eight digits.

THE LCD CALCULATOR WATCH

In 1977, three years after Casio released the Casiotron (see page 168), Seiko caused a sensation by unveiling the C-153, the first calculator watch with an LCD display. Other brands rapidly followed suit, but Casio, the authority in the field, had no illusions about what was at stake. It knew it had to fight back if it wished to maintain its lead and, in 1980, it revealed the C-80 model featuring a keypad that summed up all the brand's IT expertise. While this was an appealing design, Casio felt that it had to be taken a step further: the watch should no longer just tell the time and do simple sums, it should also become a true database, and so, in 1984, the CD-40 was born. With its 16 buttons, it could store up to 10 messages (text or phone numbers), becoming in effect a portable telephone directory. Contemporary sales brochures called it a micro-computer for the wrist. A whole host of variants appeared a year later under the name Databank.

THE DATABANKS

The first Databanks were called the DBC (Data Bank Computer) and housed the 563 module, providing the exceptional storage (for the time) of 50 entries that could include up to 9 characters of text and numbers up to 12 digits. In addition, there was also a secret note function, protected by a four-digit password, and appointments were automatically deleted once they had passed. The more luxurious DBX-100 (Data Bank Extended), fitted with the 261 module, appeared in 1988. The majority were made of steel or gold-plated but, crucially, they could now store up to 100 pieces of text that could be retrieved at will. The screen of the DBX could also display a week-by-week view, with a planner that detailed the start and end times of events. This display was undoubtedly the most sophisticated of all the Databank watches.

A SIX-MILLION UNIT SUCCESS

In 1989, the simpler and more powerful 676 module was introduced to the Databank series. This upgrade included a countdown function and a world time feature (see page 236). The display could be optimized by operating certain buttons. Databank watches evolved over the years as their technology was refined, their design perfected and new calibres were released. More than six million units were sold between 1984 and 1989. Although the exact figures have not been released to the public, these watches (including the 'Calculator', 'World Time', and 'Alarm' versions with the data bank function) are still highly successful and are still available for sale, appealing to many collectors of neo-retro watches.

ALARM SIG ON·OFF/RESET
CASIO
DATA BANK
DBX-112
WORLD TIME
ADJUST
MODE
SHIFT
SECRET/C
12·24HR
THIS
NEXT
WEEK
S M T W T F S
SAT '23 9-30
13:17 46
SCHEDULE
TELEMEMO

G-SHOCK

CASIO – 1983

Casio rocked the world of LCD watches to its foundations in 1983 with the first model in its new G-Shock range. With shock-resistance, waterproofing and battery life far superior to its competitors, the watch heralded the dawn of a new era.

SEE OPPOSITE	1996 MODEL
MANUFACTURER	CASIO
MODEL	G-SHOCK
CALIBRE	MODULE 1548
MOVEMENT	LCD
PRODUCTION	SOLD COMMERCIALLY + MILITARY
MATERIAL	RESIN + STEEL
STRAP	POLYURETHANE

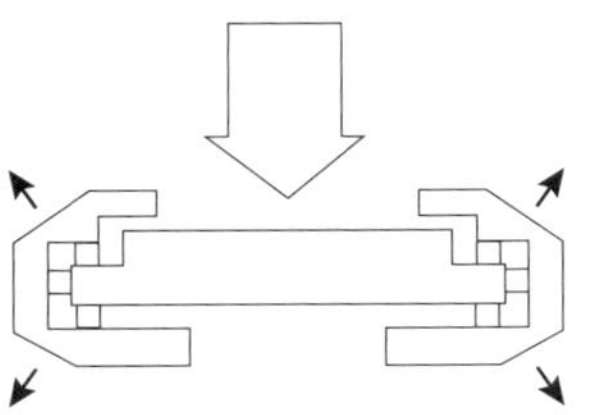

THE G-SHOCK'S STRUCTURAL TECHNOLOGY

Unlike a traditional watch, the module seems to float within the case, an ingenious design that allows it to absorb shocks.

IBE KIKUO, FATHER OF THE G-SHOCK

In 1981, Japanese engineer Ibe Kikuo designed the G-Shock, a watch of such robust durability that it was supposedly able to survive any fall. This brilliant mind had been recruited by Casio five years earlier and drew his inspiration from a distressing family experience when his father's precious watch had been dropped and smashed before his eyes – or at least that's how the story goes. The engineer himself attributed his design to watching some workmen outside his office. They were not wearing watches, and for good reason, as the potential shocks from the use of their tools and the vibrations from machinery such as pneumatic drills are the worst enemies of the wristwatch. Whichever story is true, the management at Casio was convinced and decided to develop the project.

THE TRIPLE 10 RULE

Ibe Kikuo headed up this new venture and assembled a stripped-down project team to bring it to life. From a methodological perspective, Kikuo instituted an innovative, results-based rule. Complex technical suggestions were to be shown the door if the outcome failed to achieve the triple ten – the watch had to survive a fall of 10m (32ft), be waterproof to ten bars of pressure (that is, a depth of 100m/328ft) and have a battery life of ten years. The only hitch was that there was no laboratory at the time that had the equipment necessary for such shock testing, so the analytical methods adopted were rudimentary – around a hundred prototypes found themselves being thrown out of Ibe Kikuo's office window to evaluate their solidity. He was watching children play with a rubber ball one day when inspiration struck – he needed a hollow structure within which the module would be kept in place by a minimal number of contact points. The engineer carried out some tests using a ball like the one used by the children, and a miracle came to pass. All that was left to do was miniaturize the design to make it viable.

ENGINEERING AND THE CONQUEST OF AMERICA

The G-Shock DW-5000 came along two years later (in 1983). Its famous shock resistance was achieved through an ingenious arrangement of ten different layers that formed a protective shield around the quartz module. This suit of armour included a polyurethane shock absorber, a stainless steel shell, reinforced mineral glass and a screw-down stainless steel caseback. The quartz module floated freely, with the mechanism nestled in polyurethane foam, while the exterior buttons and the module's LCD screen were connected by flexible wires. Although the range struggled to appeal to the Japanese market (where some stores had no appetite for selling a watch considered unbreakable), it was a success in the West, with a memorable publicity campaign in the United States making it particularly popular (including an ad in which the G-Shock was used as an ice hockey puck). It was initially adopted by professionals (firefighters, soldiers and even astronauts) before finding favour with skateboarders accustomed to falling and surfers in search of waterproofing. It was then carried along by a wave of popularity that had its roots in streetwear. Some 130 million G-Shocks have been sold around the world since the first model was released.

PROTECTION
CASIO
WATER 200M RESIST
TIMER RESET
ADJUST
START·STOP
10 20 30 40 50
WE 9-20
24
16:06 05
SELECT
12/24HR
MODE
LIGHT
ILLUMINATOR
SHOCK RESIST
G-SHOCK

WORLD TIMER

CASIO – 2010

At the time of writing, the world's best-selling watch is the F-91, a Casio LCD released in 1989. It has become an eternal symbol of the Casio brand and reigns supreme in the Timeless collection, alongside such other invincible classics as the World Timer (nicknamed the Royale).

SEE OPPOSITE	2010 MODEL
MANUFACTURER	CASIO
MODEL	AE-1200 WORLD TIMER
CALIBRE	MODULE 3299
MOVEMENT	LCD
PRODUCTION	SOLD COMMERCIALLY
MATERIAL	RESIN
STRAP	POLYURETHANE

CASIO
F-91

The F-91, a Casio LCD unveiled in 1989, is the world's best-selling watch at the time of writing.

A NEW CLASSIC

The World Timer, a variant of the AE-1000 series, was launched in the 2010s as part of Casio's Youth Series range, a collection intended to appeal to younger consumers. Its appeal soon spread beyond its target audience, however, as an older demographic took an interest in its many functions and it became one of the brand's essential models. It has a nicely balanced layout, with a display of a map of the world at top right, an analogue display to the left, and the time and date on a six-digit screen in the centre. It was ideal for travelling – a display of times for two cities could be read at a glance. The whole package was enclosed in a vaguely rectangular resin case furnished with metal push-buttons on either side. Despite its many functions, it was very easy to read, and its sleek design delivered a durability approaching that of the G-Shock, without any of the latter's aesthetic harshness.

FROM 17 TO 35 DOLLARS

The AE-1200 was presented as a multifunction watch built for adventure. Although it lacked the robust armour plating of the G-Shock, it still boasted waterproofing to a depth of 100m (328ft) and a battery life of ten years, and so fulfilled two of the triple ten criteria (see page 176) underlying the creation of its shockproof elder sibling. Although knocks and scratches might leave the occasional mark on the black coating of its resin case, its reasonable price was enough to allay owners' concerns; costing anything from $17 to $35 (depending on the model), it was far cheaper than a standard watch of reasonable quality.

'CASIO ROYALE'

Keen collectors have dubbed a silver version of the AE-1200 the 'Casio Royale'. There is a rather unusual reason for this – the AE-1200 does indeed bear a striking resemblance to the Seiko G757 LCD worn by Roger Moore in *Octopussy* (see page 118). It was the rather unusual association of ideas, between the release of the World Timer and the new James Bond film, that led aficionados to come up with this name. That said, the Casio World Timer and the Seiko G757 certainly have several characteristics in common, starting with a bevelled bezel and four function buttons, not to mention the feature at top left that enthusiasts call the 'radar' (in fact this is an analogue time display on the Casio and a chronometer on the Seiko).

WORLD TIME
5ALARMS
CASIO
MUTE
ALM
ADJUST
LIGHT
WR100M
MODE
SEARCH
21:03 17
10YEAR BATTERY
ILLUMINATOR

swatch
QUARTZ
swiss

THE SWATCH PHENOMENON

CHAPTER 5

DELIRIUM

ETA SA – 1979

On 12 January 1979, the Swiss watchmaking industry announced the release of the Delirium, the thinnest watch ever manufactured, developed by Ébauches SA (now known as ETA). It was to lay the future foundations for a revolution in the world of watchmaking – the Swatch.

SEE OPPOSITE	1979 MODEL
MANUFACTURE	ETA SA
MODEL	DELIRIUM
CALIBRE	ETA 999.001
MOVEMENT	QUARTZ
PRODUCTION	PROTOTYPE
MATERIAL	YELLOW GOLD
STRAP	LEATHER

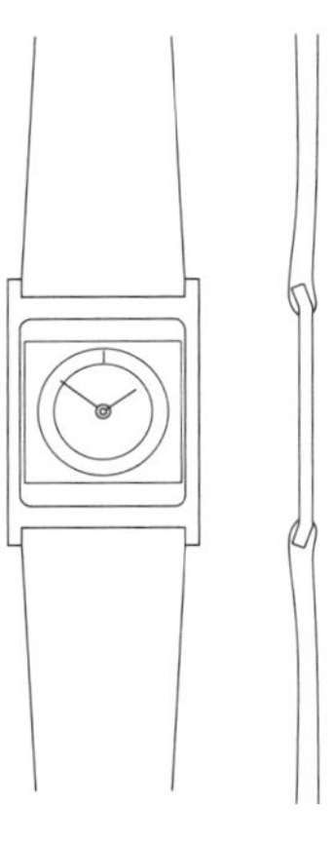

ETA SA
DELIRIUM

The Delirium I, with a thickness of 1.98mm, was revealed to the world on 12 January 1979, immediately establishing itself as the epitome of the era's watchmaking skills. Another version, the Delirium II released by Eterna, pushed the envelope further with a thickness of only 1.5mm.

ULTRA-THIN FROM JAPAN

Once they had appeared, Japanese firms made gigantic strides in simplifying and standardizing the technology of quartz watches. Seiko lowered prices to appeal to a mass market, for example, but also brought out its fair share of innovations every year, especially where thickness was concerned. In 1974, the brand brought the calibre 41 (a slim quartz movement for women's watches) to market and, when Citizen developed an ultra-thin movement four years later, Seiko lost no time in picking up the gauntlet. The watch it produced was indeed the thinnest of its time, featuring the new calibre 9320 (0.9mm thick) housed in a 2.5mm case, and though it proved a loss leader, this exceptional watch found its way into the display windows of prestigious New York jeweller Tiffany & Co – a stunning debut for luxury Japanese watches in the land of Uncle Sam.

GERRY GRINBERG

With the exception of the Rolex Day-Date, American tastes of the time seemed to run to sports watches rather than elegant, luxury models – but this would be to disregard the influence of Gedalio (known as Gerry) Grinberg, a watchmaker of Cuban origin whose North American Watch Company would shake things up entirely. As a distributor, he had established Piaget watches among the elite of New York before turning his attention to other renowned brands, including Corum with its famous Pièce models; but first and foremost among these was Concord, the brand he headed. Having seen the ultra-thin Seiko at Tiffany & Co, he decided to move into this niche area, but realized it would require a proper deal with the right people. At the end of the 1970s, a number of Swiss watchmaking companies had joined forces as Ébauches SA, which became ETA SA. Its technical director André Beyner was ideally placed to create the thin quartz watch of Grinberg's dreams. Grinberg offered him 2 million Swiss francs for ETA SA to design the model.

THE DELIRIUM TREMENS PROJECT

Movement designer Anton Bally developed a mechanism that distributed components horizontally to minimize the thickness and Beyner decided to integrate this movement into the case. These elements were crafted into a single unit designed by Maurice Grimm. In 1978, the 'Delirium Tremens' project (so called after the quest was referred to as *un delirium très mince* ('a very thin delirium'), was presented to Ernst Thomke. He had recently taken over the reins of production at ETA SA, and had been charged with turning the company around in the middle of the watchmaking crisis. He was won over, and little wonder – the Delirium held a trump card not possessed by the Japanese models in the form of a Renata battery cell that was only 1.1mm thick. It was the thickest component in the Delirium, which was unveiled to the world's press on 12 January 1979. At no more than 1.98mm from crystal to caseback, it was the thinnest watch in existence. A delighted Gerry Grinberg travelled to the United States to present his Concord at Tiffany & Co, launching an advertising campaign that boasted 'the thinnest watch ever made'. It was also to be sold by Longines, Eterna and IWC. Ernst Thomke saw the Delirium as the chance to create an affordable quartz watch able to compete with Japanese models.

ETA
Swiss Quartz
Délirium

ZAUGG

SWATCH – 1981

The first prototypes of a plastic watch that was both value for money and 100 per cent Swiss appeared in 1980. The project would become so important that it attracted support from all the players in the country's economy.

SEE OPPOSITE	1981 MODEL
MANUFACTURER	SWATCH
MODEL	ZAUGG
CALIBRE	ETA
MOVEMENT	QUARTZ
PRODUCTION	PROTOTYPE
MATERIAL	ABS PLASTIC
STRAP	N/A

ASUAG-SSIH

The quartz crisis was so grave that, by 1981, Swiss banks had started to inject more than 900 million Swiss francs into the SSIH, the owner of brands such as Omega and Tissot, and the Swiss watch industry group Allgemeine Schweizerischen Uhrenindustrie AG (ASUAG), which controlled the likes of Longines and ETA components. This was to prove insufficient, and the banks demanded an audit of the solvency of the Swiss watchmaking industry, the upshot of which was that ASUAG and SSIH, the two major syndicates of Swiss watchmakers, were obliged to merge. Ernst Thomke, the former CEO of Ébauches SA (now ETA), was co-opted to manage the new conglomerate with the support of industrialist Nicolas Hayek.

MOCK AND MÜLLER

The history of Swatch began in 1980 when ETA engineer Elmar Mock was summoned to the office of Ernst Thomke, who demanded an explanation for an outlay of 500,000 Swiss francs on a plastic injection moulding machine. Mock showed him a revolutionary drawing for a plastic watch, the results of a collaboration with his co-worker and friend Jacques Müller. Ernst Thomke took Mock by surprise, saying, 'I have been waiting for this for more than a year!' It was indeed true that a watch that would be both 100 per cent Swiss and accessible to the general public had long been the dream of the man who was the head of ETA, to the extent that he had started an in-house competition between his engineers. Mock and Müller were the perfect combination of expertise in plastics and in watchmaking skills, their genius rooted in their collaboration. The traditional structure of a watch, with a movement plate housed in a case that was closed off by a caseback and a crystal, had been replaced by a unique plastic case, injection-moulded at high pressure and fused to the glass, with not a screw in sight. Indeed, screws were supplanted by rivets fitted using an ultrasonic process. The idea was so original that the first sketches (made on a napkin) had elicited ridicule from their colleagues, but it took more than this to discourage them. Mock and Müller initially produced the first prototypes (dubbed the 'Delerium Vulgaris') by hand until the injection moulding machine made it possible to test prototypes on an industrial scale.

ZAUGG SWATCHES

The Swatch brand was trademarked in 1981. The name was a contraction of the words 'Swiss' and 'watch' but also concealed a little-known additional meaning; it could be read as 'second watch', referring to the idea of providing an alternative to traditional watches. The designer duo Marlyse Schmid and Bernard Müller brought their expertise to bear on the architecture of the watches, from the cases and dials to the straps and logo. They also brought talent in from outside the firm in the form of Hans Zaugg, who lent his name to the first prototypes. Unlike the hand-made test watches, Zaugg's designs featured a metal compartment for the Renata cells that was closed off with a metal lid, and an ABS plastic case that was shock-resistant and easy to mould when compared with other materials. These prototypes featured almost all the technological innovations to be found in future Swatches, with one exception – the design of the case did not yet allow for perfect integration of the strap.

Swatch
quartz
SWISS

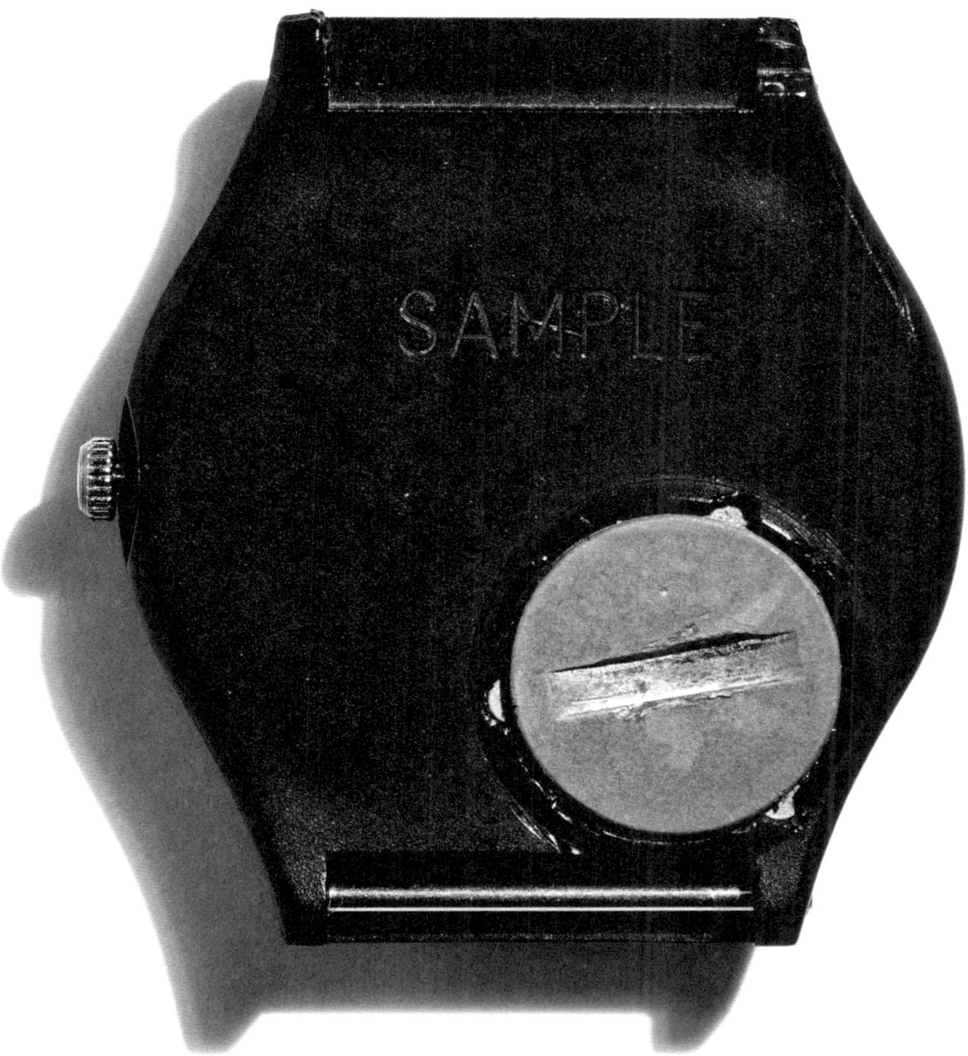
SAMPLE

SCHMÜLLERS

SWATCH – 1982

Marlyse Schmid and Bernard Müller, a renowned design duo nicknamed the 'Schmüllers', breathed life into a host of Swatch prototypes during 1982. As well as working on the logo font and the ergonomics of the case, they also gradually worked out how to integrate the strap perfectly.

OPPOSITE PAGE	1982 MODEL
MANUFACTURER	SWATCH
MODEL	'SCHMÜLLERS'
CALIBRE	ETA 500
MOVEMENT	QUARTZ
PRODUCTION	PROTOTYPE
MATERIAL	ABS PLASTIC
STRAP	N/A

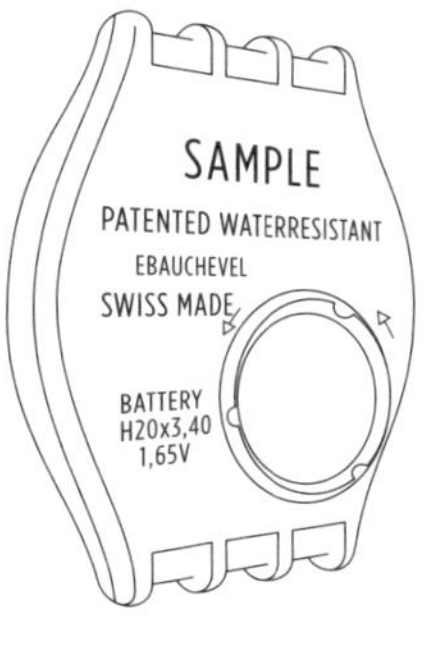

SWATCH
STRAP ATTACHMENT SYSTEM

Taking their inspiration from Lego, the Schmüllers added two central lugs to the plastic, while a new steel pin was introduced to ensure the perfect integration of the strap.

A REVOLUTIONARY CASE

The year 1982 saw Marlyse Schmid and Bernard Müller create numerous prototypes with 'Sample' stamped on the back of the case. At the same time, they also tested a number of different crowns and hands on these watches and designed versions with and without dates. The duo initially opted for the case designed by Zaugg, which had one major drawback, the difficulty of integrating the strap well. The Schmüllers then dreamed up a new case with softer curves allowing for smoother integration. The first version merely concealed the strap attachment points, but they gradually refined their research and, taking inspiration from Lego, added two central lugs to the plastic case and decided to use a new steel pin. This time it was perfect.

THINKING ABOUT THE LOGO

The Schmüllers also thought hard about the typeface for the logo, and had plenty of ideas. One of the first versions included an 'S' that dominated the other letters. They then looked at the crossing of two 'Vs' to form a 'W', before considering which way the tail of the 'Q' for 'quartz' should point. The designers even toyed with the idea of inserting a Swiss flag between the 'S' and the 'W', but strict legislation on the use of national emblems for commercial purposes scotched this bold suggestion. Every detail was meticulously scrutinized and nothing was left to chance – the logo had to be perfect.

THE FINAL DESIGN

These logos, known as big S designs, were eventually binned, with Swatch plumping for a purer, more legible typeface where all the letters were of equal size. This is the font still in use today. A rounded shape with soft contours was chosen for the case, with a discreet crown and the two central lugs, which of course appealed to the brand's decision makers. Every date complication option was considered for the first round of marketing, including versions with no date, versions with the date alone or some with a day-date display. Once these choices had been made, the watch was more or less ready. All that was left to do was to kickstart the automated industrial production that would bring it to market. A watchmaking tidal wave was in the offing.

Swatch
Quartz
SUN 29
SWISS

GN100

SWATCH – 1983

Swatch was first marketed in 1983 and rapidly turned into an unprecedented watch tsunami that engulfed the world. Nicolas Hayek, one of the architects of the phenomenon, took over the reins of ASUAG-SSIH – the company that, 15 years later, would become the Swatch Group.

SEE OPPOSITE	1983 MODEL
MANUFACTURER	SWATCH
MODEL	GN100
CALIBRE	ETA 500
MOVEMENT	QUARTZ
PRODUCTION	MARKETING
MATERIAL	ABS PLASTIC
STRAP	PLASTIC

REVOLUTIONARY ASSEMBLY

Evidence of the revolution brought about by Swatch was to be found as much in its factories as in its watches. Thanks to the delicate ballet carried out by 21 fully automated robots, as many human beings and intricate operations regulated to the last millimetre, right down to the setting of the time, this extraordinary company managed to produce 35,000 watches a day. This feat of assembly, and the speed with which it was carried out, was due in particular to the drastic reduction in the number of parts. A traditional watch required 91 components, but a Swatch worked perfectly well with 51 – a revolution within a revolution. More than anything, however, it was purely and simply the incarnation of the idea of 'design for assembly' in which each decision at the planning stage was made with manufacturing costs and assembly methods in mind. The project was pursued with great diligence and initially pointed towards a square prototype, but it was ultimately the circular version that was ready for commercial production by the end of 1982.

AMERICA BEFORE SWITZERLAND

By 1982, electronic watches (which had not even existed for public use 13 years previously) now outnumbered their mechanical counterparts, and Switzerland was forced to bow the knee and cede its pre-eminent position to Japan. It was in the midst of this global upheaval that the Swatch phenomenon was to emerge. The company's first foray onto American soil featured a range of 25 models. Under the inspired leadership of Nicolas Hayek, and bolstered by a bold marketing strategy devised by Jacques Irniger (a veteran of Colgate and Nestlé), the watches became much more than just an instrument for telling the time – they were elements of style in their own right. The advertising campaign of the time proclaimed, 'The Swatch is stylish, with a rainbow of fashion colors and styles to match whatever outfit or mood you are in'. Having conquered the United States, Swatch took on Europe, starting in Zurich in 1983, when 12 models were marketed in the Swiss city, selling for anything between 39.90 and 49.90 Swiss francs. The price was fixed at 50 Swiss francs in the autumn of that year.

THE SWATCH GROUP

Sales targets were set at 1 million watches for 1983 and 2.5 million the following year. Thanks to an aggressive marketing campaign, and its relatively low price for a Swiss product, the watch experienced an instant boom on the domestic market. Two years later, Nicolas Hayek and a group of investors purchased 51 per cent of the ASUAG-SSIH group's capital for the sum of 153 million Swiss francs – rather a modest amount, given the brand's ambitions. Six years after that, Hayek succeeded Ernst Thomke as CEO of the ASUAG-SSIH group, which was then renamed the SMH (Société Suisse de Microélectronique et d'Horlogerie SA), marking the end of the independence of several historic brands. This enforced merger was akin to a rescue mission for many, and the majority flourished in what became the Swatch Group in 1998. More than 60 Swatch shops around the world opened at about this time, selling a host of different models.

swatch
QUARTZ
SWISS

METAL

SWATCH – 1984

Just a few months after the market launch of the first Swatch, the brand's engineers were already exploring multiple options for expanding the range, looking at new materials, exploring new graphics and working on new shapes.

SEE OPPOSITE	1984 MODEL
MANUFACTURER	SWATCH
MODEL	METAL LADY
CALIBRE	ETA
MOVEMENT	QUARTZ
PRODUCTION	PROTOTYPE
MATERIAL	BRASS
STRAP	N/A

A METALLIC CAP

In 1984, after three years of research focusing on design and graphics, Swatch began a journey of innovation, exploring materials such as a range of different metals to complement the range in ABS plastic. As the engineers well knew, automating the production of solid metal cases would be a considerable challenge, especially on the scale on which Swatch operated. Marlyse Schmid and Bernard Müller, two of the boffins behind the watches, came up with a cunning solution – a metal cap, precisely machined to cover the strap lugs, which was to be fitted over the plastic case. Their aim was to give the watch the sophisticated look of a high-end timepiece without allowing costs to skyrocket. Countless materials tests were carried out, from steel to aged brass, but the outcome was invariably the same – the strap attachment system was too weak. These prototypes never made it to the mass production stage and remain one-off pieces.

A 100 PER CENT METAL CASE

In 1986, however, a handful of brass prototypes appeared. These looked very different from traditional Swatches, with prominent lugs that suggested a more adept integration of the strap (a crucial element that had previously been problematic for the metal-cap models). Once again, however, these test models failed to make it to production and were doomed to stay on the drawing board. This time round it was clear that any metal Swatch would require a new system of automated industrial manufacturing. Some of the prototype ladies' models nonetheless boasted an aesthetic that was entirely different from traditional Swatches thanks to their innovative graphic identities. These experiments were proof positive of the desire nursed by the brand's engineers to push Swatch design as far as possible, both in their choice of materials and aesthetics, and the clientele they could reach.

SWATCH IRONY

A metal-capped Swatch finally saw the light of day at the end of 1988. In the mid-1990s, the Irony series was unveiled, a range with a 100 per cent solid metal case. The first model in this collection was a chronograph (see page 111), followed by classic analogue watches. The Swatch Irony had cases made of stainless steel or aluminium and as a result were more expensive to buy than the standard models in ABS plastic. The price variation was justified by their robust construction, resistance to scratches and shocks, and their more luxurious image than the rest of the range.

swatch
QUARTZ
SWISS

KIKI PICASSO

PICASSO – 1985

In 1983, Swatch's designers took on the job of brightening up the rather sober-looking dials of the brand's first watches. Two years later, it was the turn of French artist Kiki Picasso, in a collaboration that used the Swatch as the world's smallest canvas.

SEE OPPOSITE	1985 MODEL
MANUFACTURER	SWATCH
MODEL	KIKI PICASSO TRIAL
CALIBRE	ETA 500
MOVEMENT	QUARTZ
PRODUCTION	PROTOTYPE
MATERIAL	ABS PLASTIC
STRAP	GENERIC, SIGNED BY THE ARTIST

FIRST COLLABORATION

For the launch of its 1985 summer collection in France, Swatch organized an art show to which it invited a group of 30 artists led by France's Christian Chapiron, AKA Kiki Picasso. Known for the revolutionary spirit of his lo-fi graphic design troupe Bazooka, he was a punk without a guitar, with a piercing gaze mercilessly scrutinizing his own times. The event was held at the Institut de Recherche et Coordination Acoustique/Musique (IRCAM) in the bustling heart of Paris. During this memorable evening, the artist added his signature to 120 Swatches, all completely unique, which were handed out to the French capital's prominent celebrities. To round things off, Christian Chapiron created 120 large posters featuring each of the different colour schemes of the watches. It was a way of exploring a subject that had fascinated him five years earlier when he collaborated on the sleeve design for the album *Chez les autres* by Starshooter, a punk group from Lyon.

PRODUCTION OF 140 UNITS

Although 120 watches were distributed that evening, 140 had in fact been manufactured, along with many prototypes. The designers Marlyse Schmid and Bernard Müller (see page 188) had been involved in the project from the creative stage. Their aim was to play around with transparency to reveal the mechanism of the watch. The creative team decided to print designs on thin sheets of Plexiglas to reinforce the 3D effect, and as the printed discs gradually rotated, the graphic design would reassemble itself twice a year. The first trials were made with matte black or transparent cases and a black-and-white illustration, but this rapidly evolved when a new translucent plastic developed by the brand was adopted. Depending on light levels, the case would vary in colour from green to deep purple. These touches of colour enriched the visuals but sparked heated in-house debate. Christian Chapiron presented Swatch with two different designs featuring a human face in striking poses. Swatch opted for an asymmetrical image in which the face, slightly raised and turned to one side, expressed a certain energy. The team were nonetheless left with the crucial question of which way the face should look – to the left or right? After numerous experiments, a decision was made and the left won out. The Kiki Picasso featured a translucent case and strap, with colour graphics unique to each model, complemented by delicate hands coloured accordingly.

A MUCH SOUGHT-AFTER LIMITED EDITION

The Kiki Picasso model unveiled in 1985 has become the holy grail for discerning collectors – and with good reason. It is both an iconic piece and Swatch's first foray into the world of art. The posters issued depicting the 120 dials with their combinations of unique colours are now also much sought-after. The original watches now change hands for unimaginable sums, with one being sold for more than 12,000 Euros at an auction held in 2016. The prototypes, often no longer working, have now found their way into the hands of smart collectors. In short, this collaboration was so successful that it laid the foundation for other ventures of a similar nature.

SWATCH
DON'T BE TOO LATE!

This model, unveiled in 1984, was a major milestone in Swatch history, incorporating a message that was both ironic and a little cheeky into bold and innovative watchmaking.

SWATCH
PROTOTYPE PULSOMETER

This prototype, designed in 1986, shows the brand's willingness to explore new horizons in terms of colours and watchmaking complications. Although initially intended for medical staff (with a blood-red tint), it eventually saw the light of day in a rather more discreet shade of grey.

K. Haring
© 85
swatch
SWISS

SWATCH
AN EXPERIMENTAL 'SERPENT'

Unlike the retail 'Serpent' model with its transparent body,
this unique model has a green case that showcases
Keith Haring's graphic design.

OIGOL ORO

SWATCH – 1989

The success of the artistic collaboration between Swatch and Kiki Picasso paved the way for many more. Two such ventures were of particular note: a complete collection that sprang from the mind of Keith Haring in 1986, followed by an iconic model designed by Mimmo Paladino in 1989.

SEE OPPOSITE	1989 MODEL
MANUFACTURER	SWATCH
MODEL	GZ113 OIGOL ORO
CALIBRE	ETA 500
MOVEMENT	QUARTZ
PRODUCTION	PROTOTYPE
MATERIAL	ABS PLASTIC
STRAP	PLASTIC

THE FIRST SWATCH COLLABORATIONS

- 1985 KIKI PICASSO
- 1985 ANDREW LOGAN
- 1986 KEITH HARING
- 1987 JEAN-MICHEL FOLON
- 1987 TADANORI YOKOO
- 1988 PIERRE ALECHINSKY
- 1988 VALERIO ADAMI
- 1989 MIMMO PALADINO

FROM ANDREW LOGAN TO KEITH HARING

After Kiki Picasso, Andrew Logan was the next artist to collaborate with Swatch on a model dubbed the 'Jellyfish' as it was completely transparent. In 1986, the same year that he set up Pop Shop in the SoHo district of New York, it was the turn of the well-known American artist Keith Haring to get involved. The store was a physical extension of his vision of art being accessible to everyone, far from the museums and galleries that he saw as too elitist. 'Art has meaning only if it speaks to all,' he emphatically declared at the time, a logic that applied perfectly to the idea of an extremely popular Swatch signed by an artist of his calibre. Among the first products sold at the Pop Shop was a collection of four Swatches, each a limited edition of 9,999 units: a model featuring tiny figures (see page 198), the centipede, the white on black design and the serpent (see page 199). These iconic models were to become some of the most popular pieces among Swatch collectors.

FROM TADANORI YOKOO TO MIMMO PALADINO

In 1987, the Swatch Art collection was enriched with works by the watercolourist Jean-Michel Folon and the graphic designer Tadanori Yokoo, who joined the brand and were followed in 1988 by the painters Pierre Alechinsky, Pol Bury and Valerio Adami. Lastly, in 1989, Swatch turned to Domenico Paladino, a painter and sculptor better known as Mimmo Paladino, one of the leading lights of the trans-avantgarde. This movement advocated a return to traditional forms of painting and printmaking, following a range of different conceptual and minimalist trends that were characteristic of the 1970s. Paladino designed a minimalist watch dubbed the Oigol Oro, inspired by the Latin phrase *memento mori* ('remember that you must die'). The black case and strap enclosed a brilliant white dial bearing a scary black mask with stylized hands emerging from its mouth. The minute hand was reminiscent of a scythe, eternally slicing through the flow of time as it passes.

THE RAREST SWATCH

No more than 140 numbered Oigol Oro watches were ever produced. The first was presented to the winner of a 'Create your Swatch' competition run by the brand that attracted more than 1,000 entrants, and the next 99 were handed out to celebrities from the American actor Robert Redford to the Dalai Lama. The last 40 were saved for employees at Mimmo Paladino and Swatch. They are distinguished from the others by being numbered in Roman rather than Arabic numerals. These last 40 (the most sought-after) have even more original numbering as the numbers are mirror images of standard Arabic markers. These pieces have a particular appeal for Swatch lovers, some of whom are willing to part with $10,000 or more to acquire one. Although countless collaborations were to follow, none was to achieve the same prestige as the Oigol Oro.

swatch
SWISS

SCUBA

SWATCH – 1990

With a view to expanding its range and in response to strong demand in the sector, Swatch unveiled a colourful new collection in 1990 that adopted the aesthetics of the dive watches that were so dear to the world of high-end watchmaking.

SEE OPPOSITE	1992 MODEL
MANUFACTURER	SWATCH
MODEL	SCUBA 200 SDN101 & HAPPY FISH
CALIBRE	ETA
MOVEMENT	QUARTZ
PRODUCTION	SOLD COMMERCIALLY
MATERIAL	ABS PLASTIC
STRAP	PLASTIC

A HOST OF VARIANTS

Having turned the watchmaking world upside down with its innovations, Swatch set about expanding its range by paying homage to traditional watches. In 1990, it created the Swatch Collector's Club, a turning point in the brand's history. In addition to classic watches with three hands, the company now sold chronographs (see page 204) intended for the European market and dive watches (see page 236) for the United States. The latter were so successful that they soon went into production on a global scale and were sold in all kinds of locations, not just American watersport tourist hotspots. The watches, dubbed the 'Scuba 200m', proudly featured the rotating bezel characteristic of dive watches and were marketed in a wide range of lively colours. Each component (bezel, strap and dial) was available in any number of variants, each with its own character. The names (Bora Bora, Barrier Reef, Hippocampus, Medusa, Blue Moon, Red Island and Happy Fish) hinted at the brand's limitless creativity. In Italy, the watches became so popular that the summer of 1991 was known as 'the Happy Fish era'. The range was further extended at the end of the decade with the introduction of the aluminium Irony Scuba models.

DIVING PROHIBITED!

The Scuba was touted as waterproof to a depth of 200m (656ft), which suggested that (like all watches with the same rating, also called 20atm) it was capable of withstanding 20 times atmospheric pressure. In actual fact, the most it could tolerate was a dip in the pool, so the Scuba was in no way a dive watch, despite its looks. Its rotating bezel did nothing to hide this either. The watch did not meet the rigorous criteria of the ISO standard (see page 136) – unlike most dive watches, it did without a screwed-down crown or caseback and was hardly designed to be shock-resistant. It was nonetheless a disruptive fashion piece and perfectly crafted for a couple of lengths of a pool or a zoom around the bay on a jet ski.

BOOSTING THE POPULARITY OF DIVE WATCHES

Despite its inherent limitations in quality, the Scuba played a major role in the rebirth of the fashion for dive watches in the 1990s. Watches such as these had previously been bought by professional users or die-hard enthusiasts, but Omega, a subsidiary of the Swatch Group, helped to popularize the style with the general public in 1993, when it relaunched the Seamaster 300 that had been immortalized by Pierce Brosnan as James Bond. In 2023, the Blancpain brand (also part of the Swatch Group) celebrated the 70th anniversary of the Fifty Fathoms, the first dive watch in history, with a new release – the bioceramic Scuba x Blancpain line that picked up on a design already used in the MoonSwatch (see page 208). With its automatic Sistem51 movement (see page 99), it was able to provide waterproofing to 50 fathoms (91m/298ft), much like the dive watches that inspired it.

THE SCUBA CATALOGUE

The Scuba range released in the 1990s offered a dazzling diversity, with each piece bearing a particularly imaginative name, including:

- BORA BORA
- BARRIER REEF
- HIPPOCAMPUS
- MEDUSA
- BLUE MOON
- RED ISLAND
- TIPPING COMPASS
- HAPPY FISH

swatch
SWISS
55
5
50
10
45
15
40
20
35
25
30

CHRONO

SWATCH – 1990

A crucial year in the history of modern watchmaking, 1990 saw the arrival of Swatch chronographs, some of which were sold in striking colours. This new range propelled the brand towards sales of 100 million units in 1992.

SEE OPPOSITE	1992 MODEL
MANUFACTURER	SWATCH
MODEL	FLASH ARROW SCL100
CALIBRE	ETA
MOVEMENT	QUARTZ
PRODUCTION	SOLD COMMERCIALLY
MATERIAL	ABS PLASTIC
STRAP	PLASTIC

THE CHRONO SWATCH

To satisfy the insatiable appetite of Swatch fans, the Swatch Chrono series was launched on the European market in the spring of 1990, taking advantage of the opportunity to firmly establish itself in Switzerland, Germany, France and Italy. Production was increased to a global scale and it dominated the sector until 1998, when it handed the baton to the Swatch Chrono Alarm collection. Two appealing versions were marketed, one of which featured an accurate display of hours, minutes and seconds but dispensed with an obvious date complication, while the other (more sophisticated) variant could display tenths of a second, seconds and minutes and, in some cases, featured a date window. With a diameter of 37mm, the watches were larger than the classic Swatches. Most importantly, they were available in a range of colours from the discreet to the garish – there was something for everyone.

SWATCH SELLS 100 MILLION WATCHES IN 1992

Enthusiasts were able to acquire a whole host of variants – each name as inspired as the next – including the likes of the Flash Arrow (SCL100), Jelly Stag (SCK104), White Horse (SCW100), Neo Wave (SCJ100), Skate Bike (SCB105), Grand Prix (SCJ101), Black Friday (SCB100), Signal Flag (SCN101) and Skychart (GN705). Demand exceeded supply from the moment the models were released, fuelling market speculation, and many collectors who queued outside Swatch stores were disappointed to find signs saying 'no Chronos available'. Little wonder, since with the many artistic collaborations and attractive pricing, the chronographs had mass appeal, allowing the brand to celebrate production of its 100 millionth Swatch in 1992, less than 10 years after the first had been unveiled.

CONTEMPORARY REINTERPRETATION

Once production had ceased, a number of collectors set out to track down these models, with some even preferring to keep them intact in their packaging – sacred relics or treasures to be preserved, like cigarette cards collected in a binder or ancient artefacts in a museum. Swatch eventually released a new collection, dubbed Neon, in 2023, choosing watches made from bioceramic materials rather than plastic for ecological reasons. 'Bigger. More dynamic. Cooler', as the advertising campaign accompanying the launch put it. The range comprised four models: two watches with three hands inspired by the classic Technosphere (GK101) and Skychart (GN705), and two others that were reminiscent of the White Horse and the Grand Prix, although their modules, christened 'Big Bold' and housed in imposing 47-mm cases, differed from those of the original models.

THE CHRONO CATALOGUE

The 1990s Chrono Swatch series was particularly rich and colourful, with each model given a particular name, including:

- FLASH ARROW
- JELLY STAG
- WHITE HORSE
- NEO WAVE
- SKATE BIKE
- GRAND PRIX
- BLACK FRIDAY
- SIGNAL FLAG

swatch
SWISS
60 Base 1000
HOURS
MINUTES
© SWATCH AG 1990

FLIK FLAK

SWATCH - 1987

In 1987, the Swatch Group launched Flik Flak, a new brand to run in parallel with its Swatch watches. Now known all over the world, from the outset the company has specialized in plastic quartz watches designed to teach children to how tell the time.

SEE OPPOSITE	2018 MODEL
MANUFACTURER	FLIK FLAK
MODEL	STAR WARS DARTH VADER FFLP005
CALIBRE	ETA
MOVEMENT	QUARTZ
PRODUCTION	PROTOTYPE
MATERIAL	ABS PLASTIC
STRAP	PLASTIC

CHILD-PROOF WATCHES

- Machine-washable at 40°C (104°F): just put it in a sock and start the wash cycle.
- No hazardous chemicals: each component was checked to ensure that it was durable and presented no risk to children.
- Shock-resistant: the Swiss-made watch movement was safely housed in a solid plastic case and hidden away behind a protective plastic dial.
- Waterproof to 30m (98ft): children could swim and wash wearing their watches.
- Made in Switzerland: every component, including the movement, was manufactured entirely in Switzerland.

DESIGNED WITH THE HELP OF TEACHERS

Flik Flak watches were launched in Biel in 1987, the city in which the already famous Swatch manufacturing group had its roots. They were manufactured in ETA's workshops, created using the experience and expertise of Swatch designers combined with input from teachers to appeal to a new target audience – children. Flik Flak relied on two key elements that were different yet closely connected: colourful designs combined with a playful educational approach that would help young people to tell the time. As a result, they soon became the most popular and the most well-known watches for children.

The range was divided into two categories: Story Time models for toddlers and Power Time for older children. Story Time had two hands representing Flik (Mr Minutes) and Flak (Ms Hours). Flik counted the minutes and moved every 60 seconds, while it was Flak's job to remind her brother that there were 60 minutes in an hour; she would wait until he had taken 60 steps before moving in her turn. Power Time watches had three standard hands and the dials clearly displaying all twelve numerals.

SWISS MANUFACTURING

Flik Flaks were high-end Swiss watches designed to take everything their small owners could throw at them. Before the launch, they spent a month in a specialized quality control laboratory where they were subjected to a battery of chemical and mechanical tests. When they were finally ready to be sold, their quality far exceeded statutory requirements and they bore a mark showing compliance with the US Consumer Product Safety Improvement Act (CPSIA).

INNOVATIVE COLLABORATIONS

The Flik Flak series was stylishly and cleverly extended with a stunning range of watches dedicated to the world of childhood, with princes rubbing shoulder with princesses, pirates, superheroes and explorers in a universe all their own. This abundance of choice gave rise to one particular nugget – the Star Wars Darth Vader watch, in which the dreaded Death Star turns into an educational dial, a lesson in watchmaking and marketing for young people drawn to the dark side of the Force.

STAR WARS
flik flak

MOONSWATCH

SWATCH - 2022

The historic alliance of Swatch and Omega, two eminent members of the Swatch Group, took the world of watchmaking by storm in 2022 with an innovative new venture – the MoonSwatch – making it possible for thousands of fans to access high-end watchmaking at an affordable price.

SEE OPPOSITE	2022 MODEL
MANUFACTURER	SWATCH X OMEGA
MODEL	MOONSWATCH MISSION TO MARS
CALIBRE	ETA
MOVEMENT	QUARTZ
PRODUCTION	SOLD COMMERCIALLY
MATERIAL	BIOCERAMIC
STRAP	N/A

THE MOONSWATCH CATALOGUE

With the exception of some limited editions, the MoonSwatch range comprised 11 variants, each named for a space mission:

- **YELLOW** | MISSION TO THE SUN
- **DARK GREY** | MISSION TO MERCURY
- **PINK** | MISSION TO VENUS
- **BLUE-GREEN** | MISSION TO EARTH
- **STEEL GREY** | MISSION TO THE MOON
- **RED** | MISSION TO MARS
- **BRONZE** | MISSION TO JUPITER
- **BEIGE** | MISSION TO SATURN
- **SKY BLUE** | MISSION TO URANUS
- **DARK BLUE** | MISSION TO NEPTUNE
- **BURGUNDY** | MISSION TO PLUTO

A SENSATIONAL LAUNCH

On 26 March 2022, the union between the highly popular Swatch brand and the iconic Omega company resulted in the MoonSwatch, an exceptional watch that was only available for sale at selected stores and which became an immediate sensation on social networks. Discussion groups were swamped with chat about the watch and it featured in every watchmaking blog. This marketing coup resulted in stock bottlenecks and endless queues of customers (who were initially allowed to buy only two watches – a limit that was then reduced to just one).

JUST 11 MODELS AND 11 MISSIONS

When the range was unveiled, it featured 11 chronograph wristwatches, all signed Swatch, each named after a space mission and styled in a different colour. The Sun model shone out in a dazzling gold, as if caressed by solar rays; Mercury was a deep grey; Venus powder pink; the Earth mixed shades of blue and green; the grey and jet-black Moon disappeared into darkness; Mars was a mixture of red and white, with sub-register hands borrowed from the Speedmaster Alaska model; Jupiter was a glittering bronze with an orange second hand; Saturn was beige, but sported its famous rings at 6 o'clock; Uranus was pale blue; Neptune a darker shade; and Pluto, the last in the series, was picked out in shades of grey and burgundy. These quartz Speedmasters remained true to the watchmaking inspiration of the original models, with a diameter of 42mm and the same Super-LumiNova luminescence on their indices and hands as their predecessors. Other special editions had individualized second hands and colour accents, or unique luminescent features.

BOOSTING SPEEDMASTER SALES

The enthusiasm with which the specialist discussion boards welcomed the watch on its release was a sign of the unmistakable triumph of this collaboration. It had succeeded in giving both brands a high profile while also preserving their individuality. And with good reason – the MoonSwatch appealed to novice watch fans and the most discerning connoisseurs alike. It was even the choice of well-known auctioneer Aurel Bacs when he was asked to name his favourite watch under 500 Euros. Swatch Group CEO Nicolas Hayek has stated that this collaboration boosted sales of the Omega Speedmaster by nearly 50 per cent.

TACHYMÈTRE
OMEGA
swatch
Speedmaster
MOONSWATCH
SWISS MADE

F.P.JOURNE
Invenit et Fecit

ADVANCED QUARTZ

CHAPTER 6

QUARTZ IN ALL ITS GUISES

FACT SHEET N°7

Under pressure from quartz, the boundaries of the possible were constantly being pushed back, clearing the way for technological and ecological progress, new and sophisticated watchmaking complications, luxury finishes and previously undreamt of feats of electronics.

TV & RADIO CONTROL

Seiko made headlines in 1982 with the T001, the first watch to feature a television (see page 214) with a 32-mm screen that brilliantly combined two technologies – LCD display and cutting-edge analogue TV signal reception. Although analogue transmission has now ceased, the watch is still popular among the most nostalgic collectors. In a similar way, the Junghans Mega set the bar with its advanced reception of radio waves (see page 216) and, by extension, the bar for atomic time as well.

BATTERY SAVING

The irresistible rise of quartz watches forced brands to address the issue of the need to replace batteries, which has harmful consequences for the environment. Manufacturers vied to come up with creative solutions, starting with Bulova which, in 1982, launched the Thermatron (see page 218), which used body heat to recharge the battery for its quartz movement. In 1988, Seiko introduced AGS Kinetic technology (see page 136), which transformed the motion of the wearer's wrist into energy that was stored in a durable battery. This invention followed the development (also by Seiko) of the calibre 8T23, the only quartz movement to be wound manually (see page 220), thus dispensing with the need to replace the battery altogether. An automatic quartz watch finally put in an appearance in the form of Jean d'Eve's Samara, which had a power generator system that used a rotor and was produced in very small quantities before being swept into oblivion by Seiko's AGS technology.

COMPASS AND WORLD TIME

Although quartz watches are often thought of as more downmarket devices, there are some that make use of prestigious materials and combine utilitarian modules with sophisticated complications. This was notably the case with the Seiko Field Master, launched in 1984, the three versions of which housed compass, odometer and/or LCD modules (see page 222). IWC and Porsche Design's World Time models and Louis Vuitton's Monterey stood out for their use of titanium, in the former, and gold or ceramics, in the latter (see pages 224 and 226).

HIGH-END WATCHMAKING

The Shellman brand has been bucking convention since 1996 by providing top-end complications at affordable prices (see page 228). As one of several brands that helped to bring the taboo against quartz to an end, the technology was now being built into prestigious electric watches. The luxurious Grand Seiko range made use of Spring Drive technology that worked without a battery thanks to its regulated mainspring. Another striking example was the calibre 1210 in the Elegante from master watchmaker François Paul Journe. Although it had batteries, its highly decorated movement featured a sleep system with a motion detector that, as if by magic, allowed the hands to realign to the correct time when the watch was returned to the wrist.

'TACT' WATCHES AND CONNECTED WATCHES

Now we come to the Apple Watch, seen as an essential accessory today and one of the world's most popular watches. Even though it is not a traditional quartz watch, its accuracy is based on a temperature-compensated quartz oscillator. As the result of a technological evolution stretching back more than 70 years, it embodies the quintessence of electronic miniaturization (see page 232). In a completely different, and almost poetic vein, quartz is now being used to revive old display methods, as in the famous Nixie and 'tact' watches (see pages 230 and 231).

BATTERY-SAVING

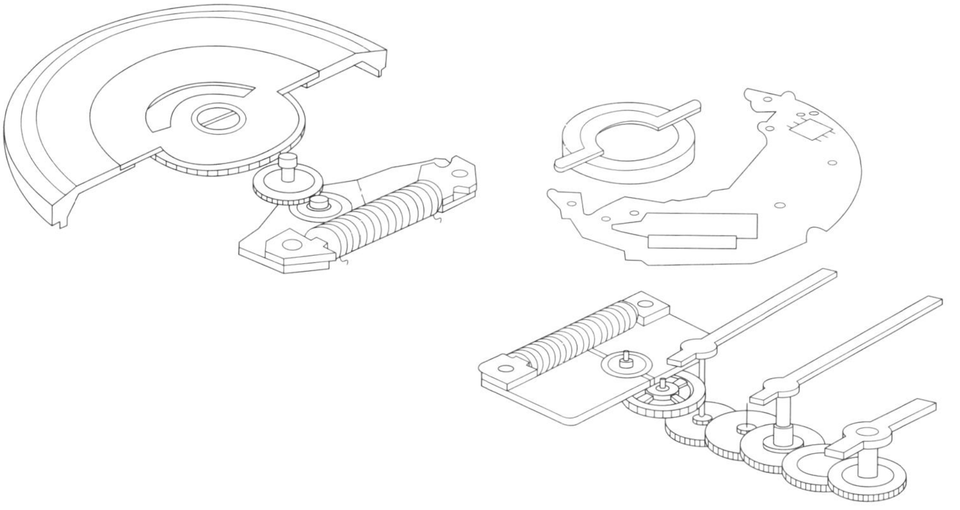

SEIKO AGS

The Automatic Generating System (AGS), the predecessor of Kinetic technology, made use of ingenious engineering to convert the natural movements of the wearer into electricity to power the watch. The energy was stored in a rechargeable battery, eliminating the need for traditional button batteries that have to be replaced.

QUARTZ 2.0

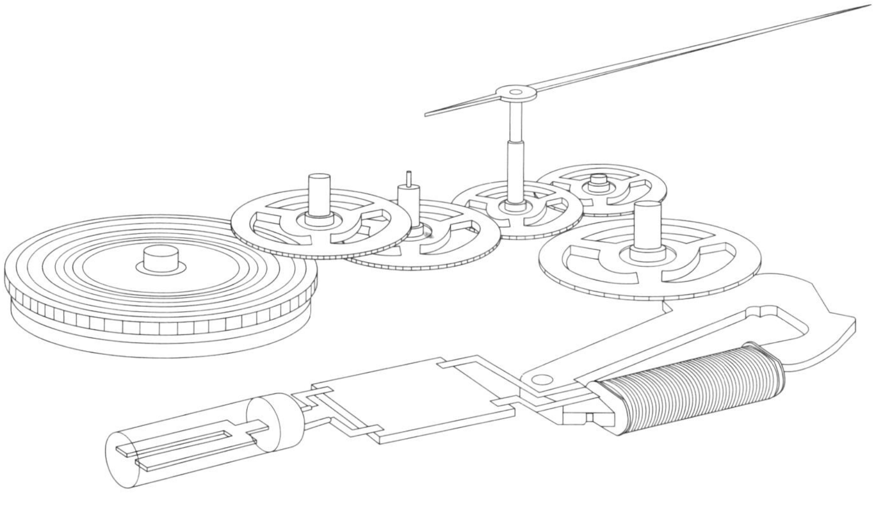

SEIKO SPRING DRIVE

Can quartz really compete with mechanical watchmaking? It can indeed, both technically and aesthetically. Spring Drive technology is notable for its use of a spring-driven motor to power the wheel train and a rotor to generate the energy required by the quartz crystal oscillator. From an aesthetic perspective, master watchmaker F P Journe also made use of quartz to create mechanisms with dazzling finishes.

TV WATCH

SEIKO - 1982

When the Seiko TV wristwatch was released in 1982, it was the first to be able to receive a television signal. Although now entirely obsolete in a world flooded with smartphones, it is a true relic of its time and testament to the boldness of the watchmaking industry, even though its functions are long outdated.

SEE OPPOSITE	1983 MODEL
MANUFACTURER	SEIKO
MODEL	TV T001-5019
CALIBRE	T001
MOVEMENT	QUARTZ
PRODUCTION	SOLD COMMERCIALLY
MATERIAL	STEEL
STRAP	INTEGRATED

THE WORLD'S SMALLEST TELEVISION

Throughout the 1970s and 1980s, the wristwatch was one of the main outlets for innovation aimed at the general public, who took a lively interest in watches thanks to manufacturers' ability to produce reliable and affordable quartz movements on a large scale. The visionary Japanese engineers at Seiko, past masters of miniaturization, organized a show-stopping new release every single year and, in 1982 (three years after Sony had sparked the Walkman revolution), Japanese watchmakers offered the world the unique experience of watching television on your wrist. The appropriately named Seiko TV was initially reserved for the Japanese market, but went on to conquer the United States in 1983 as the reference T001-5019, priced at $495. Its popularity skyrocketed when it appeared on the wrist of Roger Moore as James Bond in *Octopussy* that same year, although it should be noted that its true functions were slightly amended for the film. It was recognized as the world's smallest television by Guinness World Records a few months later.

AN INDEPENDENT RECEIVER

With its two separate LCD screens, the Seiko TV was particularly ahead of it time. The first display was discreetly located at the top of the watch, showing the time and date with remarkable accuracy, along with its alarm and chronometer functions. The second, slightly more impressive 32-mm screen, was dedicated to video output. However, the watch did not contain a device capable of receiving a television signal. This required a separate accessory, about the size of a Walkman, that could pick up analogue VHF and UHF frequencies and stereo FM. The receiver was supplied with the watch in a leather pouch, along with a connecting cable and a pair of headphones. The intention was for the wearer to slip it into a jacket pocket or a bag, much as they would have been used to doing with the portable cassette tape players of the time. The instruction manual even presented the receiver as a stylish accessory and suggested hiding the headphone wires down one sleeve. Despite its limited contrast, LCD technology had been chosen for its economical use of battery power. The receiver unit was powered by two AA batteries that enabled more than five hours of uninterrupted viewing.

A NOSTALGIC RELIC OF THE PAST

The Seiko T001 is a perfect illustration of the epic quest of watchmakers through the ages, as they come up with ever more ingenious and innovative ideas to appeal to the public. Of course, it is the inevitable fate of all innovation that television reception on this type of watch is entirely obsolete these days – the analogue signals it could receive have disappeared into oblivion and taken the Seiko TV with them. The watch now sits in silence, not even responding when its receiver is switched on, as it can no longer receive any signal. What was once a symbol of modernity is now a relic of a time gone by, a sacred artefact of another age before the smartphone even existed in the human imagination. As inoperable as it now may be, however, the watch is highly sought-after among collectors who are prepared to spend a small fortune on its beautiful LCD screens.

OFF ON OFF ON VIDEO
MONO STEREO FM
FM 76 80 84 88 91 MHz
VHF L 1 2 3 CH
H 4 6 8 9 10 11 12
UHF 13 20 30 40 50 62
SEIKO
FM
TV
VHF
UHF
SEIKO LVD
5:17 34
STOP. W ALARM TIME SET
LVD MODE SELECT START · STOP
SET SPLIT · RESET
SEIKO
LVD TV & FM STE

MEGA RADIO CONTROL

JUNGHANS – 1991

Junghans revolutionized the reception of atomic time when it launched the first radio-controlled desk alarm clock in 1985. This technology had been sufficiently scaled down by 1990 to make a digital wristwatch possible, followed by a digital/analogue watch in 1991.

SEE OPPOSITE	1994 MODEL
MANUFACTURER	JUNGHANS
MODEL	MEGA II
CALIBRE	W605
MOVEMENT	QUARTZ
PRODUCTION	SOLD COMMERCIALLY
MATERIAL	STEEL + GOLD-PLATED
STRAP	LEATHER

JUNGHANS
MEGA 1

The pioneering Mega 1 model with its digital screen appeared in 1990, marking the advent of a wristwatch capable of receiving atomic time via its revolutionary radio-controlled technology.

ATOMIC TIME

Radio-controlled clocks synchronize their time with a single atomic clock, one of several that are installed around the world. Atomic clocks are capable of automatically adjusting their time and date and are set up as part of satellite GPS systems or in radio masts to guarantee broadcasting at precise and uniform times. Six masts are in operation on Earth, tirelessly transmitting the exact time: two in Europe (in Mainflingen in Germany and Anthorn in the UK), two in Japan (in Fukushima and Fukuoka), one in the United States (in the state of Colorado), which covers all of Canada and America to the tip of Tierra del Fuego, and one in China (in Shangqiu).

JUNGHANS MEGA

In 1985, the Junghans brand took the world by surprise by introducing this technology into everyday life when it released the first radio-controlled desk alarm clock. Five years later, its engineers managed to miniaturize the technology to the extent that it would fit into the Mega I, a digital wristwatch. A year after that, Junghans brought out the Mega II, the world's first radio-controlled watch, elegantly combining traditional hands with an LCD display. On its release, its partially gold-plated stainless steel case and immaculate white dial caused a sensation, with many wondering how this technology could be fitted into such a watch. The trick was an aerial hidden in the strap that allowed the watch to pick up time signals in an area of a radius of 1,500km (932 miles) around the DCF77 transmitter in Mainflingen. That was not all, however. The watch also featured functions such as a time zone setting, a perpetual calendar (day of the week, date, month), an internal time memory, a signal strength indicator, a call button for the transmitter and a digital seconds display.

UNRIVALLED ACCURACY

The delay between encoding the atomic time and its radio transmission inevitably entailed slight inaccuracy on the receiving side, but the lag could be kept to a minimum by means of regular synchronization with the signal, and the watch's accuracy remained excellent. The Junghans Mega synchronized with the transmitter to which it was linked between 2 and 3 o'clock every day, and if reception was poor, the watch would repeat its attempts to synchronize every hour until 6 o'clock. This was so effective that radio-controlled Junghans Mega wristwatches boasted an accuracy of +/- one second in a million years.

JUNGHANS MEGA
30. 9. 15
mo tu we th fr sa su
GERMANY

THERMATRON

BULOVA – 1982

The Thermatron, released in 1982, was a watch that made use of the wearer's body heat to recharge its battery and power its quartz movement. Despite this innovative design, which was way ahead of its time from an environmental perspective, problems of reliability rapidly turned it into a commercial flop.

SEE OPPOSITE	1982 MODEL
MANUFACTURER	BULOVA
MODEL	THERMATRON
CALIBRE	2467.10
MOVEMENT	QUARTZ
PRODUCTION	SOLD COMMERCIALLY
MATERIAL	STEEL + PVD
STRAP	INTEGRATED

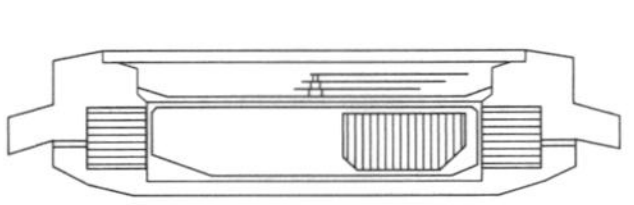

BULOVA
THERMATHRON

The watch made use of the disparity in temperature of the caseback, which was in contact with the warmth of the skin, and the watch-face, exposed to the air in the surrounding atmosphere, to generate a current that powered the quartz movement.

AN ECOLOGICAL WATCH

Just when Swiss manufacturers were facing up to the massive boom in quartz watches from Asia, Bulova unveiled the Thermatron, its flagship project, at the 1980 Basel trade fair. This revolutionary watch, the result of considerable investment in terms of both expertise and Swiss francs, drew energy from the natural warmth of the wrist, which it used to charge the battery of its quartz movement. This technological and ecological advance was intended to free quartz watches from the annoying constraint of constantly having to have their batteries replaced. The Thermatron was developed in Biel, Switzerland, and two calibres in six different designs were created. When the watch was officially launched in 1982, it was sold in a wide variety of styles, with an angular, square case in a range of finishes from metal to black PVD.

THE SEEBECK EFFECT

The technology used in the Thermatron, which had been developed in collaboration with the CEH (see page 41), was based on a thermoelectric generator that powered its quartz movement via a rechargeable back-up battery. This design made use of the Seebeck effect (named after Thomas Seebeck, who discovered it in 1821): the tendency of two metals at different temperatures to generate electric current when placed in contact with one another. Here, the caseback was warmed by the wrist, and the face of the watch cooled by the ambient air temperature. The energy generated was directly proportional to the temperature difference between these two points. The greater the disparity, the greater the output. Unsurprisingly, the watch stopped producing energy altogether when the temperature of the wearer's body and the air were too close.

A COMMERCIAL DISASTER

After years of research and considerable financial difficulties, the rush release of the Thermatron in 1982 led to a resounding flop. It was highly unreliable and, even though the battery could be recharged, it still had to be replaced every ten years. In a further blow, its asking price of $2,000 was prohibitive for a brand like Bulova and kept potential purchasers at bay. As a last nail in the coffin, an increasing number of watches were being returned for repair. Bulova failed to make a return on its investment and was well on the way to bankruptcy. With only 500 units sold, the company shuttered its business activities in Europe and refocused its efforts on North America. The Thermatron inventory was eventually sold on to STW, a company that reinvented the watch by replacing the battery with a capacitor that could be topped up with a small battery-powered wand or recharged by removing it from the case entirely. This valiant attempt to revive the Thermatron's fortunes was still unable to prevent the arrival of new technologies from burying it completely. Despite the many faults that consigned it to oblivion, it nonetheless demonstrates manufacturers' constant efforts to compete with Asian quartz watches.

BULOVA
SWISS 7456 T

8T23

SEIKO – 1986

In 1986, as part of a cutting-edge ecological undertaking, Seiko carved a niche for itself by designing a manual-wind quartz movement that reduced energy consumption and extended battery life.

SEE OPPOSITE	1986 MODEL
MANUFACTURER	SEIKO
MODEL	8T23-8020
CALIBRE	8T23
MOVEMENT	QUARTZ MANUEL
PRODUCTION	SOLD COMMERCIALLY
MATERIAL	METAL COAT + STEEL
STRAP	LEATHER

SEIKO
LE PHARE-JEAN D'EVE SAMARA

This quartz watch featured an energy-generation system. The result of three years of research, it featured a flywheel coupled to a power generator, freeing it from any dependence on an external energy source such as a battery.

MANUAL QUARTZ

The massive boom in quartz watches during the tumultuous years of the 1980s led to the unbridled use of batteries, with devastating ecological repercussions. To combat this excessive energy consumption, the eternally innovative Seiko developed the calibre 8T23, the world's first manual-wind quartz watch movement. A simple action from the wearer could recharge it – they just needed to wind the crown to make a small generator activate a capacitor. The quartz movement could therefore continue to function without depending on traditional batteries. The 8T23 watches powered by this innovative system, which was a real technical and ecological advance, were released in 1986.

AN OUTSIZE CROWN

To simplify winding, Seiko designed an outsize crown that was inspired by the first aviators' watches. The Japanese firm recommended three minutes of winding for a complete recharge, which would provide seventy-five hours of battery life. Once the battery was fully charged, a red LED (see page 143) located at 6 o'clock would light up to tell the wearer that no further winding was required. The watch also featured a low-battery indicator – it was time to recharge when the second hand advanced two seconds at a time. It should be noted that, unlike a traditional mechanical watch, the crown was able to generate energy when turned in either direction.

QUARTZ AUTO

The short-lived calibre 8T23 was sold commercially for no more than a year.

Customers did not find the ritual of three minutes' winding for a battery life of three days particularly appealing and, in any case, in 1988 a new technological era had dawned with the advent of the automatic quartz movement when Le Phare-Jean d'Eve unveiled the Samara, with its Kinetron system. The watch had no batteries, sourcing energy from the motion of the wearer's wrist. Each movement of the wrist was converted into an electrical impulse and stored in a capacitor, guaranteeing a battery life of ten days. This innovation was soon to be eclipsed in turn by Seiko's AGS (Automatic Generation System, renamed Kinetic, see page 136), which came out the same year. With its integrated generator, the AGS could also capture kinetic energy from motion of the wrist and store it in a rechargeable battery, but it also promised greater practicality and battery life than the Samara. It should be noted that the Kinetic system made it possible to recharge the power source (the generator, in this case) with a rotor, just like a traditional automatic movement, although the birth of Direct Drive technology in 2007 made it possible to wind a Kinetic movement manually.

SEIKO
THU 4

FIELD MASTER

SEIKO – 1984

One outcome of the creative frenzy that took hold of Seiko in the 1980s was the Field Master, a multifunction quartz model. This discreetly sized modular watch could do much more than just tell the time.

SEE OPPOSITE	1984 MODEL
MANUFACTURER	SEIKO
MODEL	FIELD MASTER
CALIBRE	2C21
MOVEMENT	QUARTZ
PRODUCTION	SOLD COMMERCIALLY
MATERIAL	STEEL + PVD
STRAP	POLYURETHANE

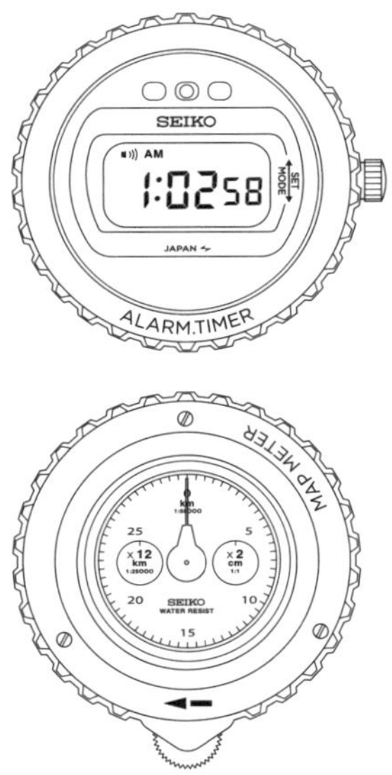

SEIKO
COMPLEMENTARY MODULES
OF THE FIELD MASTER

Shown here are the LCD time display module and the odometer module to measure distance.

THE BOLD FIELD MASTER

Seiko designed a multitude of quartz watches during the 1980s, juggling its ranges to adapt to the various needs of the market. It was during this intense period of innovation and bold experimentation that the Field Master first appeared. With its two compartments, both 28 x 28mm, the watches featured a quartz movement traditionally associated with ladies' watches, but its compact appearance was deceptive as it was certainly not short of functionality. The Field Master essentially combined two stainless steel cases: the first was fixed, with an analogue display of the time, while the second could be easily swapped out using the crown at 4 o'clock. Numerous options were available to the wearer, depending on their preferences and lifestyle.

A MODULAR TIMEPIECE

The Field Master first appeared on the market in 1984, in three versions that were as different as they were intriguing. The first featured a compass module or an odometer (which could be used to measure distances on maps). The second had compass, odometer and LCD modules, and the last, a rare version reserved for the Japanese market, the JDM (see page 112), comprised the watch and all three modules listed above. It was available in olive PVD and featured a gold bezel insert.

A GUERILLA WATCH

The Field Master was taken on all kinds of expeditions, from the icy wastes of the poles to the dizzying heights of the Himalayas, to prove its robustness and the life-saving prospects of its compass and odometer modules. Despite its performance, however, its small size and discreet accessories made it look more like a toy than a piece of professional equipment, which discouraged potential purchasers. However, at the end of the 1980s, an unusual level of demand caused sales of the watch to surge. The American administration of the time happened to be financing the Contras, a pro-US counter-revolutionary group fighting the Communist revolution in Nicaragua. The guerrillas were sent a wide range of equipment, including surplus Field Masters straight from Japan. This was enough to earn them the name 'Seiko Contra' among discerning collectors.

SEIKO
QUARTZ
SEIKO
N
NE
E
S
W
NW

TRAVEL WORLD TIME ALARM

IWC & PORSCHE DESIGN – 1993

IWC and Porsche Design began a collaboration in the 1970s that was intended to stand up to the rising power of quartz by creating luxuriously appointed, minimalist mechanical watches. The two brands eventually changed their tune and succumbed to the new technology in the 1990s.

SEE OPPOSITE	1995 MODEL
MANUFACTURER	IWC X PORSCHE DESIGN
MODEL	TRAVEL WORLD TIME ALARM
CALIBRE	2C21
MOVEMENT	QUARTZ
PRODUCTION	SOLD COMMERCIALLY
MATERIAL	TITANIUM
STRAP	LEATHER

FERDINAND ALEXANDER PORSCHE

Ferdinand Alexander Porsche (nicknamed Butzi) was the grandson of Ferdinand Porsche, founder of the famous automobile brand, but this heir to the company was also a renowned car designer in his own right. Having taken over the firm's design studio in 1962, he took barely a year to develop the legendary Porsche 911. Ten years later, he founded Porsche Design as a studio and a brand, with the exceptional finishes of its products rapidly establishing the company's reputation. For him, the spirit of Porsche Design could be summed up in a single sentence: 'If you analyse the function of an object, its form often becomes obvious.' Forever seeking new challenges, he designed his first watch in 1974 in collaboration with the Orfina brand owned by his friend Umberto Maglioli. And it was not just any old watch – they created the first steel chronograph to be entirely coated with black PVD.

IWC AND TITANIUM

Encouraged by this triumph, Porsche aspired to even bolder moves, although he was obliged to part ways with Orfina because of its limited resources. To bring his ideas to life, he teamed up with IWC, a brand that had been hit hard by the quartz crisis and needed to strike a major blow in return. The IWC board found Porsche's designs to be both distinctive and likely to help the firm. The Kompass Uhr, IWC's first Porsche Design watch, was a triumph of ingenuity that fully justified this ambitious alliance. The watch, which was launched in 1978, concealed a magnetic compass beneath its dial, while the materials chosen by the always cutting-edge Porsche Design studio included anodized black aluminium, which is lighter and more robust than PVD-treated steel. Porsche Design revolutionized the watchmaking world once again at the end of 1980 with the Porsche Design Titan. Although titanium is a super material and handling it remains a technical challenge, this first mass-produced titanium watch seemed to make light work of it. The IWC watchmakers and the Porsche Design studio had in fact drawn on aeronautical expertise for the design. By 1985, titanium case watches had begun to sell sufficiently well to prove lifelines for IWC and Porsche Design as they weathered the storm conjured up by the quartz crisis.

LATE USE OF QUARTZ

During this rather difficult period, mechanical watchmaking was stuck between its somewhat conservative relationship with tradition and an almost artisanal approach to production. However, the minimalist shapes, unique materials and high-end finishes of IWC's Porsche Design collection stood out radically enough to slow things down a little. The collection even made up 20 per cent of IWC's sales. The two brands eventually succumbed to the temptations of quartz at the turn of 1990s, and even the famous Titan chronograph would appear in a small-diameter quartz version. The Porsche Travel Worldtimer, which made an appearance in 1993, was a watch with a world time complication and an alarm, housed in an exquisite titanium case and powered by a quartz movement.

GMT
AZORES
PARIS
CAIRO
MOSCOW
DUBAI
KARACHI
DACCA
BANGKOK
HONGKONG
TOKYO
SYDNEY
NOUMEA
date line
SAMOA
HONOLULU
ANCHOR.
LOS ANG.
DENVER
CHICAGO
N.YORK
CARACAS
RIO DE JAN.
PORSCHE DESIGN
IWC
SWISS

MONTEREY I

LOUIS VUITTON – 1988

While Louis Vuitton owes its watchmaking reputation to La Fabrique du Temps, a facility in Switzerland established in 2002 to bring together the great watchmaking professions under one roof, its interest in the sector goes all the way back to 1988 and the release of the Monterey, a quartz watch signed by Gae Aulenti.

SEE OPPOSITE	1988 MODEL
MANUFACTURER	LOUIS VUITTON
MODEL	MONTEREY I
CALIBRE	QUARTZ IWC
MOVEMENT	QUARTZ
PRODUCTION	SOLD COMMERCIALLY
MATERIAL	WHITE GOLD
STRAP	LEATHER

DESIGN BY GAE AULENTI

The eminent Italian architect Gae Aulenti settled in Paris at the end of the 1980s, beginning one of the most notable chapters of her career with the transformation of the Gare d'Orsay railway station into a museum that has since become an iconic symbol of the French capital. Aulenti was a true virtuoso in the management of public spaces and had a similar reputation as a designer, with some of her creations considered among the most timeless of the 20th century. Examples include the Pipistrello lamp (1965), designed for Martinelli Luce, or the Tavolo con Ruote table on castors (1980) for Fontana Arte, where she was also the company's artistic director. Aulenti also turned her creative genius towards watchmaking, a sector that was totally new to her. She began a unique collaboration with Louis Vuitton to design a watch that would be fitting for the brand and its famous monogram.

LV & IWC

The name Louis Vuitton is highly evocative, instantly conjuring up visions of the world's most famous luxury goods, but few would associate the company with watchmaking. It nonetheless took the plunge into this new world in 1988 with the Monterey I, a world time-style watch (a complication developed by Louis Cottier in the 1930s), whose curvaceous silhouette, shunning sharp angles, summoned up an elegance reminiscent of the pocket watches of a bygone age. Despite its quartz movement, the Monterey I featured an alarm function, a date complication and the phases of the moon. The watch was designed for an up-market clientele and was housed in an 18-carat yellow gold case (although some extremely rare models appeared in white gold). And the story did not stop there. The collaboration between Louis Vuitton and Aulenti continued with the Monterey II. While still powered by a quartz movement with an alarm function, the watch had been simplified and now featured only a date display. It was the bold choice of ceramic as the material for the case that set this watch apart, however, and Louis Vuitton teamed up with IWC (which had proven its expertise in the use of the material) for the design. The watch became the secret favourite of discerning connoisseurs and is found on the wrists of leading collectors such as Jean Arnault, director of Louis Vuitton's watch department.

LA FABRIQUE DU TEMPS

Louis Vuitton made a rather more public entry into the world of watchmaking in 2002 when the company opened La Fabrique du Temps, a new factory that brought together the best artisan watchmakers in a stimulating environment combining tradition with cutting-edge technology. The Tambour, the first watch to emerge from these workshops, was a bold departure. It underwent an elegant metamorphosis 21 years later, joining the ranks of luxury sports watches with panache by using a skilful blend of exceptional finishes and an integrated strap. Might the Monterey, so dear to the heart of the brand's young director, be in line for a similar resurrection?

AZORES
PARIS
LONDON
CAIRO
MOSCOW
MAURITIUS
KARACHI
DACCA
BANGKOK
HONGKONG
TOKYO
SYDNEY
TAHITI
ANCHORAGE
LOS ANG.
DENVER
CHICAGO
NEWYORK
SANTIAGO
RIO DE JAN.
LOUIS VUITTON
PARIS
date line

MINUTE REPEATER

SHELLMAN – 1996

An expert in the sale of vintage collectible watches in Japan, since 1996 Shellman has also created a superb range of watches with grand complications that are a little out of the ordinary. Equipped with quartz movements, they benefit from impeccable finishing.

SEE OPPOSITE	1999 MODEL
MANUFACTURER	SHELLMAN
MODEL	SIDE SLIDE MINUTE REPEATER
CALIBRE	CITIZEN CALIBRE 6890
MOVEMENT	QUARTZ
PRODUCTION	SOLD COMMERCIALLY
MATERIAL	STEEL
STRAP	LEATHER

A SPECIALIST IN COLLECTIBLE WATCHES

The great luxury watchmaking companies all have a presence on Chuo-dori, one of the prestigious streets in the bustling Ginza district of Tokyo. You will find the likes of Audemars Piguet, Cartier and even the Nicolas G Hayek Center, the impressive headquarters of the Swatch Group there. Just around the corner from these watchmaking giants, however, is a more discreet address known to every true enthusiast – Shellman Times. Since 1971, this store has been an essential haunt for lovers of vintage watches from the 1930s to the 1970s. There's no ostentatious luxury here – the decor is sober, with marble floors and dark wood panelling – and the treasure it guards is a unique collection of vintage watches, with all the great brands represented: Patek Philippe, Rolex, Omega, Audemars Piguet, IWC, Jaeger-LeCoultre, Longines, Vacheron Constantin, Zenith and many more besides. The name Camille Fournet, a prestigious manufacturer of watch straps who teamed up with Shellman in 1992, completes the list. Four years later, Shellman unveiled a series of original watches featuring exceptional finishes and high-precision quartz movements.

QUARTZ WITH COMPLICATIONS

In the public imagination – and in the minds of many novice collectors – quartz watches are, by necessity, cheap and cheerful. While mechanical watches are the fruit of precise craftsmanship (quite unlike industrially produced quartz watches), and are often entirely beyond the reach of mere mortals. Those that feature impressive complications such as minute repeaters, second-splitting chronographs or perpetual calendars can cost exorbitant amounts, sometimes in excess of $100,000. Mechanical marvels they may be, but they are destined to remain the exclusive preserve of a privileged few. Shellman's skilled experts have therefore developed a series of models with grand complications and quartz movements to make these functions accessible to more people. The mechanical movement may have been replaced with an electric one, but the finishes are still immaculate, with steel or gold-plated cases and dials (some of which are *guilloché* decorated) to rival those made by greatest names in watchmaking. Each watch is assembled by hand, as demonstrated by the four months required to make 300 examples of the Grand Complication model. The Side Slide Minute Repeater model uses a quarter-second stepping motor for its accurate chronograph function and the sound of its minute repeater is as clear and pleasant as that of many mechanical watches.

PRIZE-WINNING CREATIONS

The Shellman Grand Complication was released in 1997, winning two prestigious Watch of the Year prizes awarded by Japan's leading specialist publications. This spectacular and prestigious achievement was topped the following year when the same watch, accompanied by a model with a *cloisonné* enamel dial, went on permanent display at the renowned International Museum of Horology at La Chaux-de-Fonds in Switzerland – total vindication for these quartz watches with complications.

SHELLMAN&CO.
Minute repeater

CATHODE CORNER
NIXIE WATCH

Nixie tubes, gas-filled electrical discharge devices that can be used to display numerals, were discovered by Haydu Brothers Laboratories in the 1950s. Their renaissance in the modern world has taken shape in various watches, such as the Cathode Corner.

EONE
BRADLEY WATCH

This quartz watch, designed by Eone as a tribute to two-time Paralympic gold medallist Bradley Snyder, is reminiscent of old 'tact' watches. Its two metallic ball bearings rotate elegantly via a magnetic system that makes it possible to tell the time by touch alone.

APPLE WATCH

APPLE – 2015

Is the Apple Watch even a watch? Although this question remains unanswered, it is undeniable that it is a technological and commercial – indeed, almost a social – achievement. As well as simplifying the lives of its users in many ways, it also offers timekeeping accuracy to the millisecond.

SEE OPPOSITE	2017 MODEL
MANUFACTURER	APPLE
MODEL	APPLE WATCH SERIES 3
CALIBRE	APPLE
MOVEMENT	TCXO
PRODUCTION	PROTOTYPE
MATERIAL	ALUMINIUM + CERAMIC
STRAP	N/A

A NON-EXHAUSTIVE TIMELINE OF APPLE WATCH FUNCTIONALITY

2015	SERIES 0
2016	SERIES 1: WATERPROOFING
2016	SERIES 2: WATERPROOFING + GPS
2017	SERIES 3: MOBILE PHONE CONNECTIVITY + IMPROVED BATTERY LIFE
2018	SERIES 4: ELECTROCARDIOGRAM (ECG)
2019	SERIES 5: PERMANENT DISPLAY + COMPASS
2020	SERIES 6: BLOOD OXYGEN SATURATION SENSOR
2021	SERIES 7: EXPANDED DISPLAY AREA + IMPROVED BATTERY LIFE ENABLING SLEEP TRACKING
2022	SERIES 8: TEMPERATURE SENSOR ENABLING OVULATION CYCLE TRACKING + CRASH DETECTION

FROM DESIGN TO REALITY

The notion of a smart watch (see page 172) had been in the ether at Apple for quite some time. Jonathan Ive, the brand's head designer, had been exploring this avenue under the leadership of Tim Cook as early as 2011, the year of Steve Jobs' death. As Jobs' successor, Cook needed to make his mark, the aim being not so much to create a watch but to design a device that could bring together the management of communications, notifications and functions for health and sports monitoring. The Apple Watch had been kept top secret for a long time before it was officially announced on 9 September 2014. Its launch in April 2015 was based on an innovative strategy that saw it distributed to upmarket outlets such as Isetan in Tokyo and Colette in Paris, in addition to Apple Stores and some traditional mobile phone stores. The watch was presented in a very careful, almost ritualized manner, as if in a high-end jeweller's, and its success was staggering. Within 3 months, 4 million units had been sold, immediately propelling the Apple Watch to the top of the still nascent connected watch market.

PRECISE TIMEKEEPING

As connected as the Apple Watch may be, it is still first and foremost a precise timekeeper – but how does it manage this? According to the Cupertino-based company, the watch is carefully adjusted to a deviation no greater than 50 milliseconds from world time thanks to a network of 15 NTP (Network Time Protocol) servers strategically distributed around the globe. These are housed in buildings fitted with GPS antennae that pick up satellite signals sent from the United States Naval Observatory in Washington. The Observatory houses an ultra-precise atomic clock that uses electron transition frequency to measure time. Apple servers then transmit the time to iPhones around the world, which in turn ensure synchronization of the time with Apple Watches via Bluetooth. In addition, every Apple Watch is equipped with a temperature-compensated quartz crystal oscillator known as a TCXO (where X stands for crystal) that keeps it at the right temperature to guarantee accuracy.

HEALTH TECHNOLOGY

The Apple Watch was partly the vision of Steve Jobs, who had been fascinated by the design and influence of the G-Shock (see page 176). During his years battling cancer, the Apple founder had been engaged on a quest for technological solutions to address the shortcomings of the American healthcare system, which led to the idea of a device dedicated to monitoring health. As each version was unveiled, components and functions were added to bolster this aspect and, from Series 4, the monitoring of well-being became a key element, thanks in particular to the electrocardiogram (ECG). This was followed by a blood oxygen saturation sensor, sleep monitoring and even blood pressure measurement. Series 8 introduced a temperature sensor with useful applications for women's health, and a car crash detector. In less than ten years, the Apple Watch had revolutionized not only smartwatch design but also the way we interact with technology.

WATCH • 42MM CASE • 316L STAINLESS STEEL • SAPPHIRE CRYSTAL • CERAMIC BACK • SERIAL FH7R303UH3V4

MAKES & MODELS

FACT SHEETS

WHO'S WHO

ARBIB, RICHARD: industrial designer who helped create the Hamilton Ventura model.

ARNAULT, JEAN: heir to the Arnault luxury goods dynasty and head of Louis Vuitton's watchmaking department.

AULENTI, GAE: Italian architectural theorist who helped design the Monterey model for Louis Vuitton.

BAUER, GÉRARD: Swiss political figure and sometime president of the Fédération Horlogère.

BENNETT, WILLIAM O: American engineer working at Bulova who helped to put the finishing touches to the calibre 214 tuning-fork movement.

BESSON, RENÉ: watchmaking engineer in charge of development at Ébauches SA.

BEYNER, ANDRÉ: watchmaking engineer who became technical director and then deputy CEO of Ébauches SA.

BIEMILLER, PHILIP E: head physicist at Hamilton who helped to develop the calibre H500.

BLUM, EUGÈNE: co-founder of the Ebel brand.

BLUM, PIERRE-ALAIN: a family member of the founders of Ebel and a former boss at the brand whose reputation he established in the 1980s.

BRAUN, MAX: German engineer, inventor and entrepreneur who founded the multinational Braun brand.

COOK, TIM: CEO of Apple.

DARGIER DE SAINT-VAULRY, PAUL: LIP engineer who helped to develop the calibre R27.

FORRER, MAX: senior manager at the Centre Électronique Horloger (CEH) who supported the Beta project.

FREI, ARMIN: scientist, inventor and member of the CEH.

FROIDEVAUX, RAYMOND: designer of the Omega Chrono-Quartz, the world's first digital and analogue chronograph, featuring the Albatross calibre developed by Norbert Henry.

GIUGIARO, GIORGETTO: one of the most prolific Italian car designers in history who was involved in designing iconic watches for the Seiko brand.

GOLAY, BERNARD: watchmaker who headed up the company of the same name and contributed to the boom in electric watches.

GRINBERG, GERRY: watchmaker of Cuban origin and CEO of the North American Watch Company who breathed life into the idea of the Delirum, the forerunner of the Swatch.

HARLAN, TIAN: German artist who came up with the concept of the Chromachron.

HATTORI, KINTARO: founder of the company that became Seiko.

HATTORI, SHOJI: descendant of the founder of Seiko, the company of which he was CEO when the Astron was released.

HAYEK, NICOLAS: Swiss entrepreneur and founder of the Swatch Group.

HEILMEIER, GEORGE HARRY: American engineer and businessman, and one of the inventors of LCD using the dynamic diffusion method that preceded the field effect.

HERMANN, JEAN: engineer at the CEH responsible for the prototype CEH 1020.

HETZEL, MAX: Swiss engineer and inventor of tuning-fork electric watches.

IVE, JONATHAN: Chief design officer at Apple, involved in designing the Apple Watch.

JOBS, STEVE: American inventor, co-founder of Apple.

KASHIO (FAMILY): founding family of Casio.

KIKUO, IBE: Casio engineer and inventor of the G-Shock.

LAVIOLETTE, JEAN-GEORGES: technical director at LIP who helped to develop the calibre R27.

LEVY, ALICE: co-founder of the Ebel brand.

LIP, FRED: visionary head of the LIP company.

LOCHINGER, ROLF: scientist and inventor, member of the CEH.

LUBS, DIETRICH: German designer who worked in close collaboration with Dieter Rams at Braun.

LUCKEY, GEORGE: head of R&D at Hamilton who supervised the design of the calibre H500.

MOCK, ELMAR: engineer at ETA who designed the first sketches for the Swatch with Jacques Müller.

MOORE, GORDON: co-founder of Intel, the first global manufacturer of microprocessors.

MÜLLER, BERNARD: designer directly involved in the final design of the Swatch with Marlyse Schmid.

MÜLLER, JACQUES: engineer at ETA who designed the first sketches for the Swatch with Elmar Mock.

NIKLÈS, FRANÇOIS: engineer at the CEH responsible for the prototype CEH 1020.

OGUEY, HENRI: watchmaking engineer at the CEH.

PERRIN, ALAIN DOMINIQUE: French businessman and former president of Cartier who popularized the Tank by incorporating a quartz movement.

POMMIER, JEAN: engineer at LIP who helped to develop the calibre R27.

PORSCHE, FERDINAND ALEXANDER: German designer and son of the founder of Porsche, head of the Porsche Design studio.

RAMS, DIETER: German contemporary industrial designer closely associated with products created at Braun.

REESE, JAMES H: technician at Hamilton who helped to develop the calibre H500.

SASAKI, KAZUNARI: designer of the Seiko Astron.

SCHMID, MARLYSE: designer directly involved in the final design of the Swatch with Bernard Müller.

SCHMID, RODOLPHE: Swiss watchmaker residing in Japan who was instrumental in transforming the Shokosha Watch Research Institute into Citizen.

SCHNEIDER, HENRI: watchmaking engineer at the CEH.

TALLON, ROGER: French industrial designer who worked with LIP to create the Mach 2000 model and its LED variants.

TANAKA, TARO: industrial designer employed at Seiko who created the grammar of design and set out the brand's aesthetic precepts.

THOMKE, ERNST: Swiss business personality and board member at Ébauches SA, ETA and then ASUAG-SIHH.

VAN HORN, JOHN: head of research at Hamilton who supervised project X for the calibre H500.

VERMOT, CHARLES: Zenith employee who saved the blueprints for the El Primero calibre when the brand was acquired by an American consortium that ceased production of mechanical watches.

VUFFRAY, GEORGES: electronics engineer who helped to perfect quartz Girard-Perregaux watches by setting their frequency at 32kHz.

WALDBURGER, HEINZ: director of project Alpha at the CEH.

WELLINGER, ROGER: Swiss-American scientist and first head of the CEH.

ZAUGG, HANS: designer instrumental in creating some of the first Swatch prototypes.

WHAT'S WHAT

ALTERNATION: the displacement of a balance wheel between two extreme positions. In quartz watches, this refers to the vibrations of the quartz crystal.

AMPLITUDE: the angle described by the balance wheel of a watch, from its position of rest to one of its extreme positions. In quartz watches, this refers to the extent of the oscillations of the quartz crystal.

ANALOGUE: a type of watch that shows the time by means of dials with moving hands, generally one for hours, one for minutes and sometimes one for seconds.

ATOMIC CLOCK: a timekeeping device of extreme precision based on the transition energy of atoms (usually caesium), providing exceptional temporal stability.

BALANCE WHEEL: a moving, circular component that oscillates about its axis of rotation and acts as a regulator in a mechanical movement. In an electric movement, it acts as both a motor and a regulator for the mechanism.

BEZEL: a ring fitted to the top of the case that may be used to measure additional data such as the duration of an event.

BRIDGE: a component attached to the plate on which one or more of the rotating pivots for the movement's moving parts may be fixed.

CALIBRE: a term designating the type of movement in a watch.

CAPACITOR: a component that stores and releases electric power, helping to even out fluctuations in voltage and ensuring the circuit works properly.

CASE: the main protective layer of a watch, shielding the mechanism from shocks, humidity and dust.

CASE MIDDLE: one of the three main parts of the enclosure protecting a watch. It holds the movement and is located between the bezel and the caseback of the watch.

CHRONOGRAPH: an accurate watch with sub-registers that allow the user to measure and display intervals of time by pressing its push-buttons.

CHRONOMETER: a highly accurate watch certified by the COSC.

CMOS: complementary metal-oxide semiconductor. High-performance integrated circuit technology with low power consumption that makes use of field-effect transistors to control functionality.

COIL: in an electric watch, a coil is made of many windings of conductive wire that generate a magnetic field when a current is passed through them. This is often used to move the hands or to activate other mechanical components.

COMPLICATION: any other function a watch may possess apart from displaying the hours, minutes and seconds.

COSC: Contrôle Officiel Suisse des Chronomètres – the official Swiss chronometer testing institute.

CROWN: a winder located on the exterior of the case with which the movement can be wound and the time set.

DATE: an indication of the numbered day of the current month, either by means of a rotating disc or a hand.

DIGITAL: a digital watch is a watch with a numeric display. However, some purists claim that digital refers only to those that require use of the fingers (for example, calculator watches and connected watches).

DIVE WATCH: a waterproof watch rated to a certain depth.

ÉBAUCHE: all the unassembled pieces of a movement, often sold in such a form.

ELECTRIC: in an electric watch, the power source is an electric current rather than a mainspring.

ELECTROMECHANICAL: electromechanical watches are electric watches whose timekeeping is based on a balance wheel or a tuning fork.

ELECTRONIC: electronic watches make use of an electronic oscillator controlled by a quartz crystal resonator, hence the nickname 'quartz' watch.

FREQUENCY: in a mechanical movement, one vibration equates to one oscillation of the balance wheel. The number of these per second defines the frequency, measured in Hz. In an electronic watch, this is based on quartz and the standard frequency is 32kHz.

GMT: Greenwich Mean Time. Refers to a function whereby local time and a reference time can be displayed simultaneously.

GUILLOCHAGE: a watchmaking technique for decorating the dial.

HERTZ (HZ): a unit of frequency indicating the number of alternations in a second. In watchmaking electronics, this represents the frequency of the oscillations of the quartz crystal.

INDEX: a mark located on the dial of a watch to indicate the hours.

INTEGRATED CIRCUIT (IC): a miniaturized component that controls timekeeping accuracy, the display and power consumption. It may also manage supplementary functions such as alarms, chronometers and connectivity.

JUMPING HOUR: a display of the time via a window, rather than with a hand.

KINETIC: a technology that uses the wearer's movements to charge an internal battery, thus powering the watch mechanism, generally combining kinetic energy and an electrical generator.

LCD: a type of watch that uses a liquid crystal screen to display the time and other digital information.

LED: a type of watch that uses light-emitting diodes to display the time and other digital information.

LIGNE: a traditional unit of measurement used to indicate the diameter of watch movements. It is equivalent to approximately 2.256mm.

LUG: located at either end of the case and used to attach the strap.

LUG WIDTH: the distance between the lugs of a watch case.

MANUFACTURER: a company that in theory should control 100 per cent of the production of its watches without recourse to sub-contractors. Since many companies have started to use *ébauches*, the stricter sense of the term has been relaxed.

MECHANICAL WATCH: a watch based on a mechanical movement that has no need of a battery to run.

MODULE: in an electronic watch, module may refer to all the integrated electronic components on a single chip or functional unit.

MOON PHASE: a watchmaking complication displaying the various phases of the moon on the dial.

MOVEMENT: all the components that enable a watch to function.

OSCILLATION: the full displacement and return of a balance wheel between two extreme positions. In an electronic watch, oscillation is performed by the quartz crystal and no longer by the balance wheel.

PLATE: a component on which the bridges and other parts of a mechanical movement are located, on top of which the dial is placed.

POWER RESERVE: how long a movement will run. Although they are less able to charge themselves independently, electronic watches have a comparatively longer power reserve than mechanical watches.

PRINTED CIRCUIT (PCB): a plate to which electronic components are connected, including the integrated circuit, resistors and capacitors. It ensures that all the components work together properly.

PROTOTYPE: an initial model or preliminary example of a watch before mass production.

PUSH-BUTTON: a button to be pressed to activate a mechanism.

PVD: physical vapor deposition. A kind of coating for watch cases.

QUARTZ: a mineral with the property of vibrating at a precise frequency when stimulated with electricity.

RAILWAY TRACK: a scale showing the minutes, printed on the dial and resembling the rails of a railroad track.

REPEATER: an acoustic device that can indicate the time (the hour, or the quarter hours and minutes), either automatically or on demand, or which can function as an alarm at a set time.

RESISTOR: a component limiting the flow of electric current, allowing it to regulate the other electronic components of a watch.

RESONANCE: a phenomenon whereby a quartz crystal exposed to a voltage vibrates at a precise and stable frequency.

RUBY: jewel used in watchmaking to reduce friction to a minimum.

SECOND: the seconds may be displayed on a sub-register located at 6 o'clock or 9 o'clock, or using a hand located at the centre of the dial.

SECOND HAND: the hand indicating the passing of seconds.

SEMICONDUCTOR: a material (such as silicon) that has an electrical conductivity between that of a conductor (such as copper) and an insulator (such as plastic), used in the manufacture of electronic components (transistors, diodes, ICs) to modify electrical signals.

SMARTWATCH: a connected watch featuring advanced functionality such as a link with a smartphone, health notifications and messaging updates.

THERMOCOMPENSATION: in a watch, this involves adjusting the frequency of the oscillator (generally a quartz crystal) to compensate for temperature variations and to preserve stable and accurate timekeeping in a range of thermal environments.

TRANSISTOR: an electronic component that controls and amplifies an electric current, enabling a range of functions such as power management and control of displays.

TUNING FORK (DIAPASON): a small, fork-shaped component, 24.85mm long, that replaces the balance wheel in electric watches. Watchmaking technology developed by Max Hetzel.

WHEEL TRAIN: part of a watch movement.

WINDOW: an aperture in the dial in which information can be displayed.

WORLD TIME: a complication invented by Louis Cottier (and then simplified) that allowed a watch to display the time in the world's 24 time zones simultaneously.

XO: standard abbreviation for crystal oscillator.

ABOUT THE AUTHOR

Clément Mazarian was born in the late 1980s and has nursed a strong passion for watchmaking ever since receiving his first watch, a Seamaster, given to him by his grandfather. Having learned the ropes from more experienced collectors and dealers, he put the finishing touches to his expertise via the internet and dedicated discussion forums. He both buys and sells watches, his discoveries attracting the attention of discerning collectors. He founded his company in 2015 and began to trade vintage watches on his Instagram account (@collection.personnelle).

Although Clément has diversified over time, watches have always been at the heart of his activities. He has worked as a consultant and written articles for the fashion magazine *L'Étiquette* since 2020.

Clément published his first book *Exceptional Watches* in 2022 (originally published as *Collection Personelle*, Éditions du Chêne), sharing his love for watchmaking and 20th-century design by telling the stories behind the iconic watches of our era. The public and critical success achieved by this first volume has allowed him to continue his research and create a second book, this time examining the period known as the 'quartz crisis'.

WATCHMAKING LITERATURE

- *Exceptional Watches*, C Mazarian, Mitchell Beazley, 2024
- *Die Elektrifizierung der Armbanduhr*, L F Trueb, G Ramm, P Wenzig, Ebner Verlag, Germany, 2011
- *Die Elektrische Armbanduhr*, Band 1, H-R Bramaz, H Baumann, Verlag Stutz Druck AG, Switzerland, 2013
- *Die Elektrische Armbanduhr*, Band 2, H-R Bramaz, H Baumann, Verlag Stutz Druck AG, Switzerland, 2013
- 'Die Entwicklung der Schweizer Quarzarmbanduhr, neue Erkenntnisse', G Colcicco, *Chronometrophilia*, No. 92, December 2023
- *Watch: Modern Wristwatch Design*, P Doensen, Snoeck-Ducaju & Zoon, Belgium, 1994
- *L'Aventure de la montre à quartz*, M Forrer, R Le Coultre, A Beyner, Centredoc, Switzerland, 2002
- 'La Montre électrique', M Hetzel, *Bulletin Annuel de la Société Suisse de Chronométrie*, 1964
- *Lip, des heures à conter*, M-P Coustans, Éditions Glénat, France, 2022
- *Mister Swatch: Nicolas Hayek and the Secret of his Success*, J Wegelin, Free Association Books, UK, 2010
- 'Rapport sur le concours chronométrique', Neuchâtel Observatory, Switzerland, 1967
- *Rattraper et dépasser la Suisse*, P-Y Donzé, Éditions Alphil, Switzerland, 2014
- *Swatch: A Guide for Connoisseurs and Collectors*, F Edwards. Firefly Books, UK, 1998
- 'Technische Rundschau', No. 19, M Hetzel, 1963

WEBSITES AND BLOGS

apple.com
astropa.inaf.it
blog.nbb.com
casio.com
cathodecorner.com
chronographes.net
cliniquehorlogere.ch
collectability.com
computerworld.ch
crazywatches.pl
digital-watch.com
doensen.home.xs4all.nl
electric-watches.co.uk
electricwatchprototypes.com
europastar.ch
forumamontres.forumactif.com
fpjourne.com
fratellowatches.com
grail-watch.com
grand-seiko.com
hamiltonwatch.com
hautehorlogerie.org
hodinkee.com
iknowwatches.com
iwc.com
journaldugeek.com
lesrhabilleurs.com
letemps.ch
lip.fr
moonphase.fr
omegaforums.net
omegapassion.com
phillips.com
plus9time.com
seiko7a38.com
seikowatches.com
shellman.com
shs.cairn.info
swatch.com
swatchprototypes.com
tomshardware.fr
toques2toquantes.unblog.fr
uhrforum.de
ukwatches.com
vintageradar.com
wadokei.me
watch-wiki.net
watchonista.com
worldtempus.com
wornandwound.com

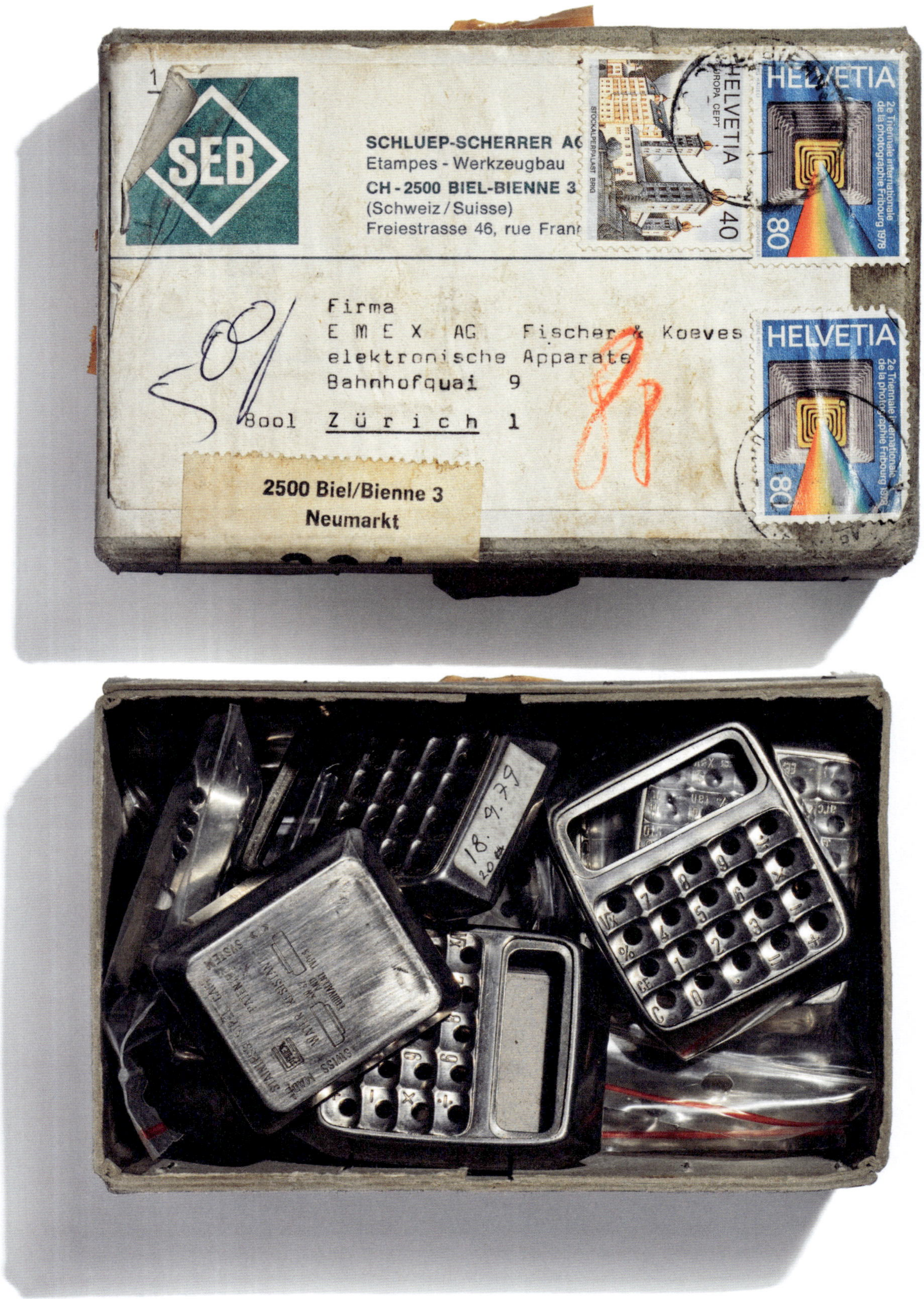
SEB
SCHLUEP-SCHERRER AG
Etampes - Werkzeugbau
CH-2500 BIEL-BIENNE 3
(Schweiz / Suisse)
Freiestrasse 46, rue Fran
HELVETIA
40
HELVETIA
80
2e Triennale internationale de la photographie Fribourg 1978
HELVETIA
80
Firma
E M E X AG Fischer & Koeves
elektronische Apparate
Bahnhofquai 9
8001 Zürich 1
2500 Biel/Bienne 3
Neumarkt
18. 9. 79

CONTRIBUTORS

I would first like to express my deep gratitude to James Dowling. Thanks to his invaluable help, we had the privilege of travelling to London to photograph some of the rarest and most iconic watches from the quartz era. His expertise and generosity were all-important in bringing this project to fruition.

Thanks are also particularly due to Giovanni Colacicco, whose contribution throughout this watchmaking journey has been essential. Giovanni assembled an exceptional team of watch collectors – Yves Wenger, Guillaume Chappuis, Sandy D'Ambrosio, Piotr Pasierbek, Sophie Masneuf and Jérôme Piguet – who ensured that unique pieces and exceptionally rare Swatches could be photographed in Zurich.

Above all, Giovanni has been my constant companion during the writing of this book, patiently checking every detail and ensuring the accuracy of my research day after day. His unwavering support and infectious passion for quartz watches have enriched this book far beyond my expectations.

My eternal thanks to both of you, James and Giovanni. Without your dedication and commitment, this book would never have seen the light of day in all its glory.

FOLLOW THEIR WORK:

WEBSITES

electricwatchprototypes.com
omegaprototypes.com
ukwatches.com

INSTAGRAM

@electricwatchprototypes
@jamesdowlingswatches
@omegaprototypes
@misterrolex

ACKNOWLEDGEMENTS

Thank you to the professional and private collectors who have allowed me to complete this selection.

Many thanks indeed to Michael Sonderegger for his invaluable assistance during the photo shoot with my friend Henry Leutwyler.

Thanks to the whole team at Les éditions du Chêne: to Emmanuel for his faith in me, Benoit for his graphic design talents, Sabine for her infallible sense of style, and Faris for his friendship and support in dealing with the ups and downs of this project.

Thank you also to Jean-Baptiste who was able to preserve and corral my hyper-energetic writing style.

Particular thanks go to Julie, who works so hard, and was always on the ball, whatever the hour.

Thank you to my friends Louis and Maxime, and to Nicolas Godin, for their electrifying vision of the project.

Thank you to Marc and all the team at *Étiquette* magazine for their constant support.

A huge thank you to my family, in particular to my parents and my brother, to Anahite, Mireille, Christine and Roluce, and to my nephew Jules and my neice Léona, whose passion for watchmaking is beginning to grow.

Lastly, I dedicate this book to Marilyn, the lady in my life.

Originally published as *Collection Électrique* by Éditions du Chêne – Hachette Livre

First published in Great Britain in 2025 by Mitchell Beazley,
an imprint of Octopus Publishing Group Ltd,
Carmelite House, 50 Victoria Embankment, London EC4Y 0DZ
www.octopusbooks.co.uk

An Hachette UK Company
www.hachette.co.uk

The authorized representative in the EEA is Hachette Ireland, 8 Castlecourt Centre,
Dublin 15, D15 XTP3, Ireland (email: info@hbgi.ie)

Distributed in the US by Hachette Book Group, 1290 Avenue of the Americas,
4th and 5th Floors, New York, NY 10104

Distributed in Canada by Canadian Manda Group, 664 Annette St.,Toronto,
Ontario, Canada M6S 2C8

ISBN 978 1 84091 967 7
eISBN 978 1 84091 968 4

A CIP catalogue record for this book is available from the British Library.

Printed in China
1 3 5 7 9 10 8 6 4 2

For Éditions du Chêne:
Editor-in-Chief: Emmanuel Le Vallois
Editor: Faris Issad
Editorial Operations: Julie Mege
Art Directors: Sabine Houplain and Benoit Berger
Artistic production and layout: Bureau Berger
Retouching: TJ Huff for Henry Leutwyler Studio, NYC
Illustrations: Derudderdesign and Fanny Faria
Production: Marc Chalmin

For Mitchell Beazley:
Publishing Director: Alison Starling
Senior Managing Editor: Sybella Stephens
English translation by JMS Books LLP
Copy Editor: Julie Brooke
Creative Director: Jonathan Christie
Designer: Jeremy Tilston